Christ's Person and Life-Work in the Theology of Albrecht Ritschl with Special Attention to *Munus Triplex*

Gerald W. McCulloh

UNIVERSITY
PRESS OF
AMERICA

Lanham • New York • London

Copyright © 1990 by
University Press of America®, Inc.
4720 Boston Way
Lanham, Maryland 20706

3 Henrietta Street
London WC2E 8LU England

All rights reserved
Printed in the United States of America
British Cataloging in Publication Information Available

Library of Congress Cataloging-in-Publication Data

McCulloh, Gerald W.
Christ's person and life-work in the theology of Albrecht Ritschl :
with special attention to munus triplex / by Gerald W. McCulloh.
p.   cm.
Originally presented as the author's thesis (Ph. D.—University
of Chicago, 1973).
Includes bibliographical references and index.
1. Jesus Christ—History of doctrines—19th century.
2. Ritschl, Albrecht, 1822-1889—Contributions in Christology.
I. Title.
BT198.M3988   1990   232'.092—dc20   90–38884 CIP

ISBN 0–8191–7885-3 (alk. paper)

BT
198
.M3988
1990

The paper used in this publication meets the minimum requirements of
American National Standard for Information Sciences—Permanence
of Paper for Printed Library Materials, ANSI Z39.48–1984.

JESUIT - KRAUSS - McCORMICK - LIBRARY
1100 EAST 55th STREET
CHICAGO, ILLINOIS 60615

Acknowledgement of Copyright and Permission to Reprint

"Christ's Person and Life-work in the Theology of Albrecht Ritschl:
With Special Attention to the *Munus Triplex*," University of Chicago,
Ph. D. Dissertation, 1974. All rights to a dissertation at the University
of Chicago remain with the author.

R. S. Franks, *A History of the Doctrine of the Work of Christ*, London: Hodder & Stoughton, 1918. Extract used by permission of the
publisher.

Reprinted from CALVIN: INSTITUTES OF THE CHRSTIAN
RELIGION, edited by John T. McNeil and translated for Ford Lewis
Lewis Battles (Volume XX and XXI: The Library of Christian Classics). Copyright (c) MCMLX W. L. Jenkins. Used by permission of
Westminster/John Knox Press.

Reprinted from CALVIN: THEOLOGICAL TREATISES, translated with Introduction and Notes by J. K. S. Reid (Volume XXII:
The Library of Christian Classics). Published simultaneously in Great
Britian and the U. S. A. by S. C. M. Press and The Westminster Press,
Philadelphia, Pennsylvania in MCMLIV. Used by permission.

Quotations from *The Holy Bible*. Revised Standard Version,
copyright by the National Council of Churches of Christ in the USA,
Divison of Education and Ministry, copyright 1946, 1952, 1971, 475
Riverside Drive, New York, NY 10027, used by permission.

TABLE OF CONTENTS

PREFACE

The original impetus for this study was the presentation of the prophet, priest, king Christology in the ancient and medieval Church given by Professor George Hunston Williams in lectures in Church History at Harvard University, Cambridge, Massachusetts in the Fall Semester, 1964. Questions about the significance of the theme for Reformation thought were raised by Professor B. A. Gerrish in his seminar on Calvin at the University of Chicago in the Autumn Quarter, 1965. The project grew into a dissertation proposal in relation to the work of Albrecht Ritschl under the guidance of the late Professor Joseph A. Haroutunian. Professor Gerrish graciously undertook its supervision upon the death of Professor Haroutunian in the fall of 1968.

The School of Theology of Loyola University of Chicago granted me a leave of absence from teaching duties to accept a fellowship from the English-Speaking Union for study at Cambridge University for the 1970-71 academic year. Wesley House, Westminster and Cheshunt Colleges, and Fitzwilliam College in Cambridge have provided the workspace, access to libraries and fellowship required for the completion of this study.

I am grateful for the generous support of the Henry J. Siegel Family Foundation in bringing this project to print.

The unstinting loyalty of my Karen and my family have carried me through the difficult times encountered; I owe them an unspeakable debt of gratitude.

In Memoriam. Gerald O. McCulloh. 1912-1988.

The recognition of Jesus as the Christ has for us no meaning unless through Him we know ourselves raised to kingship or dominion over the world, and to priesthood or undisturbed communion with God.

Albrecht Ritschl in *The Christian Doctrine of Justification and Reconciliation*, III, 418.

At that time the disciples came to Jesus, saying, "Who is the greatest in the kingdom of heaven?" And calling to him a child, he put him in the midst of them, and said, "Truly, I say to you, unless you turn and become like children, you will never enter the kingdom of heaven. Whoever humbles himself like this child, he is the greatest in the kingdom of heaven."

Matthew 18:1-4 (Revised Standard Version)

The phenomena in which many seek the real proof of the might of Christianity, namely, political influence and the legal authority of Church officials and ecclesiastical institutions, are the very things that come under strong suspicion of falsifying the intentions of Christ; indeed, it is only a really strong faith in the invisible that, amid the miry abominations and miserable trivialities of Church history, can trace the advancing power of Christ over this world at all.

Albrecht Ritschl in *The Christian Doctrine of Justification and Reconciliation*, III, 460.

CHAPTER I
INTRODUCTION
The Plan of the Study

The year 1989 marks a century since the final revision of the third edition of Albrecht Ritschl's best known work, the three volume study of the Christian faith from the perspective of the doctrine of justification and reconciliation.[1] In assessing the importance of Ritschl's work, H. R. Mackintosh wrote in *Types of Modern Theology*, in 1937, that Ritschl, like Tennyson, belonged to the middle distance, too far for gratitude, too near for reverence, that Ritschl was behind a passing cloud.[2] The cloud persisted in the somber tone of Karl Barth's criticism of liberal Protestant thought in general and of Ritschl in particular, as "the very epitome of the liberal German bourgeois of the age of Bismarck," for whom reconciliation meant, to put it baldly, the realized ideal of human life.[3] By 1966 the cloud cover was lifting and B. A. Reist was able to assure us that there was "Life in the Old Boys Yet," in the title of his review for *The Christian Century* of Philip Hefner's book, *Faith and the Vitalities of History* (on Ritschl), and Peter Hodgson's book *The Formation of Historical Theology* (on F. C. Baur).[4] With the articles on aspects of Ritschl's thought in *Church History*, *The Journal of Religion*, *The Scottish Journal of Theology*, and *The Lutheran Quarterly*, written by Hefner, Dan Deegan and Paul Jersild from May, 1961 to April, 1964, the publication of studies of Ritschl by Rolf Schäfer in 1968 and David Mueller in 1969, together with several recent dissertations on Ritschlian thought, we can affirm that the cloud has passed on and that the Ritschlian features of the landscape of late nineteenth century theology are once more illuminated.[5]

In the study of Ritschl's Christology we become aware of characteristic emphases in Ritschl's thought, which are: a definition of religion as a positive historical phenomenon; a critique of the place of metaphysics in theology; an assertion of the importance of the Bible for understanding the Christian faith; a view of the earthly ministry of Jesus as the only meaningful foundation for knowledge of God; and a claim for the free, active participation of man with God in justification and reconciliation.[6] Ritschl sees that his theological task includes a critical history of Christian doctrine which examines the philosophical consistency, the claims to biblical authenticity, and the historical development of Christian doctrine. This task is undertaken in order that the effect of Jesus' life and teaching upon the Christian community can be clearly seen and fully appreciated, joining the experience of the first century Christian with the experience of the contemporary Christian.[7] It is the intention of this study to show how Ritschl's reappraisal of the *munus triplex* exemplifies his historical, critical, and constructive method in theology and how it reveals his positions in both epistemology (namely, that things are known in their effects) and biblical theology (that the New Testament is the record of God's being known to man in terms of Jesus' historical life). The constructive suggestions which Ritschl makes for the modification of the *munus triplex* reflect his concern to present the Christian faith from the perspective of common human experience within a specific historical tradition, and at the same time show how the content of his dogmatic theology influences his epistemology.

Our method for this study will be to examine Ritschl's philosophical, biblical, and historical judgments concerning the *munus triplex*. First we shall follow the presentation of Ritschl's case in his account of *The Christian Doctrine of Justification and Reconciliation* and after examining the history of the *munus triplex* we shall criticize the main points of Ritschl's Christological argument, considering their validity with respect to the history of the doctrine *munus triplex*, the threefold office of Christ as Prophet, Priest, and King.[8] Finally, we shall try to draw together from the positive contributions of Ritschl and our criticism some constructive proposals for the study of Christology and the interpretation of the *munus triplex*.

Albrecht Ritschl in the Context of His Work

In a short essay entitled *Christian Perfection* which was published in 1874 at the time of completion of the last volumes of the first edition of *The Christian Doctrine of Justification and Reconciliation*, Ritschl makes use of the term life-work (*Lebenswerk*) in distinguishing between a version of the doctrine of perfection which emphasizes the overall positive direction and collective value of the life of an individual and a version which sees each individual's life as a series of moments which make ethical demands on the individual and which receive only finite and partial responses, leaving man with a life seen as a series of failures to attain the absolute.[9] In considering who Ritschl was and what his contribution to the history of Christian thought was, we will first sketch briefly his own *Lebenswerk* as it is a positive attempt to present the Christian faith intelligibly within the context of nineteenth century religious thought. We will then, later on, turn to the more critical and analytical assessment of his work.

Ritschl began his constructive theological work in the liberal context of the Tübingen school under the tutelage of F. C. Baur, publishing in 1846 *Das Evangelium Marcions und das kanonische Evangelium Lucas*, which was considered typical of the Tübingen school's application of Hegelian thought to the historical data of the early Church.[10] Ritschl withdrew from the direct influence of Baur in the second edition of *Die Entstehung der altkatholischen Kirche* in 1857 as he turned from biblical studies to the problems of historical theology and found Baur's account of the relationship between the early Christian community and the emerging Catholic Church of the third century to be unconvincing.[11] At this stage Ritschl was concerned to discover the meaning of Christ for the Church and to do so within the limits of historical knowledge of the life of Christ available in Scripture, in the traditions of the Christian community, and in the experience of the individual Christian.[12]

A series of articles from 1864-69 led into the publication in 1870 of the first volume of his major historical, critical, and systematic work, *Die christliche Lehre von der Rechtfertigung und Versöhnung*, which was completed in 1874.[13] In the introduction to the third volume Ritschl acknowledged that he did not fit into any of the existing parties in German Protestant theology and noted that he had drawn criticism of his work from all quarters.[14] His critical reaction against pietism on historical and systematic grounds appeared in *Geschichte des Pietismus* in 1880.[15] Ritschl's interest in methodology in the study of religion and the relationship of philosophy to theology, which had been a part of his earlier attraction to Hegel and Baur continued in the later volumes of *Die christliche Lehre der Rechtfertigung und Versöhnung* and in a shorter essay, *Theologie und Metaphysik*, in 1881.[16] Revision of his major work on justification continued to the third edition in 1888. This edition has become the standard for Ritschl's work.[17] Ritschl died in 1889.

His influence was strongly felt in the academic circles of his day and hotly debated in ecclesiastical circles, although Ritschl himself was not a prominent figure in the institutional structure of the Church. He was an academic theologian, serving as a professor at Bonn from 1846-64 and at Göttingen from 1864-89. The major biograpical work on Ritschl was prepared by his son Otto Ritschl in 1892.[18] There is a short piece by E. Ehrenfeuchter which contains reprints of letters from Theodor Plitt, professor of practical theology at Bonn, to Ehrenfeuchter's grandfather, Friedrich A. E. Ehrenfeuchter, at Göttingen.[19] They deal with the character of Ritschl and his suitability for appointment in systematic theology at Göttingen. Plitt's evaluation of Ritschl is that he is a talented and distinguished teacher, although he lacks a certain external manner that befits a clergyman. He is possessed of a sharp tongue that may seem unpleasant at first but which is not used lightly or with malice. Plitt regards Ritschl's work in Church History as a definite contribution to the faculty although he knows that Ritschl's early association with the Tübingen school may make him unacceptable in some quarters.[20]

G. Wayne Glick in *The Reality of Christianity* records a different view of Ritschl in some correspondence from Theodosius Harnack of Dorpat to his son Adolf Harnack.

> ...in his central thought, that of justification, and especially in the separation rather than differentiation of faith and knowledge, he has worked radically and destructively...He will not get by with it, no matter how much he gives the church to do. For as you know from church history better than I, it has been the fate of all middle parties that they have been crushed. That is the inevitable judgment of history. And because I value your work highly, I do not want this judgment to fall on it.[21]

4

Robert Mackintosh in *Albrecht Ritschl and His School* preserves evidence of the tenuous acceptance of the academic theologian when he was judged by the external canons of popular piety.

> In 1883 Ritschl and Schultz were favored with anonymous letters from some pious persons at Hermannsburg, where Ludwig Harms earlier in the century carried on his vigorous labours on behalf of evangelical religion and orthodox Lutheranism. The letters intimated that several Christians had been praying God to convert the two Göttingen theologians, but if that "could not be" to stop their teaching. After this, when he felt worse than usual, Ritschl would remark, "The people at Hermannsburg are praying."[22]

In the definitive biography by his son, Albrecht Ritschl's life and work are painstakingly chronicled beginning with the influence of his grandfather, Pastor Georg Wilhelm Ritschl of St. John's Church, Erfurt, upon the family and the care which Ritschl's own father, Bishop Georg Carl Benjamin Ritschl, general superintendent for Pomerania, took in his son Albrecht Benjamin's theological education. The details include the course of Ritschl's student years, the slow unfolding of his academic career in Bonn and its firm establishment in Göttingen. The names of his students, outlines of his courses, and the major academic disputes are recorded. The lectures, sermons, articles and books by Ritschl are listed and private correspondence is preserved from within the family.[23]

By the time of D. F. Strauss' *Life of Jesus*, which was published in 1835, German Protestant theology had divided into three major camps, each with its own inner divisions.[24] The speculative (or Hegelian) theologians generally supported the critical direction which Strauss' work had taken although they may have had reservations about some of his specific results.[25] Men like Feuerbach and Biedermann, as speculative theologians, stood opposed to a neo-Lutheran confessionalism which rejected Strauss's work as impiety and sought to reassert traditional supernatural theological categories. Representative of the various groups in the conservative camp are Philippi, Stahl and von Hofmann, as well as Hengstenberg, Harms and Thomasius. A third group was conscious of the polarities which separated the liberals and the orthodox groups and they sought to mediate the division and to provide a harmonizing appreciation of both points of view even if no universally acceptable synthesis emerged. The mediating theologians recognized the results of historical criticism of Scripture and the necessity for scientific methodology in the study of history but also felt strongly, in the tradition of Schleiermacher, the place of the individual Christian consciousness in properly expressing the Christian faith. The teachings, symbols and rituals of the Church served to impart a distinctively Christian self-consciousness. Neander, Tholuck, and Dorner are representative of the mediating theology (*Vermittlungstheologie*). The speculative, conservative, and mediating theologies were the left, right, and center against which Ritschl stood with his attempt to synthesize the experience of the traditional faith and the new knowledge of science and history, without sacrificing the continuity of the Christian faith and the fidelity which it owed to the apostolic Church. Ritschl sought to free theology from bondage to an outmoded philosophy in order that it could express itself in the language of the new age without surrendering to a rational reductionism.[26]

At first Ritschl wrote under the influence of F. C. Baur and the liberal theologians who sought to give a developmental history of religion. In *Das Evangelium Marcions und das kanonische Evangelium Lucas* Ritschl supported Baur's early dating of Matthew, found Marcion's gospel preceded Luke and had regarded Mark as a later, shortened form of the earlier traditions. Ritschl was regarded by Baur as an able advocate of his position. Ritschl shifted to accept the priority of the Gospel of Mark and to question the validity of Baur's account of the relation of parties in the early Church. As Ritschl separated himself from Baur and what was left of the Tübingen school after 1857, he remained on essentially friendly relations with the members of the school, the polemical style of German theological discussion of the period notwithstanding.[27] Ritschl could not fit himself into the conservative or neo-Lutheran group because of his acceptance of a non-supernatural worldview, limiting knowledge of God to the impact of the life and work of Christ upon the believer. His application of Kantian categories to the problem of knowing and morality brought him into closer relationship with the liberal theologians, although his concern for the historical continuity represented by the life of the Christian community would not allow him to embrace the speculative positions of the more radical Hegelians such as Bauer and Feuerbach. Ritschl sought to reconcile the divisions within the Church and within the theological world of his time by grasping the points of both sides. He sought to recover the unity of the historical development of Christian theology, Catholic and Protestant, in his understanding of the true catholicity of the Kingdom of God. He was concerned to recover the effect of the life of the historical Jesus upon the community which formed in response to his work, and to present this witness of faith as fact acceptable to the contemporary world. In this sense Ritschl is a mediating theologian. The reason for not locating him at once as a mediating theologian among the others is in order to recognize his distinctive contribution in going back to the positions of Kant and Schleiermacher which had given shape to the conflict of the period and trying his own synthesis of modern and traditional language and experience. Ritschl's attempt was important for the scope of his integrative effort at a period of intense hostility and destructive criticism. He brought together the fruits of his labors in philosophy, biblical exegesis, church history, and systematic theology. To draw on an image which served Ritschl himself, he tried to realize both rationalistic and romantic motifs, reason and faith, as the foci from which to draw an ellipse expressing the larger unity in the convergence of the witness of faith to the historical Jesus as the Christ of faith, royal prophet and royal priest of the community which is called to be the Kingdom of God. Theology for Ritschl is the study of the convergence of the truth of biblical criticism, historical theology, and systematic theology in an interpretation of the person and life-work of Jesus Christ.

During the last third of the nineteenth century the impact of Ritschl's work increased. His classes at Göttingen were the largest of his career and the numbers of English and Scottish students that were studying in Germany brought interest in Ritschl to Great Britain and the United States. Among his students and supporters may be named: Bender, Guthe, Robertson Smith, John S. Black, Duhm, Smend, Baethgen, Wellhausen, Bornemann, Loofs, Wrede, Baldensperger, Oskar Holtzmann, Simons, Gunkel, Weiss, Mirbt, Troeltsch, and Bousset. Schültz, Kattenbusch, Wendt, Schürer, Adolf Harnack and Wilhelm Herrmann were colleagues of Ritschl who identified themselves with his work.[28]

While the effects of Ritschl's influence have been termed a "school" in the usual sense, Ritschlianism did not long survive Ritschl himself. The objective sources represented by the New Testament text itself, the documents of the early Church and the historical data of the history of doctrine were more important to Ritschl than the personal style of an individual thinker. His own stance recognized the succession of philosophical systems associated with the history of theology and the revaluation of the historical data associated with the advance of critical methodology. His "school" was therefore open to development, stimulated by the advances in science, history, and philosophy which were transforming the world, and not overly bound by authoritarian dogmatism. While his personality left its mark on his students, they were encouraged to become scholars in their own fields. The advances in philology, archeology, and history in the study of religion meant that few could expect to obtain the encyclopedic knowledge or maintain the critical standards in all the fields which Ritschl himself had mastered.

The history of religions school (*Religionsgeschichtliche Schule*) pursued an ideal of history as a unity, which Ritschl had affirmed for the Christian faith, into the study of non-Christian religions.[29] They were less inclined to see Christianity as the highest evolution of ethical and philosophical forms than Ritschl was. Ritschl's historical account of the uniqueness of Jesus' life and work in founding a community that understood itself to be part of the Kingdom of God was no longer the satisfactory historical or theological ground for considering all other religious structures to be inferior when compared with the Christian faith or the Christian church. With the publication of Karl Barth's Commentary on *The Epistle to Romans* (1918) the work of the liberal theologian in expressing the positive relationship between religion and culture began to be eclipsed in favor of the neo-orthodox emphasis on the role of the divine initiative and the radical uniqueness of the salvation proclaimed by Christ.[30] Ritschl was no longer rigorous enough in his philosophy or historiography for the liberal scholars. Troeltsch surpassed him in the sociological analysis of religious structures.[31] Nor was Ritschl a strong enough advocate of the discontinuity in history produced by the person and work of Christ to suit the neo-orthodox. Interest in the Ritschlian image of the Kingdom of God as the historical goal of the Chruch, to be realized in history, found further development in more concrete social missions, and responsibility for the disciplines of academic theology in which Ritschl had labored fell upon the neo-orthodox critics who had rejected his synthesis of theology and culture for their own age.[32]

As a man Albrecht Ritschl was almost wholly absorbed in his work. Seriousminded in his approach to it, he was not without a sense of humor to appreciate its ironies. He did not travel much outside of Germany after an excursion as a student. He was closely bound to his family and although widowed after ten years, did not seek much outside of the family circle for amusement or entertainment. He did not involve himself directly in the political side of ecclesiastical affairs with the exception of an approach to the *Vorparlament* in Frankfurt in 1848.[33] He was forced to wait a long time for formal recognition and advancement in his profession. His early success with the Tübingen school was an identification which left some stigma about him for the more conservative scholars. He accepted this, burying himself in his work as an academic theologian, writing, reading and lecturing to small classes. It was within his own work that he traveled freely. He moved from the history of Israelite religion through the formation of the Christian community and its subsequent Hellenization, to the growth and the development of the Roman Church and the reaction to it in the Reformation, and to criticism of the contemporary scene in German Protestant theology with a sense of direction and purpose. He enjoyed vistas of perspective that reached across the boundaries of the Catholic, Lutheran and Reformed communities to see the intricate relationships and historical developments that bound them altogether in the service of the Kingdom of God. A clear understanding of the past was, for Ritschl, the key to full appreciation and participation in the present and hope for the future.

9

NOTES CHAPTER I

¹ Albrecht B. Ritschl, *Die christliche Lehre von der Rechtfertigung und Versöhnung* (3 vols.; Bonn: Adolph Marcus, 1870-74). All translations are my own unless otherwise specified. English translation of Vol. I from the first edition is by J. S. Black, *A Critical History of the Christian Doctrine of Justification and Reconciliation* (Edinburgh: Edmonston and Douglas, 1872) and Vol. III from the third edition, 1882, by H. R. Mackintosh and A. B. Macaulay, *The Christian Doctrine of Justification and Reconciliation* (Clifton, New Jersey: Reference Book Publishers, 1966 reprint). The references from the three volumes are hereafter cited RV, I, II, or III and the English translation is given as JR, I, II, or III. Pagination in Vol. I is for the first edition, Vol. III for the third edition, corresponding with most available English material. More extensive quotation of Ritschl's work occurs in Chapter II than any other and so some of the German text has been included in the notes in order to provide examples of the vocabulary and style of the original. A bibliography for Ritschl must be put together from several sources: Otto Ritschl, *Albrecht Ritschls Leben* (2 vols.; Freiburg: Akademische Verlagsbuchhandlung, J. C. B. Mohr, 1892); Gosta Hök, *Die elliptische Theologie Albrecht Ritschls: Nach Ursprung und innerem Zusammenhang* (Uppsala: Uppsala Universitets Arsskrift, 1942); Rolf Schaefer, *Ritschl: Grundlinen eines fast verschollenen dogmatischen Systems* (Tübingen: J. C. B. Mohr, 1968) and Philip Hefner, *Faith and the Vitalities of History: A Theological Study Based on the Work of Albrecht Ritschl* (New York: Harper & Row, 1966).

² H R. Mackintosh, *Types of Modern Theology* (New York: Chas. Scribner's Sons, 1937), p. 141.

³ Karl Barth, *Die protestantische Theologie im 19. Jahrhundert* (Zurich: Zollikon, 1952). English translation, *Protestant Thought: From Rousseau to Ritschl* (New York: Harper & Row, 1959), pp. 392-393.

⁴ B.A. Reist, "Life in the Old Boys Yet," *The Christian Century*, LXXXIII (September 28, 1966), 1179-1180. Hefner, *Faith and the Vitalities of History*,. p. 1, n. 1 above. Peter Hodgson, *The Formation of Historical Theology* (New York: Harper & Row, 1966).

⁵ Dan Deegan, "Albrecht Ritschl as Critical Empiricist," *Journal of Religion*, XLIV (April 1964), 149-160; "Albrecht Ritschl on the Historical Jesus," *The Scottish Journal of Theology*,. XV (June, 1962), 133-150, "The Ritschlian School, the Essence of Christianity and Karl Barth," *The Scottish Journal of Theology*, XVI (December, 1963), 390-414; Hefner, "Albrecht Ritschl and His Current Critics," *The Lutheran Quarterly*, XIII (May 1961), 103-112, "Baur Versus Ritschl on Early Christianity," *Church History*, XXXI (September, 1962), 259-278, "The Role of Church History in the Theology of Albrecht Ritschl," *Church History*, XXXIII (September, 1964), 338-355; Paul Jersild, "The Judgment of God in Albrecht Ritschl and Karl Barth," *The Lutheran Quarterly*,. XIV (November, 1962), 328-346; "Natural Theology and the Doctrine of God in Albrecht Ritschl and Karl Barth," *The Lutheran Quarterly*, XIV (August, 1962), 239-257; Schäfer, *Ritschl*, see p. 1, n. 1 above; David L. Mueller,

An Introduction to the Theology of Albrecht Ritschl (Philadelphia: Westminster Press, 1969); and among recent dissertations on Ritschl, George P. Guthrie, "Kant and Ritschl" (unpublished Ph.D. dissertation, University of Chicago, 1962); Robert E. Koenig, "The Use of the Bible in Albrecht Ritschl's Theology" (unpublished Ph.D. dissertation, University of Chicago, 1963); and Joseph W. Pickle, Jr., "Epistemology and Soteriology: A Study in the Theologies of Albrecht Ritschl and Karl Barth" (unpublished Ph.D. dissertation, University of Chicago, 1969).

[6] Mueller, *Introduction to Ritschl,* pp. 19-21, mentions twelve characteristic emphases of Ritschl which he has drawn from Otto Ritschl, "Albrecht Ritschls Theologie und ihre bisherigen Schicksale," *Zeitschrift für Theologie und Kirche,* N. F., 16. Jhr. (1935), pp. 44-47. The emphases which I mention are those involved in Ritschl's judgment upon the systematic and historical value of the *munus triplex.*

[7] A. Ritschl, RV, I, 1-10; III, 1-8; JR, I, 1-10; III, 1-8.

[8] A. Ritschl, RV, III, 364-455; JR, III, 385-484.

[9] A Ritschl, *Christliche Vollkommenheit* (Leipzig: J. C. Hinrichs, 1924), p. 11.

[10] Robert Mackintosh, *Albrecht Ritschl and His School* (London: Chapman and Hall, 1915), pp. 30-31.

[11] Hefner, *Faith and the Vitalities of History,* pp. 12-44, and O. Ritschl, *Leben,* I, 271-294.

[12] A. Ritschl, RV, III, 383; JR, III, 406. "Jede Wirkung Christi aber muss ihren Masstab in der geschichtlichen Gestalt seines Lebens finden."

[13] A. Ritschl, RV, I, v-vi; JR, I, vii-viii.

[14] A. Ritschl, RV, III, vii-viii; JR, III, vii.

[15] A. Ritschl, *Geschichte des Pietismus* (3 vols.; Bonn: Adolph Marcus, 1880-86.

[16] A. Ritschl, RV, III, 1-30, 203-211; *Theologie und Metaphysik: Zur Verständigung und Abwehr* (Bonn: Adolph Marcus, 1881).

[17] Cajus Fabricius, *Die Entwicklung in Albrecht Ritschls Theologie von 1874 bis 1889* (Tübingen: J. C. B. Mohr, 1909). Fabricius follows the development of Ritschl's revisions of *The Christian Doctrine of Justification and Reconciliation* from the first publication of Volume III until the last edition revised by Ritschl and issued as the third edition in 1889. He establishes the third edition as the standard edition for Ritschl's work although no complete critical edition has been prepared. Until the reprinting of the translation of Volume III of *Justification and Reconciliation* and a facsimile edition of *Geschichte des Pietismus* in the last decade, the availability of Ritschl in the English speaking world had been quite limited either in English or in German.

[18] O. Ritschl, *Albrecht Ritschls Leben,* see p. 1, n. 1 above.

[19] E. Ehrenfeuchter, "Albrecht Ritschl in der Sicht eines Bonner Kollegen 1863," *Jahrbuch der Gesellschaft für niedersächsische Kirchengeschichte,* LX (1962), 146-150.

[20] *Ibid.,* pp. 148-150. "Bonn d. 30 January 1863 . . . Ritschls Hauptcharisma ist ohne Zweifel seine wirklich ausgezeichnete Lehrgabe. Keiner von uns ist in dieser Beziehung mit ihm zu vergleichen . . . Ich halte Ritschls Lehrgabe für geradezu eminent. Uber seine konfessionelle Stellung weiss ich kaum etwas anders zu sagen, als dass er lutherisch geboren ist, aber durchaus der angehört. Sein theologischer Standpunkt ist Ihnen bekannt, und wenn Sie die irrtümliche Ansicht mancher Leute theilten, dass er der destruktiven Tübinger Richtung angehöre, würden Sie sich natürlich nicht für seine Berufung in Ihre Fakultät interessieren . . . Plitt." "Bonn, d. 14 Mai 1863 . . . Es ist ganz richtig, dass Ritschl etwas skeptisches in seiner Natur hat, eine Neigung zur Satyre. Er gilt dafür eine scharfe Zunge zu haben. Früher als ich ihn noch weniger kannte, hat mich dies von ihm zurück gestossen, jetzt, da ich weiss, dass er von aller Frivolität und Malice weit entfernt ist, nicht mehr . . . Plitt."

[21] G. Wayne Glick, *The Reality of Christianity* (New York: Harper & Row, 1967), pp. 27-28. Further material on Ritschl's effect on Harnack may be found in Agnes von Zahn-Harnack, *Adolph von Harnack* (Berlin: Hans Bott, 1936).

[22] R. Mackintosh, *Albrecht Ritschl and His School.* p. 46.

[23] O. Ritschl, *Albrecht Ritschls Leben.* Vol. I deals with Ritschl's life from 1822 to 1864 including his early education in Bonn and Halle and his relationship with Baur and the Tübingen School. An outline of his scholarly writing through 1864 is attached. Vol. II begins with Ritschl's transfer to Göttingen in 1864 and examines his theological method, the formulation of the distinctive interests of the "Ritschlian School," and his final years. The bibliography is carried to 1889 and a list of his courses and the number of students is added in an appendix.

[24] David F. Strauss, *Das Leben Jesu kritisch bearbeitet* (Tübingen: J. C. B. Mohr, 1835). English translation from 4th German edition, George Eliot, *The Life of Jesus Critically Examined* (London: Sonnenschein, 1848).

[25] Any use of labels like "liberal," "radical," "conservative," or "orthodox" is problematic. The labels often begin as pejorative or derisive characterizations and then become descriptive and denotative as the usage is generalized. I draw the characterizations here loosely for illustrative purposes The compression of individuals into groups obscures some of the distinctions made by some of the authors listed below but in general I follow the main headings suggested by them. The literature for this discussion is: F. Lichtenberger, *History of German Theology* (Edinburgh: T. & T. Clark, 1889); Otto Pfleiderer, *Development of Theology in Germany Since Kant* (London: Sonnenschein, 1890); John Herman Randall, Jr., *The Making of the Modern Mind* (Cambridge: Houghton Mifflin, 1954); A. Ritschl, RV, I, 542-638; JR, I, 557-605; Paul Tillich, *Perspectives on 19th and 20th Century Protestant*

Theology (New York: Harper & Row, 1967); Williston Walker, *A History of the Christian Church* (New York: Chas. Scribners Sons, 1959); and Claude Welch, *God and Incarnation in Mid-nineteenth Century German Theology* (New York: Oxford University Press, 1965).

²⁶ Hefner, *Faith and the Vitalities of History,* pp. 46-87, gives Ritschl's application of his method to the course of Church history.

²⁷ *Ibid.,* pp. 14-26 gives the positive effect of Baur on Ritschl and then traces the disengagement pp. 27-44. Hodgson, *The Formation of Historical Theology,* pp. 86-89, acknowledges the critical task of the "Tübingen School" and its continuity of point of view and method even if specific conclusions are modified or even reversed. Cf. R. Mackintosh, *Albrecht Ritschl and His School.* p. 273.

²⁸ R. Mackintosh, *Albrecht Ritschl and His School,.* pp. 43-45, and O. Ritschl, *Albrecht Ritschls Leben,.* II, 236-314.

²⁹ Cf. "Religionsgeschichtliche Schule" in *Religion in Geschichte und Gegenwart,* Dritte Auflage, Bd. 5, pp. 991-994.

³⁰ Karl Barth, *Der Römerbrief* (Munich: Ch. Kaiser, 1919). English translation from sixth edition by Edwyn C. Hoskyns, *The Epistle to Romans* (Oxford: Oxford University Press, 1933).

³¹ Ernst Troeltsch, *Die Soziallehren der christlichen Kirchen und Gruppen* (Tübingen: J. C. B. Mohr, 1912). English translation Olive Wyon, *The Social Teaching of the Christian Churches* (New York: Harper, 1931).

³² Johannes Weiss, Ritschl's son-in-law and student, withdrew from Ritschl's ethical understanding of the Kingdom of God by defining the eschatological context of the phrase in the preaching of Jesus without attempting to modernize it. Cf. Johannes Weiss, *Die Predigt Jesu vom Reiche Gottes* (Göttingen: Vandenhoeck & Ruprecht, 1892). English translation by Richard H. Hiers and David L. Holland, *Jesus' Proclamation of the Kingdom of God* (Philadelphia: Fortress Press, 1971); Albert Schweitzer, *Von Reimarus zu Wrede* (Tübingen: J. C. B. Mohr, 1906), English translation from the first edition by W. Montgomery, *The Quest of the Historical Jesus* (New York: Macmillan, 1962), pp. 223-253, and James M. Robinson, *A New Quest of the Historical Jesus* (London: SCM Press, 1959), pp. 26-35.

³³ O. Ritschl, *Albrecht Ritschls Leben,* I, 141-151; E. J. Passant, *A Short History of Germany 1815-1945* (Cambridge: Cambridge University Press, 1969), p. 29; A. J. P. Taylor, *The Course of German History* (London: Hamilton, 1945), pp. 46-89.

CHAPTER II
RITSCHL'S PRESENTATION OF THE PERSON AND LIFE-WORK OF CHRIST IN THE CHRISTIAN FAITH

Albrecht Ritschl's treatment of the structure and content of the Christian faith is arranged in line with his understanding of the doctrine of justification. In turn, for him, the content of the doctrine of justification is determined by the person and work of Christ. Ritschl's understanding of Christology is basic to his whole theological enterprise. In his epistemology and in his view of eschatology, there is a constant focus on the work of Christ in establishing the Kingdom of God as the central fact of Christian experience, the active moment of God's self-revelation, and the heart of the common life of the Church. In our examination of Ritschl's Christology we will present it as it appears in *The Christian Doctrine of Justification and Reconciliation* and refer to *Instruction in the Christian Religion* and *Theologie und Metaphysik* as they help to understand Ritschl's constructive position.[1]

The publication in 1889 of the third revised edition of *Die christliche Lehre von der Rechtfertigung und Versöhnung* represents the highest point of development in Ritschl's historical, biblical, and systematic statement of the Christian faith. The organization and structure of the three volumes give us insight into Ritschl's method of approach. The first volume, originally published in 1870, traces the historical development of the doctrine of justification and reconciliation from a primitive model in the early Church through two divergent forms of the doctrine in Anselm and Abelard to the conflict of Lutheran orthodoxy and speculative theology in the nineteenth century. The second volume is the biblical theology which Ritschl held to be the authentic basis of the doctrine of justification. The third volume contains Ritschl's own constructive statement of the doctrine of justification and reconciliation. In order to appreciate the perspective from which Ritschl speaks in the third volume we will look at the development of the first two volumes.

A Critical History

Ritschl opens Volume One proposing to unfold the Christian doctrine of justification and reconciliation in a scientific manner which will demonstrate it to be the real center of the theological system of the Christian faith.

> The Christian doctrine of Justification and Reconciliation, which I purpose to unfold in a scientific manner, constitutes the real centre of the theological system. In it is developed the determinate and direct result of the historical revelation of God's purpose of grace through Christ—the result, namely, that the Church founded by Christ has freedom of religious intercourse with God, notwithstanding the fact of sin, and at the same time, in the exercise of that freedom, directs the working of its own will in conformity with God's expressed design. To the religious discernment this implies in itself the moral restoration of man, and all religious blessedness.[2]

Ritschl sees his task as the scientific (*wissenschaftliche*) analysis of a cause-effect relationship which obtains between God's action, historical revelation through Christ, and the result, the life of the Church. Given the historical fact of the Christ, Ritschl sees that the freedom of man's access to God, "the moral restoration of man," and "all religious blessedness" are entailed. The consequences of the action of God in Christ will be the "moral effects of the Life, Passion, Death and Resurrection of Christ towards the founding of the Church."[3]

Ritschl is critical of the loose and unscientific form of traditional theological language. He finds that the use of the threefold office of Christ as Prophet, Priest, and King which had been employed by Protestant orthodoxy in Lutheran and Reformed theology since Luther and Calvin is "inharmonious and strange."

...the fact is, that neither our Lord Himself nor any one of the New Testament writers, has made use of the three offices as the comprehensive and only forms for expressing the saving operations of Christ, and that this use was not introduced into systematic theology until the Reformation period.[4]

Ritschl's attack on the value of the prophet, priest, king schema challenged the tolerance of Schleiermacher who had acknowledged that the use of the titles by the Church was sufficient ground to retain their usage in order to preserve continuity in dogmatic expression. Ritschl argues that only a mechanical application of biblical authority supports the use of the titles, and it does so at the cost of a harmonious relationship between doctrinal and biblical theology.[5] Ritschl's aim is to give instead a critical account of the history of doctrine in which the action of God in Christ is properly expressed and the course of development traced, in the light of the faithfulness of the doctrine to the original event, and in the modification of the doctrine by succeeding ages of men in their re-presentation of the Christian faith. For Ritschl, this is done by a careful re-reading of the documents of the Church, proceeding from the witness to the life and work of Christ in the New Testament and continuing in the writings of the Church fathers and the later Christian writers. In Volume One he begins with the post-biblical formulations of the Christian faith.

The Patristic View of the Death of Christ

The early Church fathers, Ritschl explains, developed a theory of the atonement as deceit of the devil.[6]

It is well known that a number of Greek and Latin Church Fathers view the death of Christ as a transaction in which God (from the motive of His justice) delivered over the life of the God-man as a price to the devil, who is recognized as the rightful lord over sinful humanity, and who could be induced to make surrender of his rights only on condition of receiving that as an equivalent. In this theory sin is represented merely as a *mechanical subjection to the devil* and the idea of redemption remains entirely out of relation to the notion of human will.[7]

In this passage Ritschl demonstrates for us elements of his perspective on the development of doctrine. He recognizes that the theological enterprise has been conducted in identifiable periods which may be characterized by the general view held by men in terms of which other doctrinal and scriptural materials are arranged and interpreted. In this case, the Church fathers are characterized as sharing a view of the death of Christ as part of a transaction with the devil. The problem for Ritschl with this view is revealed in the further development of the ethical and ontological background of the image.

> . . . it is found in carrying out this thought, that the issue of the legal transaction comes into collision with the idea of God's justice which had led to it: for the price paid to the devil as an equivalent for man cannot, from the very nature of the case, remain in his possession. The significance which in this connexion attaches to the resurrection of Christ from the dead is, that thereby the devil lost possession of the compensation which he had received. But while the supposition that the devil had been deceived as to the effects of the legal transaction he had entered into was inevitable, it was impossible to believe with regard to the other party to the transaction—the omniscient God—anything else than that He had intended the deception. But such an intention is inconsistent with the justice of God, which is presupposed, thus the theory is self-contradictory and is therefore untrue.[8]

The criteria of a critically sound Christology which Ritschl applied in setting aside traditional Lutheran and Calvinist dogmatics and in his characterization of patristic thought are: Biblical authenticity, either associated with the words of Jesus or the witness of the New Testament writers; appeal to the experience of contemporary man in regard to the notion of human will; and the logical consistency of a doctrine when its implications are examined.

The Middle Ages and the Work of Christ

Ritschl credits the theologians of the Middle Ages, especially Anselm and Abelard, with uprooting the transaction theory of atonement and lifting the problem of the saving efficacy of the work of Christ to a higher level in which the legal and moral aspects of sin are considered. For Anselm, according to Ritschl, man's sin is an injury done to the honor of God. The death of Christ arises out of the need for satisfaction to be given to God. The devil has no independent right over men, nor any claim against God's justice.[9] In Abelard, Ritschl finds that the work of Christ expressed in terms of his death is seen to be a demonstration of the love of God for men which is directed to awaken a reciprocal love for God by men.[10] In this case the devil never has the elect in his power nor does the devil forfeit rights over mankind by any deception. Ritschl judges this version of the atonement to be more advanced because it begins to recognize that the positive goal is the transformation of men and their reconciliation with God. The earlier theory involving ransom did not suggest any real involvement of men but regarded them as completely passive in the transaction. Ritschl finds in Anselm and Abelard that the relationship between men and God begins to be examined for its own possibilities and the devil is written off as an independent agent.

These medieval formulations do not satisfy Ritschl, however, because he holds them to be essentially negative ideas which depend on another idea, reconciliation, for a positive view of what is really at stake in the image of releasing man from the devil or debt to God. The positive activity of man and God together is the central notion which is presupposed by the atonement theories insofar as they show how Christ's actions protect and restore the possibility of this relationship. This insight gives Ritschl the distinctive viewpoint which he expresses in the title of his work.

Now, in the selection of a title, I am led by this very consideration—that the bearing of Christ's saving work on the mutual relations between the Divine and human *will* must be expressed. For this purpose the notions of justification and reconciliation at once present themselves as specially adapted. For justification removes the guilt and reconciliation the enmity of sin towards God: both notions thus include in themselves an effect upon the human will just as certainly as guilt and enmity towards God can only be understood as belonging to the human will. But now, since these effects must be conceived as proceeding from the Divine will through the instrumentality of the doing and the suffering of Christ, our title does not preclude the view that Christ's work can be regarded as efficacious in the justification and reconciliation of men only in so far as we at the same time recognize a reference of that work to God.[11]

Ritschl objects to the tendency in theology to limit Christ's actions to the propitiation of God, regarding the effect upon men as indirect and secondary. The notion of the merit of Christ involves a movement away from the full reciprocity of human and Divine will. In the work of Anselm and Abelard Ritschl finds the notion of merit which is basic to an understanding of medieval theology. The significance of the notion of satisfaction is that it seeks to express how God relates to men, who are sinners. The notion of merit is related to reconciliation as it seeks to express how Christ's actions affect the relationship between God and man. In the further development of satisfaction and merit in the work of Thomas Aquinas and Duns Scotus, Ritschl is impressed that the *de facto* result of this train of thought is a less clearly defined but widely held view of the Church as being involved in a causal relation which requires a positive response by God to the merit of Christ.

It is certain that theologians, from Augustine onwards, always assume only the causal connexion between grace as justification on the one hand. and merit on the other. Nowhere do we find it stated that justification must be just what it is according to their doctrine, *in order that* merit may be possible. I cannot, however, fully account for the practical interest in that dogma displayed by those of the Roman Catholic confession, except on the understanding that the causal relation which in their doctrine is affirmed to subsist between justification and merit is at the same time a relation of purpose. For it is only the impression (even though it be an unconscious one) of relations of purpose that dominates the feelings as an immediate motive of practical conduct. When, accordingly, in that positive religious interest which invariably controls all negations of opposing theologumena, justification is asserted in the Catholic sense, it is in full belief that merits avail with God.[12]

Ritschl claims that the example of the mendicant orders of monks who lived in a humble imitation of Christ's poverty was transformed by the theology of Scotus and his followers into a prevailing tendency towards meritorious action. As the confidence of the Church in the efficacy of merit weakened, the importance of the subjective awareness of assurance of salvation and of peace of conscience were recovered.

Ritschl portrays the Church as the bearer of the Christian faith in such a way that the continuing history of the Church corrects the distortions of the understanding of God's reconciliation in Christ that may occur in a particular age. His notion of the history of doctrine is developmental. On the one hand, he finds continuing refinement of doctrine in its ability to interpret and express the Christian faith. This is the case with his evaluation of the place of Anselm and Abelard in relation to the earlier fathers, and with post-Kantian thought in relation to earlier metaphysics. But on the other hand, this development can be seen approaching an already given norm. Ritschl finds that Christian doctrine expresses a normative standard which serves to evaluate the validity of particular doctrines or the theology of a particular age, recovering that which Ritschl himself holds to be the true understanding of the work of Christ in justification and reconciliation.[13] By including the notion of the unconscious motive in his account of the Catholic doctrine of merit, he raises the question of the ability of the Church or the individual to control the meaning of the symbols or theology which are employed in expressing religious experience. Ritschl does not explore the destructive implications here but focuses upon the positive effect of the Reformation in recovering what is for him an authentic understanding of justification.

It was understood in the middle ages that faith alone pertains to justification; that justification is bestowed freely by grace; that it does not depend on *merita de congruo* as conditions: it is only the Nominalistic theory which forsakes these positions... And what in fact the Reformers wish to establish is that the regenerate person does not owe his position before God and his assurance of salvation to the good works which he really does perform, but to the grace of God, which to his believing confidence pledges his justification through Christ.[14]

The Reformation, Justification by Faith, and the Work of Christ

By distinguishing the work of Christ as justification and reconciliation from other descriptions of the work of Christ, Ritschl is in a position to present the Reformation as an affirmation of the proper understanding of the work of Christ within the Church and not forced to reject all pre-Reformation Christianity along with the errors of some pre-Reformation doctrine.[15]

In the medieval system of doctrine, the treatment of the satisfaction or merit which Christ gave or acquired towards God on behalf of the human race or the elect was carried out in a purely objective way; the influence of this work upon man was always only alluded to in that connexion, and treated with doctrinal fulness, on the other hand, in an entirely different part of the system, in the doctrine of justification. The Reformers, on the contrary, not only take together the two thoughts in their immediate reciprocal relation to each other, but at the same time fix the chief interest upon the thought of justification, and seemingly assign the doctrine of Christ's satisfaction the position of a subsidiary doctrine, which has the function of explaining the assertion they make, that justification is conditioned exclusively by faith.[16]

Ritschl is searching for a perspective which will acknowledge the distinctions within the experience of the Christian faith in a way which will be instructive to the several parties rather than divisive. The notion of orthodoxy becomes divisive as disagreeing parties seek to excommunicate each other, invalidating each others' insights rather than harmonizing them. Ritschl explains that the Roman Catholic doctrine of justification is intended to demonstrate how and by what means an actually righteous person, who can be judged as such in consistence with truth even by God, is produced out of a sinner. The Reformation sense of justification is that the believer, who through the Holy Spirit produces good works, does not receive his standing before God because of these works as evidence of his own righteousness but rather by the mediatorial and perfectly righteous work of Christ appropriated in faith. Ritschl holds that the continuing animosity of the Catholic and Protestant parties in the Reforma-

21

tion period is dependent upon the defective development that is attributed to doctrine by ignoring the legitimate character of alternative formulations and fixing on a single formulation as the objective standard, namely one's own.

It is from his conception of the basic catholicity of the Reformers and his belief in the inherent logicality of the Christian faith that Ritschl proceeds with his analysis of the accounts of the work of Christ offered by the post-Reformation period. The effect of Enlightenment criticism undermined the viability of the Anselmic understanding of justification and reconciliation as primarily an objective relationship in either Protestant or Roman Catholic formulations. Neither the Bible nor the traditional theological formulas could provide an immediately apprehended worldview which dealt adequately with contemporary experience.

Ritschl and Historical Continuity

The history of theology is not a development *in vacuo* for Ritschl. The historical sequence formed by successive presentations of a doctrine reveals a change or progression in the manner of viewing its content. New influences can be detected and evaluated by comparison with other schools of thought. But this is not a purely logical or philosophical development alone. As a historian Ritschl is alert to the whole complex of social, institutional, and political factors which make up the life of the Church in the world.[17]

It is impossible to understand either the history of man's spiritual life as a whole, or the history of the doctrine of atonement by means of the change of relation between the logical determinations of subject and object. The history of any single Christian doctrine must be based upon the history of Christian theology; but this is influenced in its course just as much by the turns that are taken in the practical development of the Church, as by influences which originate in the development of the general ethical tone of society and in free scientific culture,—particularly in the variety of philosophical systems. Thus one cannot carry through a history of the isolated doctrines of justification and reconciliation, without having a general understanding of the changing conditions of theology at each of several steps in the development.[18]

Ritschl is disappointed by Baur's study *The Christian Doctrine of Reconciliation in Its Historical Development from the Earliest to the Latest Times* (1838) and by Dorner's *History of Protestant Theology* (1857) for their failure to present a sustained and consistent account of the development of Christian thought and their failure to answer what Ritschl felt were the important questions.

It is hard upon my *esprit de corps* as a theologian to be compelled to say that one is left in the lurch by everybody when one tries to ascertain, in a plain and intelligible way, how it is that the Reformation, notwithstanding its antagonism to the medieval Church, is rooted in medieval Christianity; or to find out who was intellectually the author of the theological scholasticism and of the ecclesiastic particularism to which the Reformation so soon fell prey; to discover what were the causes which led to the so-called "Illumination," or why again the magnificent impulse given by Kant spent itself in "Illumination" philosophy and theology; and finally, on what it is that Schleiermacher rests his claim to be leader of the German evangelical theology of this century, which is now being aimlessly frittered away and so threatened with extinction.[19]

These are the concerns that order the balance of Volume One. Ritschl traces the tendency to objectify justification in terms of a legalistic view of works and the recovery of the emphasis on transformation of the subject, which he found in Abelard, through the scholasticism of the post-Reformation period and into the controversy between neo-Lutheran orthodoxy and speculative theology in the nineteenth century. He closes his survey with a report of an emerging consensus in which his contemporary theologians agree but which had not yet been expressed as a logically ordered unity. He finds that reconciliation is deduced from the notion of the love of God and is not to be subordinated to the notion of justice nor to the transformation of God from wrath to grace by Christ's satisfaction; that the whole life and passion of Christ manifest the love of God as the ground of reconciliation; that Christ in *statu exaltationis* was the Head of humanity

23

and of the Church; that the idea of the vocation of Christ explains his suffering and doing and the notion of merit is suppressed; that where penal satisfaction is examined, the reconciliation is viewed as ethical propitiation and not as juridical *quid pro quo* of a legal code. Finally, he calls for the establishment, as a principle, of the identity of reconciliation and justification in the New Testament, thus eliminating the controversy over the priority of justification or regneration.

In these emphases, Ritschl argues that one can see a return to the understanding of justification held by Luther and in harmony with the New Testament writers. This challenges the judgments of Baur and Strauss which pointed toward an inevitable progress of doctrine in the historical process, and it is an example of Ritschl's use of the history of doctrine organized from the perspective of the doctrine of justification and reconciliation as the basis for a normative judgment. The positive development of the themes of this consensus can be detected in Ritschl's own work, and he derives a sense of direction from them, providing the basis for a reconciliation of the views of divergent theological schools upon the common ground of biblical theology and the history of doctrine, critically conceived, from his perspective. Ritschl's concern is to develop a critical approach to the Christian faith which will reveal its status as a positive reality without reducing the Christian faith to a subjective fantasy in the course of acknowledging the participation of the experience of the Christian in his knowledge of the content of faith. At the same time, Ritschl does not want to commit the modern Christian to an outmoded worldview that is indefensible in contemporary philosophy. The positive historical ground upon which doctrine should be based is the biblical witness to the historical Jesus as the bearer of reconciliation.

The Biblical Evidence

In Volume Two Ritschl originally planned to complete his study of justification and reconciliation. As the work developed, the length became unwieldy and he added an additional volume. The character of Ritschl's biblical theology is problematic. He has prepared us to expect the evidence for the verification of his account of the person and life-work of Jesus as founder of the Kingdom of God and the record of the emergence of the Church as a result of the actions of

Jesus of Nazareth. However in dealing with the biblical materials, we are not led to indisputable historical fact but rather to a series of principles which Ritschl uses to organize the biblical material in a way which, for him, reveals its unity. To what extent is Ritschl in fact supplying the structure by means of his interpretative judgments and then claiming that they are authentically and objectively "there" as evidence of God's will having penetrated the nexus of human history? To charge that Ritschl was uncritical in his use of biblical materials is not to ignore that he is aware of distinctions between the printed text, the word of God, and a coherent, factual narrative. Ritschl is attempting a critical approach to the interpretation of Scripture within the Christian tradition. The problem is that "much of his detailed exegesis failed to carry conviction."[20] The principles of interpretation which emerge from the biblical material in Ritschl's view will give us an insight into what he considered as important for historical evidence and for doctrinal development. Ritschl holds that the New Testament is to be interpreted in light of the Old Testament. There is a basic continuity between the redemptive actions of God reported in the Old Testament and the theme of justification and reconciliation in relation to the work of Christ presented in the New Testament. This may be seen in the organization of the topic headings in the chapters of Volume Two.[21] Ritschl does develop a biblical theology but it is controlled by his own doctrinal interest. He examines the New Testament material as the source of authority for the teachings of Jesus and the witness of the early Christian writers to the meaning of Jesus' life and the significance of his death. The Old Testament material is discussed in terms of the distinctive characteristics of the historical narratives, the legal codes, sacrificial law, and the later writings of the poets, psalmists and prophets. The general influence of the Old Testament writers upon the New Testament is acknowledged, but the interest of Ritschl in identification of justification with reconciliation and his aversion to substitutionary atonement theory, which was developed in Volume One, emerge as the presuppositions of his study rather than the conclusion. Volume Two, Chapter One, is directed at a presentation of the life of Jesus as evidence of the seriousness with which he accepted his vocation of founding the Kingdom of God. His death is viewed as a part of his life lived freely, in positive fulfillment of the will of God and not required by the ransom theory view of the atonement.[22] Ritschl finds that the understanding of the worship of God as the active realization of the Kingdom of God, even to the extent of one's own suffering and death, is unique to Jesus (Sections 6 and 7). In order to distinguish this from the Old Testament image of the suffering servant in Isaiah, Ritschl tries to demonstrate the moral incompleteness of the Old Testament formulation by limiting its religious context to the Jewish nation (Section 9). This is in keeping with Ritschl's view of an ethical progression from the nationalistic religion of Israel to the universality of the Christian religion as the highest form of religion. If Ritschl were to be consistent here he would have to dismiss the doctrine of God in the Old Testament as the proclamation of a tribal deity, but he is able to sustain the general continuity of the notion of the will of God for reconciliation while dismembering the notions of Old Testament theology which challenge his formulation of the unique contribution of the self-understanding of Jesus. In order to eliminate the ransom theory of atonement he has to deal with the notion of the wrath of God in such a way as not to require the death of Christ as the placation of the wrath of God. He then moves toward the positive development of an alternative view of the death of Christ (Chapter Three) and how this is related to the individual's religious life (Chapter Four).

One may argue that Ritschl distorts the Old Testament notions of sacrifice, the wrath of God, and the expectation of the day of the Lord which he is forced to deal with in exegesis, discounting their value for interpreting the New Testament and undermining their claims for biblical authority in later doctrinal formulations.[23]

In Ritschl's presentation of biblical theology the person and lifework of Christ are necessary to an over-all understanding of the Bible, the Old Testament as well as the New. Ritschl is on strong historical grounds when he asserts the importance of the Old Testament for understanding the New Testament and he avoids the tendency to a disjunction between Old Testament and New Testament that sometimes accompanies the emphasis on Law versus Gospel in Lutheran theology. But what he avoids in theory, he risks committing in practice when he uses the Old Testament so consistently as a foil for demonstrating the superiority of the revelation of God in Jesus Christ.

The New Testament is the record of the effect of the person and life-work of Christ upon the community which he formed. The details of the life of Christ in the Gospels preserve for Ritschl the events of Jesus' life and the interpretation given the events by the community which responded to them. It is the judgment of the community in response to its founder that the events of the Old Testament are continuous with the revelation of God in the New Testament. Jesus gives to the new community its basis for appreciating its relationship to Israel and to Judaism. Ritschl recognizes that Scripture should be interpreted by theologians in reference to the context of the community which employs the Scripture as the record of its experience. This view of Scripture and tradition is consistent with his view of the character of religious knowledge and affords him a basis for reconciling the traditional antithesis of Catholic and Protestant theology.[24]

> The exposition of Biblical Theology contained in my second volume was undertaken in order to ascertain what idea of the forgiveness of sins, justification and reconciliation—together with their relations—had been called into existence by Jesus as the founder of the Christian Church. . . Now it is not sufficient for my purpose to bring out what Jesus has said about forgiveness of sins attached to his Person and Death. For even if His statements might seem perfectly clear, their significance becomes completely intelligible only when we see how they are reflected in the consciousness of those who believe in Him and how the members of the Christian community trace back their consciousness of pardon to the action and passion of Jesus. . .We should pay no attention to this purpose of Jesus, nor should we seek to discover its value and meaning did we not reckon ourselves part of the religious community which first attested, through the articles of the New Testament, its possession of the forgiveness of sins as effected by Christ.[25]

Ritschl's formulation of the place of Scripture in the Christian faith moves between the use of Scripture as a historical record of the expression of human religious experience in a descriptive sense, and the selective use of Scripture as a normative standard. He distinguishes between various doctrines of sacrifice and atonement found in the biblical material and validates some at the expense of others. Thus the identification of a Scriptural basis for a doctrine is a descriptive historical judgment reporting on what the primitive community believed and a normative value judgment as well. When Ritschl describes the effect of the experience of forgiveness of sins within the Christian community as the basis for serious consideration of the person and work of Christ in the passage quoted above, he is reporting a value judgment relating the experience of the individual to the experience of the community and an interpretation of that experience. On the one hand it appears that the experience precedes the interpretation or evaluation of that experience, while on the other hand the experience itself is a form of judgment. Is Jesus divine because he is valued as a God, or is he valued as God because he is divine? Ritschl's emphasis on the historical Jesus and the role of the individual person in judging the of value of experience suggests that he would grasp the first horn of this dilemma, while his acceptance of the correspondence between the will of God, the will of Christ, and the positive reality of the Christian religion suggests the second.

Ritschl finds that the proclamation of the Kingdom of God as a present reality is the message of Jesus which has been appropriated by the Christian community to distinguish its understanding of the Kingdom of God from the notion of the Kingdom of God in the Old Testament. The Old Testament understanding of the Kingdom of God as Ritschl presents it is a future expectation and not a present historical reality. It describes the religious phenomenon which is present in the New Testament but does so from an imperfect perspective, resulting in a defective formulation. A similar ambiguity applies to the understanding of sacrifice in the Old Testament. For Ritschl, Jesus is the first who really is able fully to express the community-forming action of God in sacrifice. Jesus approaches God and is in fellowship with Him. This immediate fellowship with God is the accomplishment of the work of justification and reconciliation. Separation of men from God is because of men's ignorance of God and consciousness of guilt. Jesus' approach to God is in full knowledge of his response to the will of God. This establishes the relationship whose subjective character is recognized by men as the forgiveness of sins. This interpretation of sacrifice as the occasion of fellowship with God is, in Ritschl's view, the intention of the sacrifices described in the Old Testament but which was obscured by nationalistic views of salvation as political success for the Jewish people. The sacrifices were then falsely understood in the Jewish community, as being related to a process insuring God's favor upon Israel only as a nation and not involving the real presence of God for all men. This puts Ritschl in the position of finding in the Old Testament materials a historical description of sacrifice as a phenomenon and two contradictory views of the significance of the phenomenon. When he distinguished the Christian views on the Kingdom of God and of sacrifice from the Old Testament views, Ritschl obscured the diversity of Jewish thought about the notion of atonement, the notion of the Kingdom of God, and the relation of history to apocalyptic theology, by reducing the Old Testament materials to a single self-contradictory point of view. As Ritschl makes no attempt to describe the origin of the person of Christ in his epistemology or his historical theology, he also avoids in his biblical theology a positive statement of the historical influence of Judaism upon Jesus other than as a defective presupposition. Jesus is the one who fully expresses the will of God, which was reported in the Old Testament and understood by the prophets more clearly than the rest of Israel, but which was not fully realized until Jesus himself.[26]

Ritschl also is forced radically to adjust the interpretation of the New Testament materials to conform with his Christology. In the New Testament two ways of expressing the divinity of Christ are apparent to Ritschl. The majority of the apostles, Ritschl reports, connected the title *Kyrios* with Jesus' Lordship over the world which is realized when he is exalted to the right hand of God as the Christ. Jesus' divinity is demonstrated by his elevation to divine status after his death. The human being Jesus of Nazareth is transformed into a different status after his death, one discontinuous with ordinary human experience. Another approach which Ritschl identifies is that suggested by John 1:14 where the revealing Word which is God becomes a human person in Jesus of Nazareth. This is seen by the disciples to be the manifestation of the son of God because the divine characteristics, grace and truth, which were seen in Jesus' life could only be evidence of his divinity. These two approaches which Ritschl selects as representative of the New Testament treatment of the Godhead of Christ oppose resurrection and incarnation as the distinctive moments in the life of Christ which are the source of his saving power. Ritschl dismissed the crucifixion as the significant moment in his reworking of the doctrine of sacrifice, subordinating the crucifixion to the notion of vocation. If Jesus was not divine until after his death, the heart of the synoptic tradition in the Gospel of Mark is not a historical record of the significant moment in the existence of men or of Christ; if on the other hand, Christ is already divine at birth, he is in Ritschl's phrase *"für uns gar nicht erkennbar."*[27] An interpretative principle is required to reduce the complexity of the biblical conceptions to a unity which does not itself further confuse the interpretation of the phenomenon. Ritschl sees the distinctive character of Jesus' person and life-work to be as founder of the Kingdom of God. This understanding of Christ can, Ritschl feels, collect the diverse witness of Scripture to the divinity of Christ and to the character of his ministry into an intelligible whole for the experience of the Christian community.

. . . every form of influence exerted by Christ must find its criterion in the historical figure presented by His life. Therefore the Godhead or universal lordship of Christ must be apprehended in definite features of His historical life as an attribute of His existence in time. For what Christ is in virtue of His eternal destiny, and what the influence is which He exerts on us because of His exaltation to God would be wholly beyond our ken if we did not also experience the effects of the same in His historical existence in time. Unless the conception of His present lordship receives its content from the definite characteristics of His historical activity, then it is either a meaningless formula or the occasion for all kinds of extravagance. If, on the other hand, we are to hold fast our faith that Christ is at this moment Lord over the community of the Kingdom of God, and is working toward the gradual subjection of the world to its true end, then the lordship over the world must be recognizable as already a conspicuous feature of Christ's historical life.[28]

The biblical witness to the work of Christ in history is the key to the significance of any notion of the pre-existence of Christ or post-resurrection Christology as Ritschl interprets them. He locates himself between a supernaturalism that admits knowledge of the Godhead of Christ apart from his life, and a reductive rationalism which sees that the actions of Jesus' life are empirical facts apart from their meaning for the community which is the source of the witness to their effects. Ritschl affirms the positive historical value of the life of Christ for the Christian community as it is recorded in the Bible and confirmed in the community's own experience of forgiveness but he does acknowledge the need for an interpretative principle. In the notion of the vocation of Jesus as the founder of the Kingdom of God, he believes that he has found it in the Bible.

The Positive Development

We see that in the third volume of *The Christian Doctrine of Justification and Reconciliation* Ritschl has turned from a critical history of Christian thought and the treatment of the Bible as evidence for the historical reality of the Christian faith to develop more clearly his own positive exposition of the Christian faith from the perspective of justification and reconciliation. He outlines his approach as follows:

First, we ascertain what is meant by justification and reconciliation; through what attribute of God we are to conceive justification, in what relation to men and how far extending; finally in what subjective functions this Divinely oriented relationship expresses itself actively. Secondly, we develop the positive and negative presuppositions of the religious truth of justification, the idea of God, the view that is to be taken of human sin, and the religious estimate of the Person and life-work of Christ. Thirdly, we prove why the thought of justification by faith is necessary at all in Christianity, and why justification is dependent on Christ as the Revealer of God and the Representative of the Church. Fourthly, we show, by way of conclusion, why justification manifests itself precisely in those religious functions which come into view and what the relation is between them and moral activity.[29]

In the introduction to Volume Three Ritschl examines the character of systematic theology. He is concerned to present it as the treatment of the correct and complete idea of the Christian faith. Following the direction of Schleiermacher, Ritschl quotes Schleiermacher's definition of the Christian religion:

The Christian religion is that monotheistic form of faith within the teleological (moral) class, in which everything is referred to the redemption wrought by Jesus.[30]

But Ritschl is not satisfied without adding the modification that "if the Divine final end is embodied in the Kingdom of God, it is to be expected that the redemption which has come through Jesus should also be related, as a means, to this final end." His concern is that Schleiermacher seems to present the Christian consciousness of God by reference sometimes to redemption through Jesus and sometimes to the Kingdom of God without expressing an explicit relationship between the notions of the Kingdom of God and the Mediator. In Ritschl's view this allows a vague idea of religion and loses the teleological character of the Christian faith.

In Christianity, the Kingdom of God is represented as the common end of God and the elect community in such a way that it rises above the natural limits of nationality and becomes the moral society of nations. In this respect Christianity shows itself to be the perfect moral religion. Redemption through Christ— an idea which embraces justification and renewal—is also divested of all conditions of a natural or sensuous kind, so as to culminate in the purely spiritual idea of eternal life. . .we have in Christianity a culmination of the monotheistic, spiritual, and teleological religion of the Bible in the idea of the perfected spiritual and moral religion.[31]

Christianity, then, in its correct sense for Ritschl, has two centers of focus, the religious and the ethical. The two characteristics mutually condition each other.

Christ made the universal moral Kingdom of God His end, and thus He came to know and decide for that kind of redemption which he achieved through the maintenance of fidelity in His calling and of His blessed fellowship with God through suffering unto death.[32]

The fault of the Church has often been to emphasize the religious at the expense of the ethical.

In his examination of the basis of the doctrine of justification, Ritschl focuses his attention on the Christian's experience of forgiveness in Christ which is shared in the fellowship of the Kingdom of God. For the individual, awareness of relationship to God comes through the historical revelation of the Person and life-work of Christ. The New Testament materials preserve a record of the revelation. Individuals who have experienced justification as the result of Christ's work are bound together in the Kingdom of God. The Kingdom of God is understood to be the most inclusive description of the moral and spiritual end of the individual and of the world. Ritschl is concerned to avoid a purely individualistic or mystical account of justification. This he considers to be a distortion of the Christian faith associated with pietism. He regards it as a divisive tendency which weakens the Church wherever it appears, in Roman Catholicism, evangelicalism or in Methodism. The experience of forgiveness in Christ which Ritschl holds to be the content of justification is not limited to individual experience. The Church is the community, drawn together by Christ, which surrounds the individual, and is the bearer of the experience of justification.[33] The Church is a specific historical institution and at the same time part of the Kingdom of God. Like Schleiermacher, Ritschl has an appreciation of the different churches which have formed in the course of history around different orders of worship and different legal constitutions in response to the demands of the historical process. The action of God in forgiveness is manifest in history and is to be known through phenomena in the experience of Christians in the life of the Church. All of the churches are part of the Kingdom of God in so far as they realize the love of God. The moral and spiritual perfection of the Church as a whole is realized in terms of the Kingdom of God. The relationship of the Church to the Kingdom of God and to Christ within the experience of the individual is for Ritschl the authentic teaching of the New Testament and the proper understanding of the Christian faith which was recovered in the Reformers' emphasis on the doctrine of justification by faith.

Ritschl's definition of Christianity is directed to admit a concentration on the balance of the ethical and spiritual aspects of faith. Individual piety is channeled toward social fulfillment of the Christian faith in the Kingdom of God by the notion of "the moral organization of mankind." His definition of Christianity keeps the transcendental sense of the traditional piety in the notion of blessedness while offering a more concrete historical ground for spiritual claims in the life-work of Christ.

> Christianity, then, is the monotheistic, completely spiritual and ethical religion, which, based on the life of its Author as Redeemer and as Founder of the Kingdom of God, consists in the freedom of the children of God, involves the impulse to conduct from the motive of love, aims at the moral organization of mankind, and grounds blessedness on the relationship of sonship to God, as well as on the Kingdom of God.[34]

Ritschl continues in his introduction to try to express the relationship between religious knowledge and knowledge of things in general. This is important for him because he is concerned to be scientific and intelligible in his analysis of religious ideas and experience, but he does not want to subscribe to the view that religion demands a particular philosophy or metaphysical view. He is concerned to move from the biblical evidence to the problem of understanding that evidence in a fashion which will clarify and not obscure the transition.

> The ideas of Christ and of the apostles, which we regard offhand as substantially in agreement, often enough employ divergent means of expression, or link themselves to different Old Testament symbols. Now exegesis itself certainly deals with many particular passages in such a way as to reduce the cognate symbolical expressions they contain to one conception of the greatest possible clearness. For in part exegesis must view the particular in the light of its relationship to everything which resembles it, in part it has to fill up the chasm between our way of thinking and the Israelites' symbolical manner of speech, in part its task is to clear away false ideas forced upon certain Biblical symbols by exegetical tradition. Under these circumstances, the exposition of religious ideas furnished by Biblical Theology, which supplies the matter of theological knowledge, itself contains attempts to define these ideas. But it gives no guarantee that they are completely and distinctly defined in organic relation to the whole. Each definition can only be made

complete as it receives its place in a system of theology, for the truth of the particular can be understood only through its connection with the whole. . .The formally correct expression of theological propositions depends on the method we follow in defining the objects of cognition, that is, on the theory of knowledge which we consciously or unconsciously obey.[35]

Christ and Knowing

The problem of epistemology or theory of knowing is crucial for Ritschl's theological enterprise. His emphasis on self-consciousness and the experience of the believer as necessary for a valid theology require him to show how knowledge of God and knowledge of Christ involve the knower. Ritschl does not want to separate knowledge of God from the knowledge of Christ. The doctrine of the person and life-work of Christ poses for Ritschl the same problem of expressing the divine in human terms as does the doctrine of the knowledge of God. In his synopsis of doctrines of the Christian faith, *Unterricht in der christlichen Religion* (1875), Ritschl spends a great part of Section One on the doctrine of the Kingdom of God in discussing the role of Christ as the representative of God to men. The knowledge of God which men have is not based on an abstract *a priori* apprehension of divinity but is based upon an analysis of what God does in Christ for the salvation of mankind. The life of Jesus is the source for the knowledge of God. The effect of Jesus' ministry upon the consciousness of the Christian is complex. It imparts a religious awareness of God as the author of the world and also an ethical awareness of man's role in the attainment of the final goal, the Kingdom of God.

In *Justification and Reconciliation* when he considers Judaism as an example of a religious community, the result of experience of knowledge of God is said to be a political nationalism; when he considers Buddhism as an example of knowledge of God, Ritschl finds simply a cosmology or a view of the world as a whole which cannot be universal, without recognizing Jesus as the Christ, balancing the ethical and religious aspects of faith. Ritschl thus regards non-Christian religious experience as incomplete and of secondary value. What Jesus provides man is experience of reconciliation with God and leadership in the vocation of realizing the kingdon of God as the fulfillment of the will of God.

> Jesus is the bearer of the perfect spiritual religion which consists in mutual fellowship with God, the author of the world and its final goal. In the idea of God as the final goal of all things lies the reason why Jesus recognizes as binding upon himself for God's sake the widest conceivable aim or moral effort, namely, the union of mankind through love; while in the idea of God as author of the world lies the reason why Jesus for his own personal life repudiates every motive that is individual, worldly, and therefore less than Divine. But inasmuch as Jesus desired his own attitude to God to be shared by the rest of mankind, He laid upon his disciples as their aim also, the union of mankind through love, or in other words, the recognition of the Kingdom of God...[36]

Ritschl expresses the relationship of man to Christ and of Christ to God in terms of consciousness of a shared goal, undertaken as a personal vocation. Ritschl holds that this formulation overcomes the tendency to allow sacramentalism or a confessionalism to obscure the ethical and religious character of Christian faith for the individual. Ritschl feels that his formulation guards the place of man in the relationship with God by acknowledging man to be an active participant in a mutual fellowship.

Ritschl's address to the problem of the meaning of Christ and the nature of human knowledge is most self-consciously philosophical in his essay *Theologie und Metaphysik* (1881) and in the introduction to the third edition of *The Christian Doctrine of Justification and Reconciliation*, Volume Three. Here he distinguishes three theories of knowing in his critique of the place of metaphysics in religious thought. These theories represent not only stages in the development of thought but major logical options in contemporary Christian thought as Ritschl sees them. Platonic idealism, the first, claims a knowledge of things in themselves, of essences apart from attributes. Kantian idealism restricts knowledge to the limits of human experience and denies any claim to immediate knowledge of things in themselves. The last, a variation of Kantian thought associated with Lotze, affirms that there is a knowledge of things in themselves available within human experience in their effects.[37]

Ritschl is adapting Kant's account of synthetic *a priori* propositions in order to describe how the Christian is capable of religious knowledge and to explain how religious knowledge is related to scientific knowledge of the objective world. By making a value judgment of the synthetic *a priori* type the knower identifies a cause. The relationship of causality bridges the gap between the knower and his concepts and the objective world of things in themselves which are causes of observable effects. Pfleiderer in *The Development of Theology in Germany Since Kant, and Its Progress in Great Britain Since 1825*, describes the real contribution of Kantian thought as giving the basis for overcoming a dualism of Theoretical Reason, limited to the world of phenomena and the Practical Reason, dealing with the intelligible world.[38] Ritschl further distinguishes between scientific knowledge and religious knowledge by suggesting that scientific knowledge properly consists of specific judgments of fact while religious knowledge deals with a whole worldview. Another distinction which Ritschl offers for religious value judgments is that they deal with the value of the cause for the knower, referring not only to an object of perception but also to the relation of the perceiver to the object. Pfleiderer was not impressed with Ritschl's attempt, based on Lotze's interpretation of Kant, to provide an epistemology of religious knowledge.[39] He charged Ritschl with confusing the views of subjective idealism and common-sense realism in such a fashion as to admit no distinction between phenomena as perceived by us and the being of things in themselves. The analogy between seeing an object and describing the object and perceiving an effect and describing a causal relationship associated with the effect is strained when the object is no longer an apple which may be universalized by Newton as an example of mass but the object of a judgment of faith, i.e., the will of God. Where the rationalist might approve the spirit of the analogy, the empiricist would balk.[40]

Mueller in *An Introduction to the Theology of Albrecht Ritschl* stresses the reductionism dictated by Ritschl's epistemology (p. 169) and the extensive reconstruction in theology occasioned by his empirical and historical concerns, but at the same time holds that the Ritschlian epistemology is not the most significant element in explain-

37

ing Ritschl's theological method. Mueller is closer to expressing Ritschl's own grasp of the immediate presence of Jesus in the biblical testimony of the apostolic community in Mueller's own discussion of Friedrich Traub (p. 152). While Ritschl could initially regard science and religion as different spheres of thought, his description of Christian thought finally makes a bid for universal knowledge. It is not his epistemology but his consciousness of the impact of Christ upon his own experience, and the knowledge of himself as part of the Kingdom of God, that supports his statement. Schäfer follows Hök in his recognition that Ritschl's philosophical work, especially his notion of religion, is a critical and regulative application of a specific insight and not a rounded speculative or constructive metaphysics (p. 167).[41]

From a consideration of causes, Ritschl moves to their evaluation for the knower. Concomitant value judgments support the conclusions of scientific theory and experiment, directed at nature. Independent value judgments express the perception of moral ends and involve the will of the knower in response to the perception. Religious value judgments express the knower's consciousness of God's help in enjoying dominion over the world or a sense of loss at the lack of that sense of freedom. For the Christian, religious knowledge is based upon the acknowledgement of the effect of the vocation of the historical Jesus, reported by the Christian community in the Bible, and confirmed in the experience of the believer.

While Ritschl consciously adopts the Kantian-Lotzean philosophy for himself, he does not hold it to be constitutive of the Christian faith but rather instrumental in understanding faith in the modern period. Ritschl regards the historical truth of the Christian faith to be established independently of a particular metaphysical system. Portrayal of Ritschl as antimetaphysical or as guilty of a naive simplistic reductionism must be qualified by an appreciation of his recognition of the place of metaphysics in religious thought and his attempt to make the metaphysical presuppositions explicit so that they may be properly studied for consistency and accuracy. This is a post-Kantian understanding of metaphysics as dealing with necessary presuppositions of knowing. Ritschl does not reject all metaphysics, but rejects the solutions of past metaphysics which do not provide for him an adequate account of the role of the individual in the process of knowing.[42] God is not known to man without his being known by man. For Ritschl, man knows God only in the person and life-work of Jesus Christ. God and the divinity of Christ are experienced only as they are judged to be the cause of the effects of reconcilia-tion observed in human experience. The identification of a cause and effect relationship is the result of a judgment by the knower, which links the observable effects of his experience to that which he discerns or judges to be the cause. While this procedure allows Ritschl to af-firm the reality of Christ as the effect of God's revelation, he is forced to distinguish between religious knowledge and scientific knowledge, opening the way for criticism of his epistemology as a subjectivism which surrenders any claims to objective verification beyond the limits of the community of believers. Such criticisms challenge whether Ritschl has not surrendered theoretical knowledge of God altogether.

> . . . I speak of Christ at all only insofar as His personal character as the Bearer of the revelation of God comes into ac-count. . . But if Christ by what He has done and suffered for my salvation is my Lord, and if, by trusting for my salvation to the power of what He has done for me, I honour Him as my God, then there is a value judgment of a direct kind. It is not a judgment which belongs to the sphere of disinterested scien-tific knowledge. . . Every cognition of a religious sort is a direct judgment of value.[43]

The ability to form value judgments is evidence for Ritschl of the uniqueness of man in Nature. Man is aware of the impersonal, machine-like character of the world as a physical system, and at the same time is aware of his own participation in the world of self-conscious spirit. The awareness of the individual of his freedom from the world is expressed in terms of value judgments concerning his identity, his past, and his future vocation.

Ritschl is primarily concerned with the ability of the individual will to affirm a common vocation with Jesus, and in turn, with Jesus' achievement of conforming his will to the will of God. Ritschl locates the freedom of the individual firmly in the notion of will and causality without subordinating religious self-consciousness to determinism. The view of man which Ritschl develops is that of a self-conscious mind able to perceive cause-effect relationships in its environment and to select among these relationships in order to direct its own mental and physical activity in accord with some ends rather than others. In the case of the Christian, the awareness of Christ as the bearer of salvation is mediated through the Christian community. The community spans the historical distance from Christ to the individual believer in its literature, its self-conscious identity and its vocation. Jesus is known in the Christian community as its founder, as one who struggles for the union of mankind in love, and as one who repudiates the individual and worldly motives for action. These actions of Christ Ritschl judges to be directed toward the salvation of mankind and indicate for him the reality of God as the author of the world and its final goal.

The Christian community, as it preserves the collective witness of many individuals function as the occasion for each individual to know the effects of Christ upon the community, the effects of God upon Christ, and by this mediate process to know Christ and God. Ritschl relies on the public character of Jesus' earthly ministry as reported in the Gospels as the historical event which prevents Christian theology from being concerned with a wholly subjectivistic experience expressed in a private language. The Christian experience of forgiveness and the positive relationship with God in reconciliation is objectively grounded in the history of the Christian community and in the relationship of the community to Jesus and to His earthly ministry.

> Authentic and complete knowledge of Jesus' religious significance—His significance, that is as founder of a religion—depends, then, on one's reckoning oneself part of the community which He founded...[44]

Christ is finally necessary to knowing the world for Ritschl, for only through Christ is the full knowledge of reality possible. The witness of the Christian community is that the historical Jesus is the Christ of faith. In this relationship the world is truly known and transcended, the self fully realized and completed, and fellowship with God achieved.

> The theological exposition of Christianity, therefore, is complete when it has been demonstrated that the Christian ideal of life, and no other, satisfies the claims of the human spirit to knowledge of things universally.[45]

Ritschl has taken pains to give the appearance of a logical and scientific development to Volume Three. He divides the contents into sections entitled "The Conception of Justification and Its Relations," "The Presuppositions," "The Proofs," and "The Consequences." In the first two sections Ritschl gives his definition of justification as the forgiveness of sins and examines the implications of this definition for the doctrines of God, man, sin and the person and life-work of Christ. Under "The Proofs," Ritschl examines the necessity of the forgiveness of sins or justification in general and the necessity of basing the forgiveness of sins on the work and passion of Christ. The consequences of the doctrine of justification are the religious functions springing out of reconciliation with God. These are religious lordship (dominion) over the world which the Christian exercises with Christ, patience and humility with which the Christian bears with the world, and the realization in moral action of the relationship of sonship to God. However within each section the reader struggles for a clear logical progression of the argument. What emerges is a topical treatment of the Christian faith in regard to important doctrines which either express Ritschl's perspective on the person and life-work of Christ, or which must be reinterpreted from traditional understandings in order to be in accord with Ritschl's view. Consideration of the summary statements which Ritschl supplies at the end of each chapter supplies an additional set of reference points from which to locate the notions which express Ritschl's controlling interests.

In Chapter One Ritschl presents his understanding of the doctrine of justification as the forgiveness of sins. The outstanding characteristics of justification as a religious conception are that the notion, in Ritschl's view, pre-supposes the understanding of a community, and that it expresses a relationship between God, man, and the world. All three elements are required although the Christian tradition has often been guilty of excluding the world in its consideration of the relationship between God and man. Justification is to be understood in the context of the Christian community and the Kingdom of God. The Kingdom of God, viewed as a promise and as a task, implies two different but related meanings for Ritschl.[46] On the one hand, it refers to the highest good which God realizes in man. This is the view from the perspective of the divine mind. Ritschl acknowledges that man enjoys this perspective occasionally for a limited time. On the other hand, the Kingdom of God refers to the common task of men in rendering obedience to the will of God. This dualism of perspective pervades Ritschl's work.[47] To reject the ethical perspective is to deny the community and to relapse into mysticism; to reject the religious perspective is to deny the historical fact of Jesus' ministry as the Christ. Ritschl holds the ethical and religious perspectives to be distinct yet related.[48] His proposal for expressing the relationship between them is the notion of alternation. Subordination of either side fails to do justice to the nature of man or the sovereignty of God. Ritschl approaches the logical problem of how man can transcend the limits of human nature to know God by referring to the knowledge of God through the knowledge of Christ. This means that contemporary knowledge of God is historically dependent on the mind of Christ. This directs the attention backwards, allowing Ritschl to give positive values to both Scripture and tradition as sources of the knowledge of Jesus Christ for the Church. But this is brief respite, for the question of the relationship of the mind of God to the mind of Christ and to the mind of the individual Christian must still be expressed in terms that do not sever the connection between the immediate sense of sin and guilt which man has apart from God and the sense of independence and responsibility for his own actions which man has as an ethical being.

> . . .a closer examination of the conception of justification reveals the fact that this Divine operation does not imply the occurrence of any mechanical process in man. For part of the significance of its relation to faith is, that this self-active faculty in man, without regard to which justification cannot be fully understood, is included under this Divine operation; part, that justification, as calling forth the reaction of faith in man, in this sense is a property of the believer, and continues to be the motive of religious demeanour which it behooves him to adopt. In both relations therefore, the conceptions of the Kingdom of God and justification are homogeneous. This holds true insofar as, for one thing, both notions express operations of Divine grace, and for another, the results of these operations manifest themselves solely in activities which exhibit the form of personal independ-

ence. They offer therefore really no obstacle to their being linked together in a complete view of Christianity. But in Dogmatics
this alternating use of the two principles cannot be avoided.
Dogmatics comprehends all religious processes in man under
the category of Divine grace, that is it looks at them from the
standpoint of God. But it is of course, impossible so thoroughly
to maintain this standpoint in our own experience as thereby
to obtain complete knowledge of the operations of grace. For
the standpoint of our knowledge lies in formal opposition to
God. Only for an instant can we transfer ourselves to the Divine
standpoint. A theology, therefore, which consisted of nothing
but propositions of this stamp could never be understood, and
would be composed of words which really did not express
knowledge on our part. If what is wanted is to write theology
on the plan not merely of a narrative of the great deeds done
by God, but of a system representing the salvation He has
wrought out, then we must exhibit the operations of God—
justification, regeneration, the communication of the Holy
Spirit, the bestowal of blessedness in the *summum bonum*—in
such a way as shall involve an analysis of the corresponding
voluntary activities in which man appropriates the operations
of God.[49]

Ritschl follows this explanation of the twofold viewpoint of theology
with a critique of the antagonism between Roman Catholic and
Evangelical (Protestant) theology in respect to the doctrine of justification. He argues that a semantic confusion has occurred by referring
to the single word *justification* two distinct aspects of the operation
of the grace of God. The resolution of the problem comes, for Ritschl,
in going back to the Bible and recognizing the basic harmony between the actions of God, and the response of men in Christ. Subsequent doctrinal development in terms of legal, political or ethical
models for explaining and illustrating the operation of grace can then
be seen to be a partial exposition of the larger, harmonious relation
ship, although it may appear to involve some contradictory detail.
This is true for the notions of justification, guilt, sin, pardon and
merit. Ritschl presents his own definition of justification as the result
of an examination of the biblical witness to the response to God in

Christ and a critical survey of the subsequent elaboration of the doctrine in the teaching of the Church, especially in the Reformation.

The definition we have reached only claims to be thinkable, and to stand nearer than any other to the view held by the men of the New Testament and the Reformers.
1. Justification or the forgiveness of sins, as the religious expression of that operation of God upon men which is fundamental in Christianity, is the acceptance of sinners into that fellowship with God in which their salvation is to be realized and carried out into eternal life.
2. Justification is conceivable as the removal of guilt and the consciousness of guilt, insofar as in the latter that contradiction to God which is realised in sin and expressed in guilt, works on as mistrust, and brings about moral separation from God.
3. Insofar as justification is viewed as effective, it must be conceived as reconciliation, of such a nature that while memory, indeed, preserves the pain felt at the sin which has been committed yet at the same time the place of mistrust towards God is taken by the positive assent of the will to God and His saving purpose.[50]

In part one of this definition the content of the biblical witness is recalled, that men are restored into fellowship with God. This is for Ritschl a positive historical fact and precedes the logical analysis of the relationship. Part two of the definition demonstrates the subordination of the notion of guilt to the relationship of justification and indicates how this is experienced by men as a real separation from God without admitting that there is a necessary separation which cannot be reconciled. Part three carries the notion to the subjective level of the individual who recognizes in justification his former separation from God and at the same time affirms his reconciliation with God in forgiveness of sins. The two perspectives of grace, Divine action and human cooperation, are then developed in the following chapters leading towards an understanding of the person and lifework of Christ as the occasion of the complete realization of the Divine will and the subjective experience of reconciliation with God. Justification or the reception of sinners as children of God, must be referred to God, according to Ritschl, under the attribute of Father. This is explored in Chapter Two where justification is seen to be positively connected with the historical activity of Christ and is related to the religious community founded by Christ. Individuals attach themselves to this community as they accept justification by faith in the Gospel. Chapter Three affirms that reconciliation must involve active response of the individual believer and cannot be referred to any objective criteria of merit or moral accomplishment. The doctrine of God that is proposed by this relationship is presented in Chapter Four as the revelation received through Christ, that of a loving will which assures to believers spiritual dominion over the world and perfect moral fellowship in the Kingdom of God. Absence of a sense of positive acceptance by God is sin, both as a mode of individual action and as an aspect of the consciousness of the human race. This is regarded from the perspective of God not as opposition to the will of God but as ignorance (Chapter Five). Christ's person and life-work are the occasion for the overcoming of sin and the accomplishment of reconciliation so that men are free and independent in relation to the world and restored to full cooperation with God. In Chapter Six Christ is presented as the royal Prophet, the perfect revelation of God, and as royal Priest, the perfect response of man to God. In virtue of the motive which inspires him, love, and the character of his patience and self estimate, Ritschl holds, Jesus is equivalent to God. The unbroken faithfulness of Christ to his vocation exhibits the relation to the Son of God to the Father. This is the source of the value of his priesthood.

Christ's Person and Life-work

In Ritschl's treatment of the person and life-work of Christ the value judgments which he makes about the essence of Christianity and the uniqueness of Jesus emerge most clearly. In this section we want to present Ritschl's criticism of traditional Christology and his modification of the *munus triplex* as he reworks it in line with his own historical and critical perspective. His distinctive positions in epistemology, that things are known in their effects, and in biblical theology, that the New Testament is the record of Jesus' life as the founder of the Kingdom of God, are reflected in his evaluation of the importance of the *munus triplex* in the history of theology and indicate the direction of his constructive suggestions for its improvement.

Ritschl opens this portion of his account of the person and life-work of Christ with the judgment that traditional Christology has compromised the notion of the Divine nature of Christ by affirming it formally as part of the Chalcedonian creed and as the symbol of Christian orthodoxy, but, in fact, using the doctrine of the Divine nature to discuss the human activity of Christ. Ritschl holds that the notion of the Divinity of Christ is unintelligible of itself and has served to obscure the real sequence of experience, judgment, and understanding which is entailed in the Christian faith.

> In the Greek theology, the incarnation of the Divine Word is the complete and saving revelation of the Godhead of Christ; the teaching of the God-man, and His yielding up of His human life to the death to annul the law of death, are but subordinate proofs of His Godhead for subordinate ends. In the Latin Church, the Godhead of Christ under the form of incarnation is no doubt recognized but His mediatorial and saving work— the satisfaction rendered and the merit acquired to procure for men the forgiveness of sins—is exhibited only in His human activity as such; the Godhead in Aquinas comes into account merely as constituting the essential worth for the expiation of sin of Christ's merit and satisfaction; in Duns Scotus it is not regarded at all. Luther's statements in the Catechisms amount to this, that while the Church formula is retained, it really is in Christ's human achievements that His God-head becomes for His people manifest, conspicuous, intelligible, winning our faith, not in the form of assent to an unintelligible dogma, but of personal trust for our own salvation.[51]

Following Luther, Ritschl rejects knowledge of God apart from God's relationship to man in Christ. The notion of the Godhead of Christ is relocated. Ritschl is collapsing a distinction between the person of Christ, traditionally expounded in terms of the two natures, and the work of Christ, which deals with the actions of Christ in respect to their value as the basis of salvation. For Ritschl as for Luther such a distinction no longer holds as intelligible. The metaphysical structure related to the doctrine of the two natures is not verifiable in human

46

experience. Confession of belief in the Divinity of Christ becomes on Ritschl's view not intellectual assent to, or comprehension of, a formula that is unintelligible, but rather a value judgment expressing the importance of Jesus Christ for the believer as the source of his salvation.

We must first be able to prove the Godhead that is revealed before we take account of the Godhead that is eternal. My opponents, however, being bent on getting first an acknowledgement of the latter, imagine that they can establish the Godhead of Christ upon the basis of a scientific idea, that is through an act of disinterested cognition, previous to all possible experience, and apart from all religious experience of the matter. And as representatives of a scientific conception of the Godhead of Christ they pursue an impracticable method, inasmuch as their conception of the Word of God, eternally begotten by God before the world, rests only on tradition, detached from all the circumstances of its origin. Accordingly, they would have us make confession of the Godhead of Christ in this particular formula, before even His God-head has been proved to us in His saving influence upon ourselves, aye even although the said influence cannot possibly prove His Godhead in the aspects of it here concerned. These teachers must first of all be good enough to tell us what Christ's Godhead in its eternal essence is—what it is in its eternal relation to God; then it will be time enough to discuss whether and in what way this attribute is for us savingly effective and actually revealed. The method of cognition herein applied is false, and Luther's warning against teachers who would determine the things of God *a priori,* from above downwards, previous to all definite Divine revelation, holds good for this problem also.[52]

This *caveat* closes the first section on the person and life-work of Christ. It serves to undercut the validity of much of the history of theology as the positive exposition of creeds and confessions, and it provides a conditional transformation of such traditional language from descriptive and expository language to expressive language, revealing the mind of the speaker as much as objectively representing a state of affairs. Further interpretation of the meaning of Christ will have to deal with the nature and authority of the historical witness to the life of Jesus and its effect upon the early Christians. Ritschl's own view of the essential work of Christ as communicating a distinctive point of view which characterizes the Christian community is expressed. The person of Christ described here is not eternal or transcendent, but one who speaks in space and time to his human hearers. He represents not a different form of being but a different quality of action.

> For beyond all doubt Jesus was conscious of a new and hitherto unknown relationship to God, and said so to His disciples; and His aim was to bring His disciples into the same attitude toward the world as His own, and to the same estimate of themselves, that under these conditions He might enlist them in the worldwide mission of the Kingdom of God, which He knew to be not only His own business but theirs.[53]

The value of Christ for the believer becomes the real content of the affirmation of divinity. Ritschl affirms this not only for himself, but regards it as the vital core of Christian tradition, recovered by Luther and drawn from the writers of the New Testament.[54]

> Thus what in the historically complete figure of Christ we recognize to be the real worth of His existence, gains for ourselves, through the uniqueness of the phenomenon and its normative bearing upon our own religious and ethical destiny, the worth of an abiding rule, since we at the same time discover that only through the impulse and direction we receive from Him, is it possible for us to enter into His relation to God and to the world.[55]

This leads Ritschl to a position where his epistemology and his Christology condition the rest of his theology. The subjective side of his theology is strongest here where his experience of salvation in Christ becomes the standard for his doctrine of God.

> But if Christ by what He has done and suffered for my salvation is my Lord, and if, by trusting for my salvation to the power of what He has done for me, I honour Him as my God, then that is a value judgment of a direct kind... Every cognition of

a religious sort is a direct judgment of value. The nature of God and the Divine we can only know in its essence by determining its value for our salvation.[56]

Ritschl's next step in developing the meaning of the person and life-work of Christ is to scrutinize the character of the biblical material as a source for the doctrine of the Godhead of Christ. He finds that it is a false assumption that a uniform doctrine of the Godhead of Christ can be exegetically constructed from the New Testament. In the first place, Ritschl asserts, the content of the New Testament books is not doctrine at all. He is arguing from a view of the development of the New Testament which regards the writings of the early Christians as preserving no single doctrinal system although he himself claimed that the notion of justification as forgiveness of sins can be clearly identified.[57] As we have seen, he found evidence of two notions of the God-head of Christ. The Pauline approach depends on the identification of Jesus as *Kyrios*, involving lordship over the world which Christ received by exaltation to the right hand of God (I Peter 3:22; James 2:1; Philippians 2:9-11 and Hebrews 1:3).[58] The Johannine conception depended on the moral impression made upon the community of disciples who recognized in Christ the manifestation of the Son of God. Both conceptions are found in the New Testament and are required in order to appreciate the effect of Jesus' person and life-work upon the early Church. The appearance of these different notions in the New Testament is evidence of their authority for the Christian faith, and subsequent theology must preserve their distinctions, recognizing them as constitutive parts of the evidence of the effect of Jesus. However, the fact that their development is different indicates that the use of biblical materials requires a critical appreciation of their autonomy and complexity. Ritschl supplies us with an example of how he controls his interpretation of the Gospel according to John by specifying the intention of the author. The specific textual and critical problems in Johannine interpretation are set aside in Ritschl's pronouncement about the basis of the Gospel and his understanding of it.

At this point it must be laid down clearly that the attribute of Godhead thus ascribed to Christ is based on the personal experience of His disciples. Apart from that relation it is inconceivable. This, and no other ground, is that on which John ranges the figure of Christ under the wider conception of the revealing Word—a conception which he applies to the creation of the world, etc., and for which he claims the predicate God.[59]

Ritschl places this qualification directly on John 1:14 which he uses to illustrate his case. He makes no acknowledgement of the critical problems of the prologue but is sure that he has grasped the essential meaning of the passage as intended by the author. The exegetical tradition of referring the passage to the notion of the pre-existence of Christ rather than the character of the apostolic witness is suppressed. Ritschl is just as direct about being able to supply the intention of the words of Jesus although he will not regard them directly as the source of doctrine.[60] But the historical Jesus is the cause from which Ritschl traces the effects of Christ in time. The distance between Ritschl and the historical evidence of the New Testament writers is eclipsed.

If the Godhead of Christ, or His lordship over the world in His present state of exaltation, is to be a postulate of the Christian faith, an integral part of the Christian view of the world, then it must be demonstrated to us in Christ's influence upon ourselves. But every form of influence exerted by Christ must find its criterion in the historical figure presented by His life. Therefore the Godhead or universal lordship of Christ must be apprehended in definite features of His existence in time. For what Christ is in virtue of His eternal destiny, and what the influence is which He exerts on us because of His exaltation to God, would be wholly beyond our ken if we did not also experience the effects of the same in His historical existence in time. Unless the conception of His present lordship receives its content from the definite characteristics of His historical activity, then it is either a meaningless formula or the occasion for all kinds of extravagance. If, on the other hand, we are to hold fast our faith that Christ is at this moment Lord over the community of the Kingdom of God, and is working toward the gradual subjection of the world to this true end, then lordship over the world must be recognizable as already a conspicuous feature of Christ's historical life.[61]

Ritschl moves from "Christ's influence upon ourselves" directly to "the historical figure presented by His life" and "His existence in time." This bridges over the critical problems on the diversity of points of view on the value of historical information in the gospels and in other early Christian literature, the diversity of individual points of view on a shared phenomenon as a problem in the psychology of perception, and diversity of opinion in the philosophy of history concerning the access enjoyed by the human mind to preceding historical periods. While he has incorporated a great deal of material from the history of theology, he has been quite ruthless about his view of the actual significance of the history of dogma being essentially unintelligible apart from recording the expression of trust of various Christian writers in Jesus as Lord no matter what epistemology or metaphysics they expouse. Ritschl does not let conflicting critical problems paralyze his own constructive attempt to present his view of a Christian personal identity, world view and representation of the reality and historical character of the person of Jesus as the Christ, revealer of the will of God. Ritschl sets aside both Lutheran and Calvinist doctrine in their post-Reformation forms as wrongly based on the nature of God, as the starting point for theology. What Ritschl does offer is an account which presupposes a positive, intelligible, and coherent personal identity, world view, and Christology for the Christian thinker. Ritschl expects in principle a convergence of biblical theology, Church history, and philosophical theology in mutual confirmation of the Christian faith as the consummation of human history. The power of such a vision in a period which saw an analytical and critical wasteland of historical relativity, where doctrines of revelation, biblical infallibility, and the final reality of the supernatural God once offered an apparently secure world view and promise of individual immortality, should not be underestimated. Images of Marxian economic determinism and of rigid Christian supernaturalism both failed to offer an expression of the place of the free individual in the emergence of new patterns of world organization or a new sense of personal identity. Ritschl's vision of the person of Christ as the founder of the Kingdom of God as a historical reality offered a personal identity, world view and a sense of participation in the cosmic process. We can appreciate an inclusive hermeneutical ideal even if Ritschl's over-ready resolution of historical and critical problems is rejected.

The heart of the problem for Ritschl is to make available to everyone the unique relationship which he perceived between God and Jesus Christ. The picture of Jesus which Ritschl offers bears the characteristics of Ritschl's own reconstruction of Christian doctrine from the perspective of the notion of justification as reconciliation.

Jesus is the bearer of the perfect spiritual religion, which consists in mutual fellowship with God, the Author of the world and its final goal. In the idea of God as the final goal of all things lies the reason why Jesus recognizes as binding upon Himself for God's sake the widest conceivable aim of moral effort, namely, the union of mankind through love; while in the idea of God as the Author of the world lies the reason why Jesus for His own personal life repudiates every motive that is individual, worldly, and therefore less than Divine. But inasmuch as Jesus desired His own attitude to God to be shared by the rest of mankind, He laid upon His disciples, as their own aim also, the union of mankind through love, or, in other words, the realization of the Kingdom of God; and through His own personal freedom in relation to the world, He led His disciples, in accepting their view of the world from Him, to the assured conviction that human life is of more worth than all the world. By making the aim of His own life the aim of mankind, who are to be called into the fellowship of the community, He is before all else the Founder of a religion and the Redeemer of men from the dominion of the world.[62]

The way in which Jesus reveals his relationship with God is by expressing a relationship between persons which deals with motives (*Bestimmungsgründe*), goals (*Endzweck*), aims (*sittliche Aufgabe*) and attitudes. These ideas or values are in turn associated with a personal identity relating motivation and action. The ideas of God as Author of the world and of God as the final goal of the world come to the individual Christian through the activities of Jesus, as the source of the ideas and their exemplification. Ritschl does not speculate on how the motives or ideas of God reach the mind of Christ; he claims rather to know Christ as Lord and holds that knowledge of God and of the world are parts of the knowledge of Christ. This position shifts from a philosophical idealism, in which ideas are prior to material reality, to a view which may be described as ethical pragmatism in which the character of the relationship between the believer and Christ, and *mutatis mutandis*, Christ and God, replaces a consistent ontology. Ritschl stops short of a total rejection of supernatural ontology by adopting an agnostic position in respect to what is historically or ontologically prior to Christ. His elusive notion of the alternation of divine and human perspective allows him to suggest both, without finally establishing the character of the relationship between the two, or the ontological basis from which he is able to observe such a dualism. What harmonization he is able to provide is in terms of the Kingdom of God as the common goal of the religious and ethical spheres. If we have learned from Ritschl to be critical of the ability of an institution, a book, or a metaphysical system adequately to express the relation of God to man, we are well advised to be critical in turn of accepting a view of Christianity as a collection of inspired metaphors.

At this point Ritschl moves to a consideration of the problem of Christ's divinity based upon an analysis of what Christ has done for the salvation of mankind. This approach meets his epistemological requirements. The way in which this had been done in Protestant thought before Ritschl was by means of the doctrine of the work of Christ. In Lutheran and Calvinist dogmatics this meant consideration of the *munus triplex*. Ritschl recognizes that the intention of identifying Christ as Prophet, Priest and King was to present the actions of Christ as they are described in the New Testament as directed to the salvation of mankind. Ritschl believes that this doctrine as developed by most theologians has failed to preserve the unity of the historical life of Jesus. *Munus triplex*, as usually interpreted, separates Christ's life before the resurrection, termed *in statu exinanitionis*, from the resurrection and post-resurrection witness of the New Testament to Jesus as the risen Lord, *in statu exaltationis*. Such a separation violates Ritschl's epistemological concern to ground knowledge of Christ in the earthly ministry of Jesus. As we have seen, Ritschl wanted to refer all significance of Christ to the events of the earthly ministry of Jesus as reflected in the New Testament.

Following the work of Krauss and Ernesti in tracing the history of the doctrine, Ritschl identifies the titles Prophet, Priest and King as Old Testament types which were first employed collectively by

Eusebius of Caesarea in the interpretation of the person of Jesus Christ.[63] It is Ritschl's judgment that the importance of the threefold office for describing the work of Christ was established in theology only at the time of the Reformation.[64] Acknowledging Calvin's dependence on the tract *De libertate christiana* (1520) by Luther for an initial description of the Reformation view of the work of Christ, Ritschl cites Calvin as providing the fullest exposition of the doctrine in Reformation theology in the *Institutes of the Christian Religion* (1559) and in the *Geneva Catechism* (1545). In assessing the practical worth of the doctrine *munus triplex*, Ritschl affirms that "the recognition of Jesus as the Christ has for us no meaning unless through Him we know ourselves raised to kingship or dominion over the world, and to priesthood or undisturbed communion with God."[65] For Ritschl, kingship and dominion are realized in terms of the freedom of the individual to act without restriction by any bonds of nation, religion, family, or selfish motive restricting his motives for action. This is his analysis of the freedom and authority of Christ and is the model which is communicated by Christ to the Christian as the pattern for his own actions.[66] Ethical concern for the freedom of the individual Christian as one who is responsible for his own actions informs Ritschl's thought. The effect of the freedom of Christ is to produce a freedom of action in the lives of his followers.

If, in accordance with this view, the aim of Christ's activity as King and Priest is to secure for us freedom with regard to the world and with regard to sin, and freedom in our intercourse with God, then surely I am in line with the real trend of the Reformation when I bring the specific significance of the Person of Christ for the Christian view of the world into relation with the attainment of our own personal independence over against the world.[67]

Ritschl sees the effect of the freedom of Christ upon the individual as being that of giving the individual freedom to pick the motive for his actions or the ultimate goal in terms of which his actions are directed. When Ritschl considers the real effect of Christian actions in history, apart from the action of Christ in the foundation of the Church, the problem is filled with "miry abominations and miserable trivialities." No procedure for evaluating practical courses of action in political and economic terms for social action can be offered. Ritschl criticizes Calvin for losing the practical significance of the offices of Christ for the believers. In Ritschl's view, Calvin also separates the kingship of Christ from the other offices by interpreting it in terms of the *status exaltationis* and destroying the integrity of the doctrine by weakening the continuity of the person and life-work of Christ and history. Any attempt to strengthen the doctrine by suggesting that the divine and human attributes of Christ may be exchanged by virtue of Christ's *status exaltationis*, as suggested by Gottfried Thomasius in his treatment of the kenotic theory of Christology, is ruled out as being an example of the kind of meaningless formula and extravagance that has no epistemological justification.[68]

The doctrine of the threefold office is challenged by Ritschl as being defective from a systematic point of view. He finds that the doctrine is unstable. In practice it allows the kingship of Christ to subordinate the offices of Priest and Prophet, and the result is a collapse of the distinctions of the individual offices which threatens the claim of the doctrine to distinguish essential attributes of Christ.[69] Any attributes that are grounded in the authority of Christ's kingship, beyond the limits of the experience of the individual Christian to know Christ as King, are meaningless for Ritschl, because of his application of the epistemological principle.

From a historical point of view Ritschl finds that the doctrine is not an accurate arrangement of the material dealing with the life of Christ in the New Testament. He finds that the threefold office does not leave room for the distinction which Jesus was forced to make between his identification as a prophet by the people and his own perception of his vocation and identity as the Son of God and founder of the Kingdom.[70]

After examining the history of the doctrine, its systematic integrity, and its basis in Scripture, Ritschl makes suggestions for the positive reworking of the doctrine of the work of Christ in relation to the traditional offices but conceived in a new form. Rather than reject *munus triplex* entirely, Ritschl restructures the doctrine in line with his epistemology. In Volume One, Ritschl had followed Schleiermacher in reservations against the use of *metaphorical expressions* in systematic theology and lodged the complaint that

55

. . . neither our Lord Himself nor any one of the New Testament writers has made use of the three offices as the comprehensive and only forms for expressing the saving operations of Christ, and that this was not introduced into systematic theology until the Reformation period.[71]

But at the same time Ritschl concedes that there is a basis for application of these titles to Christ in the Bible. In regard to the Old Testament the conceptions of sacrifice and priesthood are important preparation for viewing the death and resurrection of Christ. In the New Testament the Old Testament offices are part of the background against which the Christian messiah reveals his own explicit nature as distinct from Jewish messianic thought.

Besides, in the New Testament these official titles are in part superceded in their application to Christ by designations which are peculiar to it; or where they are used, occur only in a metaphorical sense in such a way that the idea contained in them can also be conveyed independently of them. The character of Prophet, although Christ Himself lays claim to it, is surpassed by his designation as Son of Man and Son of God. His Kingship pertains to a sphere entirely different from that which is assigned to the expected Son of David. His Priesthood, corresponding to His sacrificial character, has, when viewed more closely, more of dissimilarity than of resemblance to the type. And, therefore, although our solution of problems in biblical theology will be dependent on our consideration of these typical notions, the framing of our leading conceptions in systematic theology cannot be regulated by such regards. These conceptions must proceed throughout upon specifically New Testament views and not upon those which, being used in a (topical) sense, are easily seen to be merely subsidiary representations so far as the New Testament sphere of thought is concerned. If the old school, in its mechanical use of Bible authority for its theological system, has disregarded this distinction in the construction of New Testament thoughts, it has set us no example that we should imitate. Rather, inasmuch as even the old school has in a majority of instances fashioned its dogmatic heads of doctrine in accordance with the fully developed ideas of the New Testament, the introduction of the three offices of Christ as a head produces, even in the old theology, an inharmonious and strange impression which ought to serve as a warning against the continued use of such titles.[72]

Ritschl makes an application of the notion of biblical authority in this instance, grudgingly acknowledging biblical authority for dealing with the *munus triplex* while denying its essential validity for systematic theology and yet at the same time insisting that systematic conceptions must be drawn from biblical sources. We have already seen that Ritschl must supply his own organizing principles to the biblical material so that the systematic and biblical formulations are indeed related. When Ritschl asks what can be properly said about Jesus' person on the basis of what, according to the historical evidence, he actually accomplished, Ritschl is able to employ the language of the *munus triplex* in a modified form. He considers the office of King to be apprehended in the priestly and prophetic activities of Jesus' life as one who founds and maintains a community of believers. It is an epistemological consideration and not an exegetical one which influences his justification of this arrangement of the doctrine. In Volume Three he writes:

The traditional scheme of the three offices is only a first step towards grasping the significance of Christ for the community which believes on Him. It is a mere attempt to reach as complete a mastery as possible of the material at our disposal. But since it offers only distinctions and contrasts without reducing these to an ultimate unity, it is far from being an exhaustive treatment of the subject which as such, is neither twofold nor threefold but one. I have endeavored to approach the truth by reducing the data to their inherent unity. From this point of view it is necessary first of all, that Christ's activity *in statu exaltationis* be conceived as the expression of the abiding influence of His historical manifestation. Further, His deeds and words must be regarded as the one common material of His prophetic and priestly activities, and His kingly office must be included in these as a modification of the same; or more correctly, His kingship must be shown to consist [be displayed] in these very same priestly and prophetic activities insofar as both are inspired by His purpose to found and maintain a community of believers.[73]

In Volume Three, then, the schema is not rejected but regarded as a first step which tries to deal with the diversity of the material in the New Testament witness. Ritschl makes a distinction between the form of the material which can be separated from the content but in "reducing the data to their inherent unity," he still employs prophet, priest and king in the new arrangement which he argues is faithful to the historical manifestation. The purpose, "to found and maintain a community of believers," is conceived by Ritschl as the key to understanding the person and life-work of Christ. Ritschl can unify the different events in the biblical account of the life of Christ by considering them from the perspective of their contribution to the foundation of the Kingdom of Heaven. Founding a community of persons with a common motive for action provided Ritschl with a description of a positive historical activity which can be brought under the notion of Christ's kingship, yet replaces the notion of Christ as an ahistorical, other-worldly king. This served to link the world of the contemporary Christian, experienced as a physical system, interpreted by scientific and empirical descriptions of time and place, with the Kingdom of God seen as the fact and promise of religious experience. It provides a relationship to God expressed in terms of a motive for action and a goal which can serve as a common description of the goal of God's action, as the definition of the work of Christ and as a purpose for the life of the individual Christian.

The ethical and religious character of life is expressed for Ritschl by the description of Jesus as royal prophet and royal priest. As royal prophet Jesus is the one who expresses the revelation of *God to man* as His presence with man through the acknowledgment of a common vocation. As royal priest, Jesus is the one who realizes the response of *man to God* by being a man in fellowship with God. Both aspects are required to express the character of salvation. This follows Ritschl's understanding of salvation as a relationship involving both God's action and man's response toward God. For the Christian this is experienced in the realization that Christ's vocation is one's own and that this involves a positive orientation toward the world as the object of a personal mission. It is realization that one is part of the

Kingdom of God that unites God and man. The work of Christ is, according to Ritschl, to establish the relationship of common vocation with God first of all for himself, in the words and deeds of his own life, in the patience and resolve with which he meets death without surrendering his vocation. Ritschl saw that the acceptance of death by Jesus had the value of the affirmation of life, and similarly, acceptance of the vocation of God (uniting all mankind in love) has the value of the presence of God in one's self. The characteristics of the life of Christ which communicate to others his unique relationship to God and generate awareness of reconciliation within the experience of the Christian community are patience, humility, and prayer. In these virtues the unity of mankind in love is realized and man's freedom and authority over the world is exercised. In the Christian community Ritschl finds the communion of God and men understood and experienced as the highest reality.

Ritschl's Understanding of the Kingship of Christ

Ritschl sets aside the demonstrations of the kingship of Christ which argue from the exegesis of the title *messiah* (or *anointed*) or from the external success of Christ's dominion over the world, seen as the pagan empire in either Roman Catholic or Puritan terms. The first he terms a mechanical application of biblical authority, and the latter he finds must await the end of history for confirmation. While Ritschl is prepared to admit a realized eschatology from the ethical perspective in respect to sharing the will of God and His final goal in the Kingdom of God, he rejects the possibility of knowing Jesus to be victorious over history until history shall have run its course. Ritschl refers to Luther and to the New Testament to support his assertion of Kingship as the primary office of Christ.

This corresponds also to the acknowledged historical facts. For when Jesus, who appeared with the marks of a prophet only, and was so regarded, sought recognition from His disciples as the anointed King, He ranged the material of His prophetic activity under a conception which must itself have had no relation to it. Hence it is a purely arbitrary analysis of the word "Christ" when theologians find expressed in it both the prophetic and the kingly office. . .Thus the analysis of the title Christ

59

which led to the scheme of the three offices is as amply refuted in argument as it lacks justification in history. For Jesus is called the Anointed solely to denote His sovereign dignity. If He is also called Prophet and Priest, it is clear that His prophetic activities afford the material for the exercise of His kingship, and, in view of the present discussion, we may surmise that His priestly activity, in freely surrendering His life, must be regarded also as a particular manifestation of His kingship, conditioned by the special circumstances of the case.[74]

It is the kingship of Christ which is the relevant identity in terms of which to express the divinity of Christ and to acknowledge the effect of His person upon believing Christians. Ritschl does not attempt to relate kingship to Jewish messianic or apocalyptic theology in the first century or to set the references to Jesus in respect to prophecy in a critical framework, but connects them directly with the real intention of the mind of Christ.

While, therefore, in our effort to grasp the significance of Christ's life, we are at liberty to follow the lines of the scheme now before us, yet this much we must regard as proved, that Christ's exercise of His Kingship, which for Himself is the chief thing, seeing He wishes to be recognized as the Christ, will find expression both in His prophetic and His priestly service. And since the kingly activity of Christ pertains to the founding and upholding of the religious community of Christ, therefore in the *statu exinanitionis* it is represented by the purpose of Christ to accomplish this end, which pervades His two other activities, and is never out of their view. On the other hand, the priestly and the prophetic offices refuse to be merged in each other, for the former moves in the direction from man to God, and the latter in exactly the opposite direction, from God to man.[75]

The concern to ground the kingship of Christ *in statu exinanitionis* is clearly a feature of Ritschl's historical interpretation of the work of Christ and not characteristic of the New Testament. Ritschl is in a difficult position: he is maintaining the priority of the office of the kingship of Christ for expressing the divinity of Christ, a view that places him with the supporters of the supernaturalist orthodoxy in asserting the kingship of Christ over against Socinian and rationalist attempts to emphasize the prophetic office, while supplying his own historicistic view of the kingship as based on the same teaching and actions as the prophetic office claims for its reference. The difficulty is compounded by the fact that no consistent view emerges from the biblical material itself. The resolution which Ritschl finds is to indicate that the content of the kingship of Christ is "his purpose to found and maintain a community of believers."

From this point of view it is necessary, first of all, that Christ's activity in *statu exaltationis* be conceived as the expression of the abiding influence of His historical manifestation. Further, His deeds and words must be regarded as the one common material of His prophetic and priestly activities, and His kingly office must be included in these as a specific modification of the same; or, more correctly, His kingship must be shown to consist in these very same priestly and prophetic activities insofar as both are inspired by His purpose to found and maintain a community of believers. Only the prophetic and priestly activities refuse to coalesce, because in the relation between God and man they run in exactly opposite directions. And yet, just because of this twofold relation, they form the unity of the *opus mediatorium*. It will be our business, by means of further elucidations, partly to substantiate, partly to complete, this unity of the prophetic and priestly functions in Christ. This, however, we can only do by analysing the purpose which may be seen to pervade Christ's life as a whole.[76]

The historical material of the New Testament concerning the life of Jesus has been brought together in Ritschl's mind to serve as a common witness to Christ as royal Prophet and Priest. The interpretative principle is the notion of the will of Christ in history to be the founder of a community and the revealer of God. The diversity of the biblical material is transcended by this "unifying purpose." It is this that distinguishes Jesus from phenomena of nature, national heroes or the Old Testament prophets as the symbol and source for the power and authority of God. It is the historical reality of this purpose of Christ being the equivalent of the will of God that is expressed for Ritschl in the witness of the New Testament to Christ, and which keeps him from idolatry in his affirmation that he regards as God the one who has the value of God for him.

. . . the religious value attached to the prophets and their words both by themselves and their countrymen is this, that they are accounted the instruments or organs of the self-revelation of God. In no way different is the estimate put by Jesus upon Himself, save only that the essential and ultimate Divine purpose, which Jesus is conscious not only of explaining in word but of realising in deed, involves His placing His own independent personality in a still closer relation to God His Father. His estimate of Himself betrays, it is true, a sort of sliding scale in the way He describes His own relation to God, not only in John, but also in the other Gospels; yet amid this variety of presentation, describing Himself at one time as a mere ambassador who has seen and heard God and executes His commands, and at another time as the Son of God who pursues God's work and in His own person exercises God's lordship over men for the ends of the Kingdom of God, Jesus attributes to His own life as a whole, in the unity which for His own consciousness it possesses, the worth of being the instrument of *the complete self-revelation of God*.[77]

Ritschl's Understanding of Christ as Prophet

Ritschl examines the offices of Christ from both religious and ethical perspectives. The religious perspective focuses on the convergence of the offices as Christ is seen to be the Son of God, establishing the kingdom. The diversity of the offices which is emphasized in different gospels and in association with different sayings of Jesus is unified in the common purpose of Christ and God. Yet in adopting this viewpoint, Ritschl still struggles with the integrity of Christ's own personality over against God and his freedom of choice as an individual in the presence of God. He recognizes this in his admission that there is, unity of purpose notwithstanding, a refusal to coalesce or merge in the priestly and prophetic offices.[78] The distinctive content which Ritschl supplies for these offices is that they express relationships of God to man (prophetic) and man to God (priestly). The ethical perspective serves Ritschl as the occasion for making a distinction between the notions of Divine and human personality and preserving the distinctions of the separate offices.

For the vocation of the kingly Prophet, to realise God's ethical lordship, is the highest of all conceivable vocations; it aims directly at the ethical as a whole; and if this aim was to be pursued as the special business of life, and firmly fixed before the mind of Him who pursued it, it had to be separated from all subordinate aims, which otherwise are meant to find a place within the whole. To fix His vocation as Christ firmly before Him, Christ had to forego all those natural conditions in the stability of which other vocations find a guarantee of their own stability—a fixed dwelling and means of support, attachment to a family, the confidence of fellow-citizens. He depended only upon the personal devotion of friends and followers and built up about Him the circle of His twelve disciples in the view that His vocation demanded the formation of a separate religious community.[79]

Ritschl's exposition of Christ as Prophet, who followed an ethical vocation, began as a statement of the unique character of Christ's vocation as distinct from the vocation of other men. The emphasis upon the work of Christ as the revelation of God and the ethical view of Christ as an independent person merge into the religious view of Christ as the obedient Son of God, the sole effective agent in the religious view of history as the working out of God's plan of salvation, establishing the kingdom of God. History viewed as an account of the organization of mankind from an ethical perspective is complemented by history viewed as the religious ideal of obedience to the will of God.

The business of His vocation was the establishment of the universal ethical fellowship of mankind, as that aim in the world which rises above all conditions included in the notion of the world. The historical connections of this idea may be left out of account; in which case it becomes all the more evident that a vocation of this kind can only be conceived under the guiding idea of one supramundane God. But for this reason Christ not merely recognises the business of His vocation to be the Lordship or Kingdom of God, He also recognises this vocation as the special ordinance of God for Himself, and His activity in the fulfillment of it as service rendered to God in God's own cause.[80]

This brings Ritschl to the intelligible limit of his Christology. The concern to formulate a rational epistemology and to present a logical exposition of the Christian faith have led to a confrontation in which the ethical and distinctive religious perspectives are seen as complementary notions within a larger unity.

The problem here presented to theology is solved when we have shown that there is no contradiction between the ethical and religious apprehension of Christ, that the former finds its necessary complement in the latter, and that there is nothing here inconsistent either with the Christian idea of God, or with the complete conception of moral freedom. The origin of the Person of Christ—how His Person attained the form in which it presents itself to our ethical and religious apprehension—is not a subject for theological inquiry, because the problem transcends all inquiry. What ecclesiastical tradition offers us in this connection is obscure in itself, and therefore is not fitted to make anything clear. As Bearer of the perfect revelation, Christ is given us that we may believe on Him. When we do believe on Him, we find Him to be the Revealer of God. But the correlation of Christ with God His Father is not a scientific explanation. And as a theologian one ought to know that the fruitless clutching after such explanations only serves to obscure the recognition of Christ as the perfect revelation of God.[81]

After this rejection of traditional theological language and the objections which Ritschl raises to the *munus triplex*, it comes as a surprise to find that Ritschl is ready to recover the traditional interpretation of the title "Prophet" as essentially equivalent to his own without totally surrendering the claims he has made for limiting his knowledge of Christ to the historical evidence.

The ethical view of the life of Christ in the light of His vocation found its appropriate sequel in the religious estimate of His life as the revelation of the love of God, and of that freedom which, as the characteristic power over the world is the mark of Godhead. This discussion has followed essentially the point of view expressed in the kingly Prophethood of Christ; it diverged from the traditional interpretation of that title only in this, that the whole moral conduct of Christ, as the presentation of the Divine grace and truth, was included in Christ's activity as Prophet.[82]

Ritschl's Understanding of Christ as Priest

Under the title of Priest, Ritschl explains, the old theology attempted an ethical interpretation of the work of Christ as obedience. The opposition of Law and Gospel understood as righteousness and grace led traditional theology into the danger of inconsistency in the presentation of the Divine will as both requiring righteousness and offering grace. Christ's priestly work can be duly and logically combined with the religious value attached to His life, for Ritschl, only by remodelling the traditional doctrine of Christ's priesthood and sacrifice in keeping with biblical theology (as reconstructed by Ritschl in Volume Two) and with the ethical consideration that what Christ achieves for others must be achieved first for Himself. The first step is to clarify the notion of sacrifice as "properly" understood in the Old Testament. Ritschl asserts that God's righteousness is His self-consistent and undeviating action in behalf of the salvation of the members of His community and that the righteousness of God is identical with His grace. Therefore, it is unbiblical to assume that the Old Testament sacrifices move God from wrath to grace.

On the contrary, these sacrifices rely implicitly upon the reality of God's grace toward the covenant people, and merely define certain positive conditions which the members of the covenant people must fulfill in order to enjoy the nearness of the God of Grace. . . Because the priest draws near to God when he brings near the gift, therefore he represents before God those in whose behalf he is acting; it is not meant that because the priest and the sacrifice come to God, that others may remain at a distance from God. These relations hold even when it is sins of ignorance which give occasion for the sacrifices; in the latter case forgiveness results from the fact that, with the sacrifice, the priest has indirectly brought the sinners also into the presence of God.[83]

The ethical condition of the work of Christ as priest is met by the fact that "Christ is first of all a Priest in His own behalf before He is a priest for others."[84] This establishes for Ritschl the guarantee that the relationship which Christ forms between Himself and mankind is real in terms of the limits of human experience and is the same one which exists between Christ and God as the basis of salvation. Ritschl believes that the traditional concept of the Godhead of Christ has obscured the fact that all the specific action of God upon Christ, "in virtue of which Christ reveals the Father and accomplishes His work, depends upon that spiritual interaction which appears in Christ's intercourse through prayer with God as His Father."[85] This gives an account of the Priesthood of Christ that emphasizes an activity, prayer, which is continuous with the behavior of the ordinary Christian while at the same time serving to indicate in what way Christ is unique in His realization of prayer in expressing His own will as that of the Father.

If, then, Christ is to be thought of as Priest, the fundamental form for this priestly activity is contained in each moment of His unique consciousness, that as the Son of God He stands to God as Father in a relationship of incomparable fellowship, which is realised in His knowledge of God, in the surrender of His will to God's providential guiding, and in the security of feeling which accompanies the same. When, in prayer especially, He collects Himself for this fellowship, He asserts the nearness of God, and assures Himself of the love of God as the ground of His own position as God's Son.[86]

As priest, Christ establishes fellowship with God for Himself and makes it available through Himself to all men. The response of men to God's revelation in Christ is their approach to God in prayer through Christ and their identification with His vocation in the character of their own lives. In the life of the Christian community the vocational ideal is transmitted. The goal is expressed as Christian perfection and is understood as a means and as an end of action.

...thus—faith in God's fatherly providence and patience correspond to the kingly dignity, humility and prayer to the priestly dignity of the Christian. The believer, however, occupies a position of lordship over the world, in the religious sense meant here, because he stands so near to God, and belongs so peculiarly to God as to ensure his independence of all elements of the world. That independence is determined by his adoption of the end of the Kingdom of God, which is seen to be the end of the world and at the same time the most personal end of God Himself. These functions are the proper manifestation of the reconciliation and the Divine sonship accomplished in Christianity; where they appear, they represent our personal realisation of Christianity as a religion; . . . at the same time they constitute the norm which should determine whether other religious functions—or what are practised as such—possess merely the subordinate value of auxiliary actions, or no value at all.[87]

Conclusion

In the three volumes of *The Christian Doctrine of Justification and Reconciliation* Ritschl gave his account of the Christian faith. His presentation was controlled by several principles in terms of which we have seen him order, organize and evaluate the significance of the biblical material, the history of Christian theology and the institutions which have emerged in the history of the Church. The criteria which Ritschl employed in evaluating the soundness of doctrine were: its biblical authenticity when related to the words or actions of Jesus, the thoughts of the New Testament writers, especially Paul and the author of the Gospel According to John; its appeal to the experience of contemporary man in regard to the notions of the human will and individual freedom and to the logical consistency of doctrine when its implications were drawn out and extended toward further conclusions.

In addition Ritschl made several judgments about the character of the history of Christian thought which served him as conclusions upon which further judgments could be made. He held that the Reformation theologians, particularly Luther and Calvin, were basically in line with the New Testament writers in their understanding of the Christian faith and enjoyed no less catholicity in this respect than Roman Catholic theologians. He held that the Christian faith demonstrated a logical consistency of the highest order of universality when properly understood. He held that the influences of history are reflected in the form and content of doctrinal statements in response to practical problems of Church administration, the philosophical views of different ages of thought, and the ethical character of the general society beyond the Church. He held that a consensus of thought was appearing among his contemporaries with which he agreed and which he struggled to express in his own work. The points of this consensus were: that reconciliation is to be deduced from the love of God and not controlled by notions of wrath or justice; that the life and passion of Christ manifest the love of God; that Christ even *in statu exinanitionis* was the Head of humanity and of the Church; that the vocation of Christ and not the notion of merit explains his suffering; that where penal satisfaction is examined it must be as part of an ethical vocation and not as a forensic formula; and finally, that reconciliation and justification are identical in the New Testament and should be so understood in Christian theology.

These considerations were in force in Ritschl's evaluation of the *munus triplex* as an example of the formulation of the doctrine of the Person and life-work of Christ. He judged the doctrine to be a distortion of the biblical evidence regarding the life of Jesus Christ, a failure in preserving the historical unity of the life of Jesus, and in making available the significance of Christ's life to individual Christians. He found the doctrine to be a defective formula from a systematic standpoint in allowing the offices to separate from each other in respect to their epistemological basis, and he declared that its prominence as a systematic formula was due primarily to the Reformation. Ritschl proposed replacing the treatment of the three offices of Christ as Prophet, Priest, and King with a consideration of the function of Christ as kingly Prophet and kingly Priest in fulfillment of His vocation as the perfect revelation of God and the Founder of the Kingdom of God.

It has been the task of this chapter to follow Ritschl in the presentation of his case, indicating the importance of his distinctive approach to Christology for his presentation of the Christian faith, allowing him as much as possible to speak for himself. In Chapter Four we shall move to our criticism of Ritschl's Christology and his analysis of the *munus triplex* in particular. First we will trace the history of the *munus triplex* in the sources of Christian thought, examining its claims to biblical authenticity and its place in the ancient and medieval Church. Then, we will consider its place in reformation thought in order to ascertain the accuracy and fairness of Ritschl's judgments. We will then move to our own critical response to Ritschl's Christology and a consideration of the reception which his Christology has received.

NOTES CHAPTER II

[1] A. Ritschl, *Unterricht in der christlichen Religion* (Leipzig: J. C. Hinrich, 1924). English translation by Alice M. Swing, *Instruction in the Christian Religion*, in A. T. Swing, *The Theology of Albrecht Ritschl* (London: Longmans, Green and Co., 1901).

[2] A. Ritschl, RV, I, 1; JR, I, 1. "Die christliche Lehre von der Rechtfertigung und Versöhnung, welche ich wissenschaftlich darzustellen unternehme, bildet die concrete Mitte des theologischen Systems. In ihr wird die bestimmungsmässige directe Wirkung der geschichtlichen Offenbarung des göttlichen Gnadenwillens durch Christus entwickelt. Dieselbe besteht darin, dass die von Christus gegründete Gemeinde die Freiheit des religiösen Verkehrs mit Gott ungeachtet der Sünde ausübt, und darin zugleich die Richtung des Willens auf Gottes offenbaren Zweck innehält, welche für die religiöse Erkenntniss die sittliche Wiederherstellung des Menschengeschlechtes und die religiöse Seligkeit in sich schleisst."

[3] A. Ritschl, RV, I, 4; JR, I, 4. "...die ethischen Wirkungendes Lebens, des Leidens und des Todes und der Auferweckung Christi zur Begründung der Gemeinde."

[4] A. Ritschl, RV, I, 3; JR, I, 3. "Allein die Thatsache ist die, dass weder Jesus noch einer der Schriftsteller des N. T. die drei Aemter als die umfassenden und ausschliesslichen Formen für die Heilswirkungen Christi in Gebrauch gesetzt hat, und dass dieser Gebrauch in der systematischen Theologie nicht vor der Reformationsepoche eintritt."

[5] A. Ritschl, RV, I, 3-4; JR, I, 3-4.

[6] A. Ritschl, RV, I, 20; JR, I, 19.

[7] A. Ritschl, RV, I, 5; JR, I, 5-6. "Eine Reihe griechischer und lateinischer Kirchenväter deutet bekanntlich den Tod Christi als das Ereigniss, in welchem Gott aus dem Motive seiner Gerechtigkeit das werthvolle Leben des Gottmenschen dem Teufel übergeben hat, welcher als der berechtigte Herrscher über die sündhaften Menschen anerkannt wird und nur dadurch zur Freigebung derselben bestimmt worden sein soll, dass ihm jenes Aequivalent überlassen wurde. In dieser Theorie ist die *Sünde* nur als die mechanische *Abhängigkeit von dem Teufel* vorgestellt, und der Gedanke der Erlösung in voller Gleichgültigkeit gegen den Begriff des menschlichen Willens gehalten."

[8] *Ibid.* "Ueberdies ergiebt sich bei der Durchführung des Gedankens, dass der Ausgang des Rechtshandels in Widerspruch mit dem leitenden Begriff der Gerechtigkeit Gottes tritt, da das dem Teufel für die Menschen gebotene Aequivalent wesentlich ungeeignet ist, in seinem Besitz zu bleiben. Die Auferweckung Christi vom Tode gewinnt dann in diesem Gedankenzussammenhange die Bedeutung, dass der Teufel seinen Ersatz für die Menschen aus seinem Machtbereich verloren hat. Indem also unumgänglich war anzunehmen, dass der Teufel sich über die Consequenzen des mit ihm eingegangen on Rechtshandels getäuscht habe, so konnte dem

andern Paciscenten dem alles wissenden Gott, nichts anderes vorausgesetzt werden, als dass derselbe die Täuschung des Teufels beabsichtigt habe. Diese Absicht aber steht in Widerspruchmit der Voraussetzung der Gerechtigkeit Gottes; also ist die Theorie ein Widerspruch, in sich, also ist sie unwahr."

⁹ A. Ritschl, RV, I, 23-36; JR, I, 22-35.

¹⁰ A. Ritschl, RV, I, 37-42; JR, I, 35-40.

¹¹ A. Ritschl, RV, I, 9; JR, I, 8-9. "Bei der Wahl der Bezeichnung für die vorliegende Aufgabe leitet mich nun eben diese Rücksicht, dass die Beziehung der nothwendigen Heilswirkungen Christi auf das wechselseitige Verhältniss zwischen dem göttlichen und dem menschlichen *Willen* zum Ausdruck komme. Hiezu erscheinen die Begriffe der Rechtfertigung und der Versöhnung der Menschen in Voraus als geeignet. Denn die Rechtfertigung hebt die Schuld, die Versöhnung die Feindschaft der Sünde gegen Gott auf; beide Begriffe schliessen also eine Wirkung auf den menschlichen Willen in sich, so gewiss Schuld und Feindschaft gegen Gott nur als Attribute des menschlichen Willens verstanden werden können. Sofern nun aber diese Wirkungen aus dem göttlichen Willen durch die Vermittlung des Thuns und Leidens Christi begriffen werden sollen, ist durch jene Bezeichnungen der Aufgabe nicht ausgeschlossen, dass Christus nur so zur Rechtfertigung und Versöhnung der Menschen wirksam gedacht werde, dass zugleich eine Beziehung seiner Leistungen auf Gott anerkannt werde."

¹² A. Ritschl, RV, I, 95-96; JR, I, 92-93. "'Allerdings stellen die Theologen von *Augustin* her immer nur die causale Verbindung zwischen der Gnade als *iustificatio* und dem *meritum* auf. Niemals findet sich der Satz ausgesprochen, dass die *iustificatio* gerade so beschaffen sein müsse, wie sie gelehrt wird, *damit* Verdienst möglich sei. Jedoch vermag ich das praktische Interesse, welches die Bekenner der römischkatholischen Kirche an jenem Dogma nehmen, vollständig nur zu erklären, wenn ich die in der Lehre behauptete causale Verbindung zwischen *iustificatio* und *meritum* als eine zugleich finale verstehe. Denn nur der wenn auch unbewusste Endruck von Zweckverbindungen beherrscht das Gefühl als unmittelbares Motiv praktischen Verhaltens. Also wo man in positiv religiösem Interesse, welches stets alle Verneinungen entgegengesetzter Theologumena beherrscht, die *iustificatio* im katholischen Sinne behauptet, geschieht in dem Glauben an die Geltung von Verdiensten vor Gott."

¹³ Cf. James C. Livingston, *Modern Christian Thought: From the Enlightenment to Vatican II* (New York: Macmillan, 1971), p. 251. Livingston points to Ritschl's ambiguity in regard to the historical Jesus. "It is just at this point that the ambiguities of Ritschl's hermeneutic become apparent. Ritschl appears to want to say that the "back to Jesus" movement erred in seeking to derive the normative Jesus Christ solely from the historical facts and yet he himself proceeds to make judgments as to what traditions concerning Jesus Christ are normative for faith on the basis of the criterion of the historical figure presented by His life (JR, III, 406). It is clear that Ritschl wants to infer Christological normativeness only from certain strata of the historical traditions."

[14] A. Ritschl, RV, I, 94-95; JR, I, 91-92. "Es ist auch im Sinne des Mittelalters, dass der Glaube allein zur *iustificario* gehört, dass dieselbe durch die Gnade gratis verliehen wird, dass sie nicht bedingt ist durch *merita de congruo*,—wovon nur die nominalistische Theologie abweicht;...Und zwar handelt es sich für die Reformatoren darum, dass der Widergeborene nicht durch die guten Werke, welche er wirklich leistet, seine Geltung vor Gott und die Gewissheit seines Heils besitze, sondern durch die Gnade Gottes, welche seinem gläubigen Vertrauen die Rechtfertigung durch Christus verbürgt.

[15] A. Ritschl, RV, I, 9-10; JR, I, 9-10.

[16] A. Ritschl, RV, I, 126; JR, I, 121. "In der mittelaltrigen Lehrbildung erfolgte die Deutung der Genugthuung oder des Verdienstes, welche Christus an Gott für das menschliche Geschlecht oder für die Erwählten geleistet hat, in rein objectiver Weise; die Beziehung dieser That auf die Menschen war in jenem Zusammenhange stets nur angedeutet, hingegen lehrhaft an einem ganz andern Orte des Systems, in der Lehre von der *iustificatio* ausgeführt worden. Die Reformatoren hingegen fassen beide Gedanken nicht nur in ihrer directen Wechselbeziehung auf einander zusammen, sondern richten zugleich das vorherrschende Interesse auf den Gedanken von der Rechtfertigung, und verleihen, wie es scheint, der Lehre von der Genugthuung Christi die Stellung einer Hülfslehre, welche ihre Bestimmung darin hat, die behauptete auschliessliche Bedingtheit der Rechtfertigung durch den Glauben zu erklären."

[17] Otto W. Heick, *A History of Christian Thought* Vol. II (Philadelphia: Fortress Press, 1966), p. 239. Heick refers to Ritschl's teaching on sin as bearing a sociological stamp.

[18] A. Ritschl, RV, I, 16; JR, I, 15.

[19] *Ibid.* "Meinem theologischen Gemeinsinn fällt es schwer, dass ich nicht umhin kann auszusprechen, dass man von Allen im Stiche gelassen wird, wenn man klar und deutlich erfahren will, wie die Reformation trotz ihres Gegensatzes gegen die Kirche des Mittelalters in dem Christenthume dieser Epoche wurzelt; wer der intellectuelle Urheber der theologischen Scholastik und des kirchlichen Particularismus ist, denen die Reformation so bald verfällt; aus welchen Motiven die sogenannte Aufklärung hervorgegangen ist; warum der grossartige Impuls von *Kant* sich wieder in Aufklärungs—Philosophie und—Theologie verlief; endlich worin eigentlich *Schleiermacher*'s Anspruch beruht, die deutsch-evangelische Theologie dieses Jahrhunderts zu leiten, welche jetzt in zielloser Weise zersplittert und deshalb mit dem Untergang bedroht ist."

[20] R. Mackintosh, *Albrecht Ritschl and His School,* p.102.

[21] A. Ritschl, RV, II, v-vi.

McCulloh

Table of Contents

73

35. The Presentation by Paul of the Mosaic Law.
36. The Concept of Justification by Faith.
37. The Effects of Justification according to Paul and the Analogical Presentation of the Other Apostles.
38. How a Dependence of the Basis of Faith on Moral Activity Would be Presented.
39. The Consciousness of Paul of Moral Perfection.
40. The Active Moral Struggle as the Condition of the Value of the Religious Function, according to John.

[22] Ritschl tries to avoid the implications of atonement theory which would leave man as a passive object who takes no part in the relationship of reconciliation with God. In the notion of ethical or moral activity (*sittliche Selbstthätigkeit*) Ritschl finds a way to suggest the active participation of man with God in the relationship of reconciliation and to suggest a way of looking at the person and life-work of Christ which will point to the independent and unique personality of Jesus as a source of action without characterizing the uniqueness of Christ in terms of older metaphysical notions of substance. Ritschl finds that these notions which are related to substance are quickly abused, resulting in a mechanistic view of atonement. Cf. RV, II, 1-10; 383-386; RV I, p. 9; and RV, III, 1.

[23] The character of Ritschl's biblical theology is problematic. He has led us to believe that the key to the success of his theological method is the high degree of correspondence between the historical facts found in the biblical narrative and the explanation of the growth of the Church and its theological traditions as the result of the actions of Jesus of Nazareth as founder of the Kingdom of God. However, in dealing with the biblical material, instead of deriving his categories for interpretation from the historical data, Ritschl employs several interpretative principles to organize the biblical material in such a way as to reveal its controlling ideas. The reader must question to what extent Ritschl in fact supplies the controlling ideas himself, claiming them to be authentically "there" as evidence of the positive effect of God's will in revelation. The claim of Ritschl, to be able to penetrate the historical obscurity of the New Testament materials and to demonstrate coherence and consistency in terms of their relationship to the self-understanding of Jesus' own mind, must be examined more closely. While proposing that the Old Testament is required as background for interpretation of the New Testament Ritschl in fact judges the validity of the Old Testament materials, selecting as normative those that confirm his own notion of the mind of Christ. Cf. R. E. Koenig, "The Use of the Bible in Albrecht Ritschl's Theology," and R. Mackintosh, *Albrecht Ritschl and His School*, pp. 102-130. What we find is that Ritschl reads directly from the Gospel narratives an account of the decisions of the mind of Christ in accord with Ritschl's own notion of the vocation of Christ as the founder of the Kingdom of God which ignores the different tendencies of the individual Gospel traditions and harmonizes them to present a picture of Christ similar to the Johannine Gospel. In doing this, Ritschl has not only collapsed the historical distance between the various Old and New Testament traditions themselves, he has also removed the distance between himself and the mind of Christ which he had to admit in dealing with contradictory traditions elsewhere in the New Testament (RV, 378; Jr, III, 400). Cf. James Barr, *The Semantics of Biblical Language* (London: Oxford University Press, 1961), pp. 9ff. and 72ff.

74

[24] On the relationship between Scripture and Tradition in the history of Christian thought see Heiko A. Oberman, "Quo Vadis, Petre?" *Harvard Divinity School Bulletin*, July, 1962, and Georges Florovsky, "Scripture and Tradition: An Orthodox Point of View," *Dialog.* II (1963), 288ff.

[25] A. Ritschl, RV, III, 1-2; JR, III, 1-2. "Die biblisch-theologische Darstellung war unternommen worden, damit festgestellt werde, welche Vorstellung von Sündenvergebung, Rechtfertigung, Versöhnung und in welchen Beziehungen dieselbe von Jesus als dem Gründer der christlichen Religionsgemeinde hervorgerufen... Für den Zweck, den ich verfolge, genügte es nun nicht, die Andeutungen Jesu über die an seine Person und an sein Sterben geknüpfte Sündenvergebung nachzuweisen. Denn auch wenn dieselben als vollkommen durchsichtig erscheinen sollten, so wird ihre Bedeutung erst dadurch vollständig klar, wie sie sich in dem Bewusstsein der an ihn Glaubenden reflectiren, und wie die Glieder der christlichen Gemeinde ihr Bewusstsein von Sündenvergebung auf die Person und das Wirken und Leiden Jesu zuruckführen... Denn wir würden überhaupt weder auf jene Absicht Jesu aufmerksam sein, noch nach ihrem Werthe und ihrer Bedeutung fragen, wenn wir uns nicht in die *religiöse Gemeinde* einrechnen dürften, welche ihren Besitz der Sündenvergebung als Wirkung Christi durch die Schriftsteller des Neuen Testaments zuerst bezeugt hat."

[26] *Ibid.* Cf. RV, III, 421-424; JR, III, 447-450; and RV, II, 29-30; RV, III, 9, for Ritschl's view of the political basis of Jewish morality and its subordination to the "nation."

[27] A. Ritschl, RV, III, 383-384; JR, III, 406. Ritschl is trying to resolve the problem of the meaning of the resurrection and crucifixion from the point of view of his soteriology and his epistemology. In so doing he erodes the meaning of the resurrection and subordinates it to his epistemology. Ritschl's attempt to deal with a positive religion on historical grounds while struggling to find a unifying principle seems to force divergent theological traditions into one formulation, disabling or discarding doctrines which he rules irrelevant.

[28] *Ibid.* "Jede Wirkung Christi aber muss ihren Massstab in der geschichtlichen Gestalt seines Lebens finden. Also muss die Gottheit oder die Weltherrschaft Christi in bestimmten Zügen seines geschichtlichen Lebens, als Attribut seiner zeitlichen Existenz begriffen werden. Denn was Christus nach seiner ewigen Bestimmung ist und gemäss seiner Erhöhung zu Gott auf uns wirkt, wäre für uns gar nicht erkennbar, wenn es nicht auch in seinem zeitlich—geschichtlichen Dasein wirksam wäre. Wenn nicht die Vorstellung seiner gegenwärtigen Herrschaft mit den bestimmten Merkmalen seines geschichtlichen Wirkens ausgefüllt werden kann, so ist sie entweder ein wertloses Schema oder der Anlass zu allen möglichen Schwärm'ereien. Sollen wir hingegen den Glauben festhalten, dass Christus gegenwärtig über die Gemeinde des Gottesreiches herrscht und zur fortschreitenden Eingliederung der Welt unter diesen ihren Endzweck wirksam ist, so muss die Weltherrschaft schon als hervostechendes Merkmal des geschichtlichen Lebens Christi erkannt werden können.

²⁹ A. Ritschl, RV, III, 25; JR, III, 25-26. "Erstens wird festgestellt werden, was unter Rechtfertigung und Versöhnung gemeint ist; von welchem Attribute Gottes aus, in welcher Relation auf die Menschen, und in welchem Umfang die Rechtfertigung gedacht werden muss; endlich in welchen subjectiven Functionen diese von Gott abzuleitende Verhältnissbestimmung zu wirksamen Ausdruck kommt. Zweitens sind die positiven und die negativen Voraussetzungen der religiösen Wahrheit der Rechtfertigung zu entwickeln, die Idee von Gott; die Beurtheilung der menschlichen Sünde; die religiöse Schätzung der Person und des Lebenswerkes Christi. Drittens ist der Beweis zu führen, warum der Gedanke der Rechtfertigung im Glauben innerhalb des Christenthums überhaupt nothwendig, und warum dieselbe von Christus als dem Offenbarer Gottes und als dem Vertreter der Gemeinde abhängig ist. Viertens, wird in der Weise der Folgerung erwiesen werden, warum die Rechtfertigung gerade in den religiösen Functionen erscheint, welche in Betracht kommen und wie sich zu denselben die sittliche Selbstthätigkeit verhält."

³⁰ A. Ritschl, RV, III, 9ff; JR, III, 10. F. Schleiermacher, *The Christian Faith*. I, 31-52.

³¹ A. Ritschl, RV, III, 10; JR, III, 10. "Im Christenthum nun ist das Reich Gottes so als der für Gott und die erwählte Religionsgemeinde gemeinsame Zweck dargestellt, dass sich derselbe über die natürlichen Schranken der Volksunterschiede zu der sittlichen Verbindung der Völker erhebt. In dieser Beziehung erscheint das Christenthum als die vollendete sittliche Religion. Die Erlösung durch Christus, so wie dieser Begriff auch die Rechtfertigung und Erneuerung umfasst, ist ebenfalls von allen Bedingungen natürlicher und sinnlicher Art enkleidet,...spitzt die monotheistisch geistige und theologische Art der biblischen Religion im Christenthum zu dem Begriff der vollendeten geistigen und sittlichen Religion zu."

³² A. Ritschl, RV, III, 10; JR, III, 10.

³³ Cf. A. Ritschl, RV, III, 167-168, 201, 633-634; JR, III, 175, 211, and 670.

³⁴ A. Ritschl, RV, III, 13; JR, III, 13. "Das Christenthum also ist die monotheistische vollendet geistige und sittliche Religion, welche auf Grund des erlösenden und das Gottesreich gründenden Lebens ihres Stifters in der Freiheit der Gotteskindschaft besteht, den Antrieb zu dem Handeln aus Liebe in sich schliesst, das auf die sittliche Organisation der Menschheit gerichtet ist, und in der Gotteskindschaft wie in dem Reiche Gottes die Seligkeit begründet."

³⁵ A. Ritschl, RV, III, 15-16; JR, III, 15. "Die Vorstellungen Christi und der Apostel, welche wir kurzer Hand als sachlich übereinstimmend beurtheilen, bedienen sich oft genug abweichender Mittel des Ausdruckes, oder lehnen sich an verschiedene alttestamentliche Symbole an. Nun verfährt freilich schon die Exegese an vielen einzelnen Stellen so, dass sie die verwandten symbolischen Ausdrücke auf einen möglichst klaren Begriff bringt. Denn theils muss sie das Einzelne nach seiner Verwandtschaft mit allem Gleichartigen beurtheilen, theils muss sie den Abstand zwischen der symbolischen Redeweise der Israeliten und unserer Denkart ausgleichen, theils hat sie die Aufgabe, falsche Begriffe abzuweisen, welche die ex-

egetische Ueberlieferung an gewisse biblische Symbole herangedrängt hat. Unter diesen Umständen enthält schon die biblisch-theologische Darstellung der religiösen Vorstellung, welche dem theologischen Erkennen den Stoff liefert, Ansätze zur Definition derselben, sie bietet aber nicht die Bürgschaft ihrer Vollständigkeit und Deutlichkeit in systematischer Beziehung auf das Ganze. Jede Definition nämlich kann erst im Zusammenhange der systematischen Theologie vollzogen werden, weil die Erkenntniss der Wahrheit auch des Einzelnen durch das Verständniss seines Zusammenhanges mit dem Ganzen begründet wird...

Die formell richtige Ausprägung theologischer Sätze ist aber auch abhängig von der Art, in welcher man bei der Abgrenzung der Erkenntnissobjecte verfährt, d. h. von der Erkenntnisstheorie, welche man sei es mit, sei es ohne Bewusstsein befolgt."

[36] A. Ritschl, RV, III, 391; JR, III, 414. "Jesus ist der Träger der vollendeten geistigen Religion, der in der gegenseitigen Gemeinschaft mit dem Gott steht, welcher der Urheber der Welt und ihr Endzweck ist. In der letztern Beziehung der Gottesidee ist es gegründet, dass Jesus die denkbar allgemeinste sittliche Aufgabe, die Verbindung der Menschen durch die Liebe als giltig für sich um Gottes willen anerkennt; in der eresten Beziehung ist es gegründet, dass er für sein persönliches Leben alle Bestimmungsgründe von sich ablehnt, welche particular, weltlich und deshalb untergöttlicher Art wären. Aber indem er seine Stellung gegen Gott auf die anderen Menschen übertragen wollte, so hat er die Verbindung der Menschen durch die Liebe oder das Reich Gottes als das Ziel für seine Jünger geltend gemacht,..."

[37] A. Ritschl, RV, III, 20; JR, III, 20. Ritschl also picks this up in his discussion of the cognitive truth of value judgments in Chapter IV. Our survey of criticism of this topic is in Chapter IV.

[38] Pfleiderer, *The Development of Theology,* pp. 7-9, 12.

[39] *Ibid.*, pp. 183ff. Cf. Rudolph Hermann Lotze, *Microcosmos*, English translation by Elizabeth Hamilton and Constance Jones (4th ed.; Edinburgh: T. & T. Clark, 1897).

[40] Cf. Deegan, "Albrecht Ritschl as Critical Empiricist," pp. 151-154.

[41] Livingston, *Modern Christian Thought*, pp. 249-250

[42] Cf. supra, n. 40.

[43] A. Ritschl, RV, III, 376; JR, III, 397-398. "...ich über Christus überhaupt nur rede, sofern sein persönlicher Character als Träger der Offenbarung Gottes in Betracht kommt,...
...Ist aber Christus durch das, was er zu meinem Heil gethan und gelitten hat, mein Herr, und ehre ich ihn als meinen Gott, indem ich um meines Heiles willen der Kraft seiner Wohlthat vertraue, so ist das ein Werthurtheil directer Art. Das Urtheil gehört nicht in das Gebiet des uninteressirten wissenschaftlichen Erkennens, wie die chalcedonensische Formel...Alle Erkenntnisse religiöser Art sind directe Werturtheile."

[44] A. Ritschl, RV, III, 2; JR, III, 2. "Also die authentische und erschöpfende Erkenntniss der religiösen Bedeutung Jesu, nämlich seiner Bedeutung als Religionsstifter, ist daran gebunden, dass man sich in die von ihm gestiftete Gemeinde gerade insofern einrechnet,..."

[45] A. Ritschl, RV, III, 25; JR, III, 25. "Seine Darstellung in der Theologie wird also durch einen Beweis der Art zum Abschluss kommen, dass das christliche Lebenideal und kein anderes den Anspruchen des menschlichen Geistes an die Erkenntniss der Dinge übeurhaupt genugthut."

[46] A. Ritschl, RV, III, 36-38; JR, III, 38-40.

[47] A. Ritschl, RV, III, 14; JR, III, 14.

[48] A. Ritschl, RV, III, 2-3; JR, III, 2-3.

[49] A. Ritschl, RV, III, 33-34; JR, III, 33-34. "Umgekehrt ergiebt die genauere Betrachtung des Begriffs der Rechtfertigung, dass mit dieser Wirkung Gottes auch kein mechanischer Vorgang an dem Menschen gemeint ist. Denn ihre Beziehung auf den Glauben hat theils den Sinn, dass diese selbstthätige Function des Menschen, ohne deren Beachtung die Rechtfertigung nicht vollständig gedacht wird, unter dieser Wirkung Gottes mitbegriffen wird, theils den Sinn, dass die Rechtfertigung, indem sie die Gegenwirkung des Menschen, den Glauben hervorruft, in dieser Form dem Gläubigen eigen ist und als Motiv der eigenthümlichen religiösen Haltung, die ihm zukommt, fortdauert. In beiden Beziehungen also sind die Begriffe vom Reiche Gottes und von der Rechtfertigung gleichartig. Diese trifft insofern ein, als einmal in beiden Begriffen Gnadenwirkung Gottes ausgedrückt sind, und widerum der Erfolg derselben nur in Thätigkeiten wahrgenommen wird, die in der Form der persönlichen Selbstandigkeit verlaufen. Sie bieten also wirklich kein Hinderniss dar, sie in der Gesammtanschauung des Christenthums auf einander zu beziehen. Diese Abwechselung zwischen beiderlei Sätzen aber kann in der Dogmatik nicht umgangen werden. In derselben werden alle religiösen Vorgänge im Menschen unter der Bestimmung der göttlichen Gnade, also vom Standpunkte Gottes aus aufgefasst. Nun ist es unmöglich, diesen Standpunkt an unserer Erfahrung so durchzuführen, dass dadurch die vollständige Erkenntniss der Gnadenwirkungen erreicht würde. Denn unsere Erkenntniss findet ihren Standpunkt in der formellen Entgegensetzung gegen Gott. Nur momentan können wir uns auf den Standpunkt Gottes selbst versetzen; die Dogmatik also, welche in lauter Sätzen dieses Gepräges verläuft, bliebe unverstanden, und bestünde aus Worten, die eben nicht unser Erkenntniss ausdrücken. Kommt es darauf an, die Dogmatik nicht blos als die Erzählung der grossen Thaten Gottes, sondern als das System des von Gott bewirkten Gottes Rechtfertigung, Widergeburt, Mittheilung dies heiligen Geistes, Verleihung der Seligkeit im höchsten Gute so erkennen zu lehren, dass die entsprechenden Selbstthätigkeiten analysiert werden, in welchen die Wirkungen Gottes vom Menschen angeeignet werden." Ritschl employs the image of a circle (RV, III, 4; JR, III, 4) to suggest Christian thought properly centered in Christ. He also uses the image of an ellipse to suggest Christianity (RV, III, 11; JR, III, 11) as having two centers or foci. The equivalence of the two foci gives the image of rounding the ellipse into a circle. Cf. RV, III, 190-191; JR, III, 200.

[50] A. Ritschl, RV, III, 82; JR, III, 84-85. "Diejenige Definition, welche gewonnen worden ist, macht nur den Anspruch, dass sie denkbar ist, und dass sie der Ansicht der Männer des Neuen Testaments und der Reformatoren näher steht als jede andere. 1. Die Rechtfertigung oder Sündervergebung, als der religiöse Ausdruck der im Christenthum grundlegenden Wirkung Gottes auf die Menschen ist die Aufnahme von Sündern in die Gemeinschaft mit Gott, in welcher deren Heil verwirklicht und auf das ewige Leben hinausgeführt werden soll. 2. Die Rechtfertigung ist denkbar als Aufhebung der Schuld und des Schuldbewusstseins in der Beziehung, dass in dem letztern der in der Sünde vollzogene und in der Schuld ausdrückte Widerspruch gegen Gott als Misstrauen fortwirkt und die moralische Getrenntheit von Gott herbeiführt. 3. Sofern die Rechtfertigung als erfolgreich vorgestellt wird, muss sie als Versöhnung gedacht werden, in der Art, dass zwar die Erinnerung die Unlust an der begangenen Sünde aufbewahrt, aber zugleich an die Stelle des Misstrauens gegen Gott, die positive zustimmung des Willens zu Gott und seinem Heilszwecke eintritt."

[51] A. Ritschl, RV, III, 372; JR, III, 394. "In der griechischen Theologie ist die Incarnation des göttlichen Wortes die volle, dem Heilszweck entsprechende Offenbarung der Gottheit Christi; dazu verhalten sich die Lehrthätigkeit des Gottmenschen und die Hingebung seines menschlichen Lebens in den Tod zur Ablösung des Todesgesetzes als untergeordneten Proben seiner Gottheit zu untergeordneten Zwecken. In der lateinischen Kirche wird die Gottheit Christi in der Form der Incarnation anerkannt, aber die mittlerischen Heilwirkungen, die Genugthuung und das Verdienst zum Erwerbe der Sündevergebung für die Menschen, werden nur an seiner menschlichen Selbstthätigkeit als solcher nachgewiesen; die Gottheit kommt bei Thomas nur als die sachliche Werthbestimmung des Verdienstes und der Genugthuung in Betracht zur Deckung des Unwertes der Sünde; bei Duns gar nicht. Luther's Aufstellung in den Katechismen haben den Sinn, dass unter Voraussetzung der kirchlichen Lehrformel die Gottheit Christi gerade in seinen menschlichen Leistungen für die Gemeinde offenbar, anschaulich, verständlich ist, und den Glauben, nicht als das Fürwahrhalten einer unverständlichen Lehre, sondern als das persönliche Vertrauen um unseres Heiles willen auf sich zieht."

[52] A. Ritschl, RV, III, 377; JR, III, 398-399. "Erst müssen wir Christi offenbare Gottheit nachweisen können, ehe wir auf seine ewige Gottheit reflectiren. Die Gegner aber, indem sie in erster Linie den letzten Titel aussprechen hören wollen, meinen, die Gottheit Christi in einem seiner Herkunft nach wissenschaftlichen Begriff, also in einem Acte uninteressirten Erkennens feststellen zu können, vor aller möglichen Erfahrung und ausserhalb aller religiösen Erfahrung von der Sache. Und als Vertreter eines wissenschaftlichen Begriffs von Christi Gottheit befolgen sie eine unbrauchbare Erkenntnissmethode, indem ihren der Gedanke des ewig vor der Welt von Gott gezeugten Wortes Gottes nur durch Tradition feststeht, abgelöst von allen Gründen seiner Enstehung. Demgemäss muthen sie uns zu, in jener Formel die Gottheit Christi zu bekennen, ehe dieselbe in seinem Wirken nachgewiesen ist, ja obleich sie in seinem Wirken auf uns in den Merkmalen, auf die es ankämes, nicht nachgewiesen werden kann. Man soll an der Hand dieser Lehrer erst wissen, was

79

die Gottheit Christi ewig in sich und im Verhältniss zu Gott ist; später wird es sich darum handeln, wie und ob dieses Attribut auch für uns wirksam und offenbar ist. Der Grundsatz des Erkennens, der hierin Anwendung findet, ist falsch (s. 19), und die Warnung Luther's vor solchen Lehren, welche die göttlichen Dinge *a priori,* von oben herunter, vor aller speciellen Offenbarung beurtheilen wollen, gilt auch für dieses Problem." Ritschl follows this with a reference to Luther's comment on John 17:3 (Walch, VIII, 697).

[53] A. Ritschl, RV, III, 365; JR, III, 386. "Denn Jesus hat ohne Zweifel ein bis dahin nicht dagewesenes religiöses Verhältnis zu Gott erlebt und seinen Jüngern bezeugt, und er hat seine Jünger in dieselbe religiöse Weltanschauung und Selbstbeurtheilung einzuführen beabsichtigt, und unter dieser Bedingung in die universelle Aufgabe des Gottesreiches, welche er für seine Jünger wie für sich gestellt wusste."

[54] A. Ritschl, RV, III, 372-374, 394-395; JR, III, 394-395, 418.

[55] A. Ritschl, RV, III, 366; JR, III, 387. "Was wir also in dem geschichtlich abgeschlossenen Lebensbilde Christi als den eigentlichen Werth seines Daseins erkennen, gewinnt durch die Eigenthümlichkeit dieser Erscheinung und durch ihre normgebende Abzweckung auf unsere religiösesittliche Bestimmung den Werth einer bleibenden Regel, weil wir zugleich feststellen, dass wir nur aus der anregenden und Richtung gebenden Kraft dieser Person heraus im Stand sind, in deren Stellung zu Gott und zur Welt einzutreten."

[56] See n. 43 above.

[57] A. Ritschl, RV, III, 378ff; JR, III, 400ff. Cf. Hefner, "Baur Versus Ritschl on Early Christianity," *Church History,* XXXI (September, 1962), 259-278.

[58] See n. 43 above.

[59] A. Ritschl, RV, III, 382; JR, III, 404. "Hier ist nun nöthig festzustellen, dass dieses Prädicat der Gottheit Christi aus der Erfahrung der Jüngergemeinde heraus behauptet wird. Ausserhalb dieser Relation ist es nicht denkbar. Erst auf Grund dessen subsumirt Johannes die Gestalt Christi unter der Vorstellung vom Offenbarungswort, welche er an Weltschöpfung u.s.w. erprobt, und für welche er das Prädicat Gott ausspricht."

[60] A. Ritschl, RV, III, 367, 378, 381-382; JR, III, 400, 404.

[61] A. Ritschl, RV, III, 383-384; JR, III, 406. "'Soll die Gottheit Christi oder seine Herrschaft über die Welt in der Form des Erhöhten als nöthwendige Erkenntniss, als Glied in der christlich-religiösen Weltanschauung bewiesen werden, so muss es in dem Wirken Christi auf uns aufgezeigt werden. Jede Wirkung Christi aber muss ihren Massstab in der geschichtlichen Gestalt seines Lebens finden. Also muss die Gottheit oder die Weltherrschaft Christi in bestimmten Zügen seines geschichtlichen Lebens, als Attribut seiner zeitlichen Existenz begriffen werden. Denn was Christus nach seiner ewigen Bestimmtheit ist und gemäss seiner Erhöhung zu Gott auf uns

wirkt, wäre für uns gar nicht erkennbar, wenn es nicht auch in seinem zeitlich-geschichtlichen Dasein wirksam wäre. Wenn nicht die Vorstellung seiner gegenwärtigen Herrschaft mit den bestimmten Merkmalen seines geschichtlichen Wirkens ausgefüllt werden kann, so ist sie entweder ein wertloses Schema oder der Anlass zu allen möglichen Schwärmereien.

Sollen wir hingegen den Glauben festhalten, dass Christus gegenwärtig über die Gemeinde des Gottesreiches herrscht und zur fortschreitenden Eingliederung der Welt unter diesen ihren Endzweck wirksam ist, so muss die Weltherrschaft schon als hervorstechendes Merkmal des geschichtlichen Lebens Christi erkannt werden können.

⁶²A. Ritschl, RV, III, 390-391; JR, III, 414. See above, n. 36.

⁶³A. Krauss, "Das Mittlerwerk nach dem Schema des *munus triplex.*" *Jahrbücher für Deutsche Theologie.* XVII (1872), 595-655; and Johann August Ernesti, *Gedanken über einige Stücke in der Lehre von Jesu Christo* (Leipzig: Publisher not given, 1775). A. Ritschl, RV, III, 393-394; JR, III, 417.

⁶⁴A. Ritschl, RV, III, 393-394; JR, III, 417.

⁶⁵A. Ritschl, RV, III, 394-395; JR, III, 418.

⁶⁶A. Ritschl, RV, III, 429-433; JR, III, 455-459.

⁶⁷A. Ritschl, RV, III, 395; JR, III, 418. "Wenn Christus nach dieser Betrachtungsweise als König und Priester dahin wirkt, unsere Freiheit über die Welt, über die Sünde, und unsere Freiheit im Verkehr mit Gott hervorzurufen, so stehe ich wohl im Einklang mit dem ächten Zuge der Reformation, indem ich die specifische Bedeutung der Person Christi in der christlichen Weltanschauung und Selbstbeurtheilung mit der Erreichung der persönlichen Selbständigkeit gegen die Welt in Relation gestellt habe." This is similar to the position taken by Paul Van Buren in *The Secular Meaning of the Gospel* (New York: Macmillan, 1963), p. 134.

⁶⁸A. Ritschl, RV, III, 383-386; JR, III, 406-408ff.

⁶⁹Ritschl criticises the formal weakness of the doctrine but recognizes such an order in his own reconstruction. Cf. RV, III, 405; JR, III, 428-429

⁷⁰A. Ritschl, RV, III, 403-408; JR, III, 427-432.

⁷¹A. Ritschl, RV, I, 3; JR, I, 3.

⁷²A. Ritschl, RV, I, 3-4; JR, I, 3-4. "Ferner werden diese Amtsbezeichnungen im N. T. theils durch die demselben eigenthümlichen Prädicate für Christus überboten, theils kommen sie nur so in übertragenem Sinne vor, dass der durch sie bezeichnete Inhalt auch unabhängig von ihnen dargestellt werden kann. Der Character des Propheten, obleich Jesu selbst ihn für sich in Abspruch nimmt, wird übuerschritten durch sein Prädicat als Sohn des Menschen und Gottes. Sein Königthum bezieht sich auf ein ganz anderes Gebiet, als auf das dem erwarteten Davidssohne angewiesene. Sein

Priesterthum, indem es mit dem Opfercharakter zusammenfällt, hat, näher betrachtet, vielmehr Unähnlichkeit als Aehnlichkeit mit dem Vorbilde. Obgleich also die Lösung der biblisch-theologischen Aufgaben an die Beachtung dieser vorbildlichen Vorstellungen gebunden sein wird, so kann doch die Bildung der systematisch-theologischen Hauptbegriffe durch diese Rücksicht nicht geleitet sein. Dieselben müssen sich durchaus auf die specifisch neutestamentlichen Anschauung stützen, nicht aber auf solche, deren Anwendung in übertragenem Sinne die für die Gedankenwelt des N. T. als blosse Hülfsvorstellungen erkennen lässt. Wenn sich die alte Schule in ihrem mechanischen Gebrauche der biblischen Auctorität für das theologische System über diesen Unterschied in der neutestamentlichen Gedanken-bildung hinweggesetzt hat, so hat sie darin kein nachahmenswerthes Beispiel gegeben. Oder vielmehr, da auch die alte Schule überwiegend ihre dogmatischen Lehrtitel nach den entwickelten neutestamentlichen Ideen gebildet hat, so macht das Auf-treten des Titels von den drei Aemtern Christi auch im Zusammenhange der alten Theologie einem unharmonischen und fremdartigen Eindruck, der vor dem fort-gesetzten Gebrauch dieses Lehrtitels warnen muss."

[73] A. Ritschl, RV, III, 408; JR, III, 432-433. "Das überlieferte Schema von den drei Aemtern ist nur ein erster Schritt dazu, die Bedeutung Christi für die an ihn glaubende Gemeinde zu begreifen. Es ist nur ein Versucht, sich des Stoffes der Anschauung möglichst vollstandig zu versichern. Aber wie es nur Unterschiede und Gegensätze darstellt, und dieselben nicht wieder auf eine Einheit zurückführt, so bleibt es davon entfernt, die Sache zu erschöpfen, die als solche weder eine Zweiheit noch eine Dreiheit, sondern Einheit ist. Dieser Wahrheit habe ich nahe zu treten versucht, indem ich die verschiedenen Data der vorliegenden Darstellung auf ihren sachlichen Zusammenhang reducirt habe. In dieser Hinsicht muss zunächst das Wirken Christi in *statu exaltationis* als Ausdruck der permanenten Wirkung seiner geschichtlichen Erscheinung vorgestellt werden. Ferner muss sein Handeln und Reden als der identische Stoff seines prophetischen und priesterlichen Wirkens betrachtet, sein königliches Wirken muss als specifische Modification in diese beiden Thätigkeiten eingerechnet, oder vielmehr sein Königthum gerade im prophetischen und im priestrlichen Wirken nachgewiesen werden, sofern beides von seiner Absicht geleitet ist, die Gemeinde der Gläubigen zu gründen und zu erhalten."

[74] A. Ritschl, RV, III, 403-404; JR, III, 427- 428. "Das entspricht auch dem un-zweifelhaften geschichtlichen Thatbestand. Denn indem Jesus, der nur unter den Merkmalen eines Propheten auftrat und beurtheilt wurde, von seinem Jüngern als der gesalbte König erkannt sein wollte, stellte er den Stoff seines prophetischen Wirkens unter eine Vorstellungsform, die an sich dagegen gleichgiltig sein würde. Demgemäss erscheint es eben als eine willkürliche Analyse des Wortes Christus," wenn man in ihm Prophetenthum und Königthum nében einander ausgedrückt fand . . . Damit aber ist die Analyse des Titels Christus, welche zu diesem Schema der drei Aemter geführt hat, ebenso durch zureichende Gründe widerlegt, wie sie historisch unberechtigt ist. Denn Jesus heisst der Gesalbte nur zur Bezeichnung seiner Herrscherwürde. Heisst er nun daneben auch Prophet und Priester, so ist es deutlich, dass seine prophetische Thätigkeit den Stoff seines königlichen Wirkens darbietet, und es ist nach den bisherigen Erörterungen zu vermuthen, dass seine priesterliche Thätigkeit in seiner freiwilligen Lebensaufopferung als eine durch die Umstände bedingte Probe seines Königthums verstanden werden muss."

[75] A. Ritschl, RV, III, 405; JR, III, 428-429. "Ist also die Orientirung über die Bedeutung des Lebens Christi an der Hand des vorliegenden Schema erlaubt, so ist zunächst festgestellt, dass das königliche Wirken Christi, welches für ihn selbst als die Hauptsache gilt, indem er als der Christus anerkannt sein will, seine Erscheinung sowohl in den prophetischen wie in den priesterlichen Leistungen haben wird. Und da die königliche Thätigheit Christi ihre Relation an der Gründung und Erhaltung der Religionsgemeinde Christi findet, so wird sie in *statu exinanitionis* durch die auf dieses Ziel hin gerichtete Absicht Christi repräsentirt, welche die beiden anderen Thätigkeiten durchdringt, und ihnen stets gegenwartig ist. Hingegen lassen sich Priesterthum und Prophetenthum nicht auf einander reduciren. Denn jenes bewegt sich in der Richtung von den Menschen auf Gott, dieses in der umgekehrten Richtung von Gott auf die Menschen."

[76] A. Ritschl, RV, III, 408-409; JR, III, 432-433. "In dieser Hinsicht muss zunächst das Wirken Christi *in statu exaltationis* als Ausdruck der permanenten Wirkung seiner geschichtlichen Erscheinung vorgestellt werden. Ferner muss sein Handeln und Reden als der identische Stoff seines prophetischen und priesterlichen Wirkens betrachtet, sein königliches Wirken muss als specifische Modification in diese beiden Thätigkeiten eingerechnet, oder vielmehr sein Königthum gerade im prophetischen und im priesterlichen Wirken nachgewiesen werden, sofern beides von seiner Absicht geleitet ist, die Gemeinde der Gläubigen zu gründen und zu erhalten. Nur die prophetische und die priesterliche Thätigkeit lassen sich nicht auf einander reduciren, weil sie in dem Verhältniss zwischen Gott und den Menschen in umgekehrter Richtung verlaufen. Aber eben in diesen Beziehungen bilden sie die Einheit des *opus mediatorium*. Es wird darauf ankommen, diese Einheit des prophetischen und priesterlichen Wirkens durch andere Erörterungen theils zu bewahren, theils zu ergänzen. Dieses kann aber nur durch die Analyse der erkennbaren Lebensabsicht Christi im Ganzen geschehen."

[77] A. Ritschl, RV, III, 411; JR, III, 435-436. ". . .sie und ihre Reden von ihnen selbst und ihren Volksgenossen religiös beurtheilt werden, gelten sie als Mittel oder Organe der absichtlichen Offenbarung Gottes. Nicht anders hat auch Jesus sich selbst beurtheilt; nur bring es der Inhalt des wesentlichen göttlichen Endzweckes, den er nicht blos durch Rede verständlich, sondern auch durch Handeln wirklich zu machen sich bewusst ist, mit sich, dass er seine selbständige Person in ein noch engeres Verhältniss zu Gott seinem Vater setzt. Seine Selbstbeurtheilung verräth zwar eine gleitende Stufenfolge in der Bezeichnung seines Verhältnisses zu Gott, nicht nur bei Johannes, sondern auch bei den anderen Evangelisten; aber wie er auf—und absteigt zwischen seiner Selbstdarstellung des Gesandten, der Gott gesehen hat und gehört hat und dessen Aufträge ausführt, und der des Sohnes Gottes, der das Werk Gottes treibt und in seiner Person dessen Herrschaft über die Menschen zum Zwecke des Gottesreiches ausübt, so beurtheilt er den ihm bewussten Zusammenhang seines Lebens eben als das Mittel der *vollständigen Selbstoffenbarung Gottes.*"

[78] Cf. A. Ritschl, RV, III, 405-406, 409; JR, III, 429, 433.

[79] A. Ritschl, RV, III, 422; JR, III, 447. "Denn der Beruf des königlichen Propheten, die sittliche Gottesherrschaft zu verwirklichen, ist der höchste, welcher unter

allen Berufen denkbar ist; er ist geradezu auf das Sittliche als Ganzes gerichtet; dieser Inhalt aber konnte nur dann als die besondere Lebensaufgabe festgehalten und für die eigene Aufmerksamkeit fixirt werden, wenn derselbe von allen übrigen Besonderheiten zurückgezogen wurde, welche übrigens in diesem Ganzen ihren Platz finden sollen. Um den Beruf als Christus für sich zu fixiren, musste Christus auf alle Lebensbedingungen verzichten, in deren Stetigkeit andere Berufe eine Gewähr ihrer eigenen Stetigkeit finden, auf die Stetigkeit des Wohnsitztes und des nährenden Erwerbes, auf den Anhalt an der Familie und dem Zutrauen der Mitbürger. Er stützte sich nur auf die persönliche Ergebenheit von Freunden und Anhängern, und bildete sich den Kreis seiner zwölf Jünger in dem Sinne heran, dass sein Lebensberuf die Bildung einer besondern Religionsgemeinde erforderte."

[80] A. Ritschl, RV, III, 423-424; JR, III, 449. "Seine Berufsaufgabe war die Gründung der universellen sittlichen Gemeinschaft der Menschen als das ziel in der Welt, welches über alle Bedingungen hinausgreift, die in dem Begriff der Welt zusammengefasst werden. Man kann absehen von den historischen Zusammenhängen dieser Idee; dann wird es um so deutlicher, dass diese Aufgabe nur unter der leitenden Idee von dem Einen uberweltlichen Gott aufgefasst werden kann. Deshalb aber kennt Christus nicht nur seine Berufsaufgabe als die Herrschaft oder das Reich Gottes, sondern er kennt sie eben auch als die besondere göttliche Vorschrift für sich, und seine Thätigkeit in ihrer Ausführung als den Dienst gegen Gott in Gottes Sache."

[81] A. Ritschl, RV, III, 426; JR, III, 451-452. "Die Aufgabe, welche der Theologie auf diesem Punkte gestellt ist, ist dadurch gelöst, dass die Widerspruchslosigkeit zwischen der ethischen und der religiösen Beurtheilung Christi, und die Nothwendigkeit der Ergänzung jener durch diese, ferner die Möglichkeit derselben in der christlichen Gotteside und im vollen Begriff der sittlichen Freiheit aufgezeigt ist. Wie die Person Christi geworden und dasjenige geworden ist, als welches sie sich für die ethische und die religiöse Schätzung darbietet, ist kein Gegenstand theologischer Forschung, weil das Problem über jede Art der Forschung hinausliegt. Was dic kirchliche Ueberlieferung in dieser Hinsicht darbietet, ist in sich undeutlich, und deshalb nicht geeignet, etwas zu erklären. Als Träger der vollendeten Offenbarung ist Christus gegeben, damit man an ihn glaube. Indem man an ihn glaubt, versteht man ihn als den Offenbarer Gottes. Aber die Combination zwischen ihm und Gott seinem Vater ist eben keine Erklärung wissenschaftlicher Art. Und man darf als Theolog wissen, das durch das vergebliche Haschen nach solcher Erklärung die Anerkennung Christi als der vollendeten Offenbarung Gottes nur getrübt wird." Ritschl does not attempt to develop the basis of the "ethical and religious apprehension," or locate the source of revelation in a consistent ontology. Ethical and religious apprehension appear to stand in the same relation to revelation as Space and Time hold to experience in Kant's *Critique of Pure Reason*. The distinction which Ritschl draws between scientific, theoretical knowledge and positive religious knowledge is collapsed by his correlation of revelation with history, but not to make such a correlation risks the reduction of religion to aesthetic expression of a personal and private character. Cf. Paul Wrzecinko, *Die philosophischen Wurzeln der Theologie Ritschls* (Berlin: Topelmann, 1964); Pickle, "Epistemology and Soteriology"; Deegan, "Albrecht Ritschl as Critical Empiricist," pp. 149-160; Guthrie, "Kant and Ritschl." It is in the will of Christ that Ritschl locates his uniqueness as an individual and

his special relationship to mankind. Ritschl will not move beyond this positive judgment towards a more complete psychology (RV, III, 433; JR, III, 467-468).

[82] A. Ritschl, RV, III, 444-445; JR, III, 472. "Die ethische Beurtheilung der Lebensführung Christi gemäss seinem Berufe fand ihre sachgemässe Fortsetzung in der religiösen Schätzung seines Lebens als der Offenbarung der Liebe Gottes und derjenigen Freiheit, welche als die characteristische Macht über die Welt Merkmal der Gottheit ist. Diese Betrachtung hat im Wesentlichen den Gesichtspunkt befolgt, welcher in dem königlichen Prophetenthum Christi ausgedrückt ist; nur wich sie von der hergebrachten Auffassung dieses Titels darin ab, dass das gesammte sittliche Handeln Christi als die Darstellung der göttlichen Gnade und Treue in die prophetische Thätigkeit desselben eingerechnet wurde."

[83] A. Ritschl, RV, III, 446-447; JR, III, 474. "Vielmehr stützen sie sich unbedingt auf die Geltung der Gnade Gottes gegen die Bundesgemeinde, und bezeichnen nur positive Bedingungen, welche die Glieder derselben zu erfüllen haben, um die Nähe des gnädigen Gottes zu geniessen. . .Weil der Priester Gott naht, indem er ihm die Gabe nahe bringt, so stellt er diejenigen vor Gott dar, für welche er handelt; es ist aber nicht gemeint, dass, weil der Priester und das Opfer Gott nahe kommen, die Anderen Gott fern bleiben mögen. Diese Beziehungen gelten auch, wenn Umwissenheitssünde den Anlass zu Opfern bildet; in diesem Falle erfolgt die Sündenvergebung daraus, dass der Priester mit dem Opfer indirect auch die Sünder in die Nähe Gottes gestellt hat."

[84] A. Ritschl, RV, III, 446-447; JR, III, 474-475.

[85] *Ibid.*

[86] A. Ritschl, RV, III, 448; JR, III, 476. "Wenn also Christus als Priester vorgestellt werden soll, so ist die Grundform für diese Thätigkeit enthalten in jedem Moment des Bewusstseins, dass er als der Sohn Gottes zu Gott als seinem Vater in der unvergleichlichen Gemeinschaft steht, welche ihm in der Erkenntniss Gottes, in der Ergebung des Willens in Gottes Fügung, in der Sicherheit der begleitenden Gefühlstimmung gegenwärtig ist. Indem er sich hiezu insbesondere im Gebete sammelt, behauptet er die Nähe Gottes und überführt sich von der Liebe Gottes als dem Grunde seiner Stellung als des Sohnes Gottes (Joh. 15:10-11)."

[87] A. Ritschl, RV, III, 610-611; JR, III, 646- 647. ". . .dass der Glaube an die väterliche Vorsehung Gottes und die Geduld der königlichen Würde, die Demuth und das Gebet der priesterlichen Würde der Christen entsprechen. Die weltherrschende Stellung aber nimmt man in dem hier geltenden religiösen Sinne ein, weil man in der Gottesnähe und in der eigenthümlichen Angehörigkeit von Gott steht, welche die Selbständigkeit gegen alle Elemente der Welt sichert, weil sie bestimmt wird durch die Aneignung des Zweckes des Gottesreiches, welcher als der Zweck der Welt und zugleich als der eigenste Zweck Gottes selbst erkannt ist. Diese Functionen sind die eigentlichste Bethätigung der in der christlichen Religion vollzogenen Versöhnung und der Gotteskindschaft; sie stellen, wo sie auftreten, die persönliche Verwirklichung des Christenthums als Religion dar, . . . Aber zugleich bilden sie den Massstab, nach welchem festgestellt werden soll, dass andere religiöse Functionen, oder was man in diesem Sinne ausübt, entweder nur den untergeordneten Werth von Hülfsleistungen oder gar keinen Werth haben."

CHAPTER III
A HISTORY OF THE
MUNUS TRIPLEX IN
CHRISTIAN THOUGHT

Introduction

In this section of the study it is our task to look at references to the *munus triplex* in Christian thought in order to see how the *munus triplex* has been used. An understanding of the use of the *munus triplex* in the ancient and medieval Church and during the Reformation period will give us a background for evaluating Ritschl's criticism of the doctrine.

The Ancient and Medieval Church

First, we will examine the offices of prophecy, priesthood and kingship in the Biblical and related literature. These are the sources for the typological and allegorical development of these traditions by the early Church. Then, we will present the *munus triplex* in several forms as it has appeared in the ancient and medieval Church as a representation or indication of the work of Christ. Finally, we will consider the treatment of the *munus triplex* in the Reformation period. There the most important statement of the doctrine is that by John Calvin. We will follow Calvin's presentation of the doctrine carefully in the context of Book II of the *Institutes of the Christian Religion*. In Chapter IV we will then turn to a criticism of Ritschl's assessment of the history of the *munus triplex*, its bases in Scripture, its relation to the life of Jesus, its formal unity and its availability as a source of meaningful language for expressing the Christian faith.

Prophet, Priest and King in the Old Testament Literature

We can understand the importance of locating the sources of prophecy, priesthood, and kingship in the Bible for the ancient Church by considering the use of the Bible by the early Church fathers. In the view of the Christian apologist Justin Martyr, the authority of the Christian religion was supreme over all other religions or systems of knowledge. This supremacy was demonstrated for Justin by his view of the historical priority of the Jewish Scripture. In Justin's understanding, the ancient prophecies of the Old Testament were thought to be the oldest writings of man. The Scriptures commanded respect within the Jewish and Christian communities for their age and their faithfulness to the word of God. In the Hellenistic world, Justin felt, the Christians had claims to truth that were as impressive as those of the great philosophical traditions. Justin believed that the non-Christian world had received knowledge of God and of God's plan of salvation in distorted or abbreviated form. The plan of salvation which God had chosen for His people had been revealed to the Christian in Scripture. Christ had taught the Christians how to interpret Scripture in order to understand the prophecies more correctly than the Jews, who shared the tradition of the Scriptures, and how to understand the character of the world more completely than the Greeks. The best knowledge of the ancient Greek philosophers and poets was regarded as a dim reflection of the biblical truth. This truth was received by the Jews but fully realized in the life and teaching of Jesus Christ. The claim of the ancient Church, then, was that it possessed the true understanding of Christ and in turn the true understanding of the Old Testament as the prophecy of the coming of Christ. The appearance of the offices of prophecy, priesthood, and kingship in the Old Testament would mean for the early Church that these offices, or the institutions that represented these offices, were part of God's intention which was fulfilled in the life of Christ.

In our examination of the presence of prophecy, priesthood, and kingship in the Old Testament and intertestamental literature we wish to establish that there is a clear reference to these institutions in the biblical and related material which would have been available to the early Church for use in allegory and typology. Further, recent biblical scholarship supports the importance of these institutions in general for understanding the history and religion of Israel as it serves as the background for the emergence of the Christian faith.

The association of the offices of prophet, priest, and king with the Old Testament operates at several levels. First, major blocks of material in the canon of the Old Testament are the writings of the prophets, the history of the kings of Israel, and describe the conduct of the cultus by the priesthood. Second, critical examination of the biblical material serves to focus on the distinctive traditions of prophecy, priesthood, and kingship, finding them represented in the material but also finding the influence of these very traditions in collecting and editing the oral traditions of Israel into the literary form in which they are preserved in the Old Testament canon itself. The traditions of prophecy, priesthood and kingship are therefore formative and constitutive sources for the interpretation of the Old Testament. Third, the offices of prophecy, priesthood and kingship serve as symbols for Israel as a nation or people, in the sense of Jeremiah 32:32 where Yahweh condemns Israel and Judah and delivers Jerusalem to Nebuchadrezzar; and finally, the offices serve as sources for interpretation of the historical context of traditions, such as anointment, which formed part of the cultus.

King

The emergence of the office of king in the history of Israel came after the threat of the Philistine cities to the amphictyonic organization of the tribes of Israel in the eleventh century B.C.[2] Coming into existence long after the incursion into Canaan, kingship in Israel copied many of the elements of Canaanite royal traditions.[3] The common inheritance from Mesopotamia, Babylonia, Assyria and Egypt resulted in a theory of kingship which, with distinctive modifications due to Israel's monotheism, was widespread in the area. The king was considered as divinized, the offspring or incarnation of the god who ruled over the king on a supernatural level. The kingship was placed in a liturgical setting which employed the king as the representation of the god and the chief agent in the liturgical events which marked the celebration of the cultus. In Israel care was taken to distinguish the deity of Yahweh from the human status of the king. The king remained the religious and political representative of the people.

88

Genesis 14:18-20 recorded an early example of the priest-king tradition associated with the person of Melchizedek.

And Melchizedek king of Salem brought out bread and wine; he was priest of God Most High. And he blessed him and said,

"Blessed be Abram by God Most High, who has delivered your enemies into your hand."

The roles of Melchizedek as priest and king were clearly asserted although his appearance and identity remained mysterious. S. H. Hooke pointed to the Jebusite source of Melchizedek as a sign of the disturbed times and as evidence of the comingling of cultural traditions.[4] Later in the biblical tradition messianic interpretations were given to Melchizedek (Ps. 110:4; Heb. 7:1-17) and the text became a source for theological interpretation quite apart from the obscure historical incident that stood behind the tradition of the text.

The roles of priest and king were in tense opposition in Israel at the time of the establishment of the monarchy. The fusion of traditions in the amphictyonic structure with the laws, customs and ideals of Canaanite kingship, aimed at a comprehensive national kingship for Israel, and encountered stiff opposition.[5] This opposition was expressed in I Samuel 8, 10, 12, and 15 which opposed the ideal of monarchy under Solomon and David as God's intention with the notion that Yahweh alone should be king over Israel. When the center of cultic functions was transferred from the tribal leaders to the king, the economic and political characteristics of a despotism began to affect the national life. Circles of seers and prophets organized to conserve the traditions of the premonarchical times.[6] An example of this opposition is recorded in the confrontation at Naboth's vineyard (1 Kings 21:1-29) between King Ahab and the prophet Elijah. The eminent domain of the despotism was challenged by the standards of justice upheld by the prophets.[7] Once established, kingship in Israel continued to the beginning of the Christian era as a sign of Israel's religious heritage and became the symbol of her hope and expectation of the future. The expectation of the return of the power of the Davidic throne remained even in periods when the royal office was corrupted, captive and subordinate to a more powerful throne, or vacant.

The anointment of the king was the sign of his ratification as the elect representative of Yahweh. The anointment of kings was mentioned in the book of Judges 9:8 in a parable which Jotham used to denounce Abimelech who had made himself king at Shechem after the murder of his half brothers. Judges 9:22 reports that Abimelech ruled over Israel for three years and was destroyed by an evil spirit sent by God to avenge the crimes of Abimelech. This episode may be contrasted with the establishment of a legitimate kingship in Israel, instituted at the direction of God rather than because of the ambition of man, recorded in the earlier stratum in the book of Samuel.[8] A later stratum in Samuel (I Samuel 8 ff.) acknowledged the foundation of kingship in Israel but presented it as an expedient measure proposed by Samuel and reluctantly approved by Yahweh. In I Samuel 9:16 and 10, Saul was anointed and spoken of as the *Lord's anointed* (I Samuel 12:2, 15:1, and II Samuel 1:14). The title was extended to David in I Samuel 16:12 and II Samuel 5:3. It became the title for the king, understood as the representative of God who would be active in the restoration of Israel.[9] The Christian who read the Old Testament looking for signs of the coming of Christ could find a powerful sequence in the title *Anointed* applied to David and its translation to Greek and the identification of Jesus Christ as the Messiah. In both sources in Samuel, anointment is recognized as part of the ritual of kingship indicating divine approval, so that although the justification behind the kingship may be debated, the association of it with anointment is clear. The anointment of the king was the sign of his ratification as the elect representative of Yahweh and was the endowment of the king with the divine spirit and superhuman power.

. . ."as an envoy (angel) of Yahweh" he discerns all things, and accomplishes what he will (II Sam. 14:17 ff.). He knows the future (Ps. 2:7; II Sam. 23). "Eternal" (i.e. extremely long) life is attributed to him. Wonderful experiences are his; and he can do what others cannot do. He rules "by the strength of Yahweh" and performs mighty super-human deeds on earth. The anointing expresses Yahweh's "choice" of him "to be king over his people". . . He promises blessings and powers which. . . bestow blessing to his surroundings. . . Thus the king is the savior to whom the people look for salvation. . . [10]

The role of the king collected the power of the priests to mediate between Yahweh and the people, the wisdom of the prophets and seers to interpret events and perform miracles, and the authority of godly sovereignty over a people.

We may in conclusion sum up in the following terms the essential qualities which Israel required for a true king. The king is the natural, official leader of the public cult of a nation, even if on ordinary occasions a priest officiates in his stead. He is the channel through which Yahweh's blessings flow to the people, being conveyed primarily through his cultic functions. The pre-supposition and condition of this is that he should be loyal to the laws and justice of Yahweh. Although in virtue of his equipment (anointing) and Yahweh's spirit he is "divine" and more than an ordinary human being, and although as a leader in the cult he is the representative of the people in the presence of the Deity: he prays, intercedes, offers up sacrifice, and receives power and blessing. The covenant is concentrated in him; and through him and his line the promises are mediated. Through him the congregation stands before God and meets God.[11]

Prophet

The prophets' concern was to evaluate the performance of the king in terms of the ideal role and to speak forth their assessment of the word of God himself. This element remained in tension with the kingship until Israel's dissolution as an independent realm.

...the way in which...the king [is] regarded as protector and friend of the needy and humble reveals the influence of the prophetic movement...It is therefore also clear that the prophets did not hesitate to direct their criticism even against sacral kingship, and to assess an individual historical king in terms of the demands of Yahwism and its ideal of kingship.[12]

James Muilenburg described the functions of the Israelite prophet as a *man of God* (I Sam. 9:6-10), who was psychically related to Yahweh as an extension of the *divine holiness*, as *messenger and herald* who received the reports of Yahweh's intentions and actions with regard to the people Israel and as *Yahweh's servant* whose role was watchman,

91

assayer, and intercessor for the salvation of Israel. As *member of the council of Yahweh*, the prophet stood in the presence of the divine king and reported to the monarch of Israel the words he heard (I Kings 22:19; Isaiah 6:1ff.; Jeremiah 23:18-22).[13]

In the messages of the prophets there was not only concern for the preservation of righteousness (I Kings 21:1-29) but also there was interpretation of the historical events which spelled out the destruction of the Israelite nation and led to its bondage and captivity.[14] The words of Amos, Hosea, Micah and Isaiah held moral and political significance for the people. Isaiah and Ezekiel performed symbolic actions (Isaiah 20:3-4; Ezekiel 4:1-3) which carried the image of the prophet as one whose presence announced and enacted the historical destiny of God's will for his people. When the great prophetic teachers were absent from the Jewish people, the seers and magicians contended for the role of prophet. The return of *the Prophet* was expected as a sign from Yahweh and the initial event in the close of the age.[15]

"For behold, the day comes, burning like an oven, when all the arrogant and all the evil-doers will be stubble; the day that comes shall burn them up," says the Lord of hosts, "so that it will leave them neither root nor branch. But for you who fear my name the sun of righteousness shall rise, with healing in its wings. You shall go forth leaping like calves from the stall. And you shall tread down the wicked, for they will be ashes under the soles of your feet, on the day when I act," says the Lord of hosts.

"Remember the law of my servant Moses, the statutes and ordinances that I commanded him at Horeb for all Israel."

"Behold, I will send you Elijah the prophet before the great and terrible day of the Lord comes. And he will turn the hearts of fathers to their children and the hearts of children to their fathers, lest I come and smite the land with a curse." Malachi 4:1-5.

The Old Testament pointed to the return of the prophet as the sign of the day of the Lord and the promise of judgment and fulfillment when Israel's Lord and King, Yahweh, be in her midst.[16]

The explicit reference to the anointment of a prophet in the Old Testament was I Kings 19:16 in which Elijah received the word of God to anoint Elisha the son of Shaphat to be a prophet. I Kings 19:19

went on to offer an account of the incident of Elisha's call which was effected by casting the mantle of Elijah upon Elisha. No mention of explicit anointment is found in the later text. The casting of the mantle may represent part of the ceremony of transferring power in which anointment may have played a part. It is difficult to determine the precise limit of figurative and literal reference at this point. I Kings 19:16 is sufficient ground to serve as the basis of a typology, and the passage in I Kings 19:19 is not sufficient to destroy the image.

Priest

The office of priest was associated with the kingship of Melchizedek in Genesis 14:18-20. In this case the narration of the history of the patriarchs had just begun and the effect is to suggest a prototype of later forms. The brief mention of Melchizedek serves to introduce the theme but does not enlarge upon priesthood of Melchizedek beyond the description of receiving a tithe and blessing bread and wine in the name of God Most High. The anointment of priests is ascribed to Moses in Exodus 29:7, 30:30 and 40:13, and in Leviticus 8 and 16. Moses was to perform the rite on Aaron and his sons to ordain a priesthood and to establish a succession. The office of the High Priest was associated with the Temple in Jerusalem as the center of the official cultus and continued throughout the history of Israel until well into the first century A.D.

In addition to the understanding of priesthood in Israel associated with the tradition of Moses and Aaron in which legitimate priesthood is identified with succession from Aaron, there is a tradition of the functions of priesthood being filled by the head of the household, and the identification of Israel as a nation of priests from whom a blessing will be extended to the nations (Exodus 19:306; Lev. 11:14, Num. 15:40).[17] In reviewing the traditions of priests and levites Raymond Abba finds that the householder functioned as priest, judge, prophet and ruler on occasion and that the history of the monarchy and the building of the Temple reveal a growing concern for the authority of the Levitical priesthood and its identification with the families of Dan, Eli, and Zadok.[18] After the exile the chief priest of Israel functions as the leader of Israel as a religious nation and the kingship of Israel is reduced to a vassal position controlled by more

powerful nations who worship other gods. The restoration of Israel
as a nation is hoped for in terms of a religious and a national restoration. The motif of a priestly nation is employed typologically by the
Christian community in its use of Exodus 19:6 and Isaiah 61:6, identifying the Christian community as the holy priesthood (I Peter 2:5,9;
Rev. 1:6, 5:10, and 20:6).[19]

The source of the power of the Israelite priests, kings and prophets
was God himself. The convergence of the offices of priest, prophet,
and king was associated with the throne of David. When the hope
of Israel was expressed in the midst of her tribulations, it was for the
appearance of these offices as a sign of God's renewed presence with
his people. The traditions of Abraham, Melchizedek, Moses and
Aaron, and David and Samuel all summoned together the offices of
priest, king, and prophet as the symbols of the servant of Yahweh.

Prophet, Priest, and King in Intertestamental Literature

In the *Testament of Levi* 8:14 there was the following application
of the titles prophet, priest, and king to the person of John Hyrcanus
(134-104 B.C.).

And the third shall be called by a new name, because a king
shall arise in Judah, and shall establish a new priesthood, after
the fashion of the gentiles.

And his presence is unutterable, as a prophet of the most high,
of the seed of Abraham our Father.[20]

The use of these images in regard to John Hyrcanus was supported
by Josephus' account of the second century in *Jewish Wars* I, ii, 8.

He [John Hyrcanus] was the only man to unite in his person
three of the highest privileges: the supreme command of the nation, the high priesthood, and the gift of prophecy. For so closely
was he in touch with the Deity, that he was never ignorant of
the future. . .[21]

The powers which were ascribed to Hyrcanus carried the implication,
in the highly eschatological language of the times, of signifying the
approval of Yahweh and the initiation of the day of the Lord. Franklin
W. Young raised this point in regard to the claim of the prophetic
powers.

94

The claim of prophecy could be made only within the context of those events which herald messianic times, which were expected by all as the period when the prophetic spirit (or holy spirit) would once more be released.[22]

The same context of meaning is supplied by looking at the exegetical presuppositions of the Essenes who rejected the leadership of Jerusalem, and what was in their eyes a polluted priesthood, in order to found a new and righteous Jerusalem and await the messiah in visions of the New Age. Frank M. Cross, Jr. emphasized this in his interpretation of the Qumran documents.

The technique of exposition in all these sources grows out of the presuppositions of apocalypticism, and can be rightly understood only within the categories of this special type of eschatological thought. Two major assumptions characterize apocalyptic exegesis. All biblical prophecy is normally taken to have eschatological meaning. The "prophets," Moses as well as Amos, the Psalmist as well as Jeremiah, speak regularly in open or veiled language of the "last days." Their predictions are not to be understood in simple terms of the near future or even remote future, but apply to the crisis of the ages, the final times when the historical epoch turns to the trans-historical epoch. Secondly, it must be understood that the apocalypticist understood himself to be living in these days of final crisis, and at the end of days and the beginning of the New Age, so that the events of his own times were recognized as precisely those events forecast by the prophets of old as coming in the last days.[23]

The confluence of the roles of prophet, priest, and king was the sign of the manifestation of divine approval. In one case the threefold title was given to a priest-king, John Hyrcanus, who sought to stabilize a disintegrating political and religious situation. It was also read back into the interpretation of Moses as the one from whom the prophetic, priestly, and royal elements in Jewish tradition took authority. Moses was adopted as a symbolic prototype and the three titles which were taken to characterize the Deity at work in the history of the people Israel were assigned to him. It is in this sense on can read Philo's *De Vita Mosis*, II, i, 3.

But Moses will be seen not only to have displayed the genius of the philosopher and of the king in an extraordinary degree at the same time, but three other powers likewise, one of which is conversant about legislation, the second about the way of discharging the office of high priest, and the last about the prophetic office; and it is on these subjects that I now have been constrained to choose to enlarge; for I conceive that all these things have fitly been united in him, inasmuch as in accordance with the providential will of God he was both a king and a lawgiver, and a high priest and a prophet, and because in each office he displayed the most eminent wisdom and virtues.[24]

Philo's sense of harmony of the Greek and Hebrew worlds led him to juxtapose the ideal of philosopher-king from Hellenic culture with the role of the king in Jewish tradition. The distinction between lawgiver and prophet which he made does not obscure the essential correspondence of his thought with the three-fold office. The functions of prediction, symbolic action, member of the divine council, and lawgiver were associated in the office of prophet.[25]

Prophet, Priest, and King in the New Testament

If we are correct in tracing the development of the offices of prophet, priest, and king from a relationship with the royal theology of the Israelite throne to a later more symbolic form in apocalyptic theology, then the matrix of apocalyptic messianism in the post-exilic period was the mold in which the offices received their meaning as indicating the character of the true servant of Yahweh in immediately pre-Christian theology.

In "The Christian Prophets in the New Testament" Ruth E. Bowlin described the state of Jewish messianic theology as it related to the appearance of prophecy and found that the expectation of the apocalyptic age had focused on the arrival of a prophetic figure who would usher in the New Age.[26] The pressure of a rising sense of crisis had forced the expectation of a prophetic figure to focus on a specific figure, such as Elias or the Messiah. The weight of such specific expectations prevented any prophecy from claiming authority which did not bear some relationship to these requirements. A prophet would have to demonstrate his authority as *the* prophet of God, the Messiah, or be persecuted as a false prophet. False prophets, according to Josephus, were usually killed as dangerous revolutionaries by the Roman authorities.[27] It is in this setting that we turn to examine the role of Jesus as prophet in the New Testament.

The prophet was the sign of the Messianic Age, which involved the promises of fulfilling the royal and sacral requirements of Davidic kingship as they had become stylized in the tradition. The Jewish nation was to be raised up and her salvation accomplished. The Gospels set about to show how these expectations were met in Jesus' birth, ministry, teachings, death and resurrection.[28]

The infancy narrative in Luke 1:67, 2:25,36, took occasion to set the birth of Jesus in the midst of prophetic activity, namely, the prophecy of Zechariah upon the birth of John and the accounts of the words of Simeon and Anna when the infant Jesus was brought to the Temple.[29] The meeting with the elders of the Temple when Jesus was twelve (Luke 2:41-51), his reading from the prophet Isaiah (Luke 4:16-21) and his raising of a dead man (Luke 7:16) as a parallel to the I Kings 17:8-24 account of Elijah were all cited by Felix Gils as conscious attempts to portray Jesus with the powers, words, and bearing of a prophet.[30] Gils found that careful attention is given to placing Jesus in the lineage of the prophets and kings in the genealogy of Matthew, with an implicit comparison of Jesus and Moses as prophet of God and lawgiver. In the Gospel According to Matthew 21:11 comes the identification of Jesus by the crowd. "And the crowds said, 'This is the prophet Jesus from Nazareth of Galilee,'" and related to it is the reluctance of the chief priests and Pharisees to arrest Jesus when they feared the multitudes who regarded him as a prophet (Luke 21:46).

The identification of Jesus as prophet in the Synoptic parallels was only by report, association or implication, but not in the form of a direct assertion by the redactor. Three examples will serve to indicate the type of indirect appellation which was used. In Matthew 13:57 and the parallels in Mark 6:4, Luke 4:24, and a related passage in John 4:44, the question of Jesus' identity at Nazareth was met with the response "A prophet is not without honor except in his own country and his own house." Matthew 16:14 and 14:2 with their respective parallels answered the question of Jesus' identity with the report of several answers; John the Baptist returned to life, Elijah, or one of the prophets. Pilate was associated with the suggestion that Jesus was John the Baptist returned (Mark 6:16) while Peter affirmed him to be the Christ (Matthew 16:16). In the scene at the trial of Jesus in Matthew 26:68 and parallels, while slapping and spitting on him, the captors shouted at him to prophesy by naming who had struck him. Bowlin, Gils, Cullmann, and Davies agree that the title prophet was an early title applied to Jesus and a conception so widely known to the common people that its value for dealing with the uniqueness with which Jesus was Messiah was questionable.[31] Jesus was a prophetic figure for the Gospel writers but their affirmation is that he was *more* than a prophet. The theological emphasis of the Gospels had shifted to other titles whose implications led to a fuller expression of the meaning of the resurrection, distinguishing Jesus from the ambiguous figures who had claimed prophetic or messianic status for themselves.[32]

The Letter to the Hebrews seized the image of the High Priest to express the significance of Jesus' work, recalling the priest-king Melchizedek (Hebrews 6:20) for the basis of Jesus' office as priest. It was the action of Christ in his self offering that fulfilled his priestly office.[33]

> For it was fitting that we should have such a high priest, holy, blameless, unstained, separated from sinners, exalted above the heavens. He has no need, like those high priests, to offer sacrifices daily, first for his own sins and then for those of the people; he did this once for all when he offered up himself. (Hebrews 7:26-27)[34]

The application of the title king to Jesus occurs in the trial sequence of the passion narrative (Matthew 27:11, 30, 42 and parallels) which maintained the oblique style of reference which characterized the use of the title prophet. The Book of Revelation portrays the victory of Christ over the empire of Antichrist with the ascription of the title "Lord of lords, King of kings" (Revelation 17:14), and the image of the heavenly host behind the King of kings and Lord of lords in battle array (Revelation 19:16). The heavenly king motif is expressed in John 18:36 when Jesus declares his kingdom is not of this world.

Other titles of Christ are developed with theological advantage in the New Testament material and are analyzed in Vincent Taylor, *The*

Names of Jesus, Oscar Cullmann, *Christology of the New Testament,* and Norman Perrin, *The Kingdom of God in the Teachings of Jesus.*[35] The title prophet is primarily restricted to the earthly ministry of Jesus and opens the way for the later titles of approbation and honor.

The role of prophecy in the early Church following the crucifixion and resurrection of Jesus Christ was a problematic one. It was associated with possession of the Holy Spirit as the spirit of Christ. The most prominent tradition of the place of the Holy Spirit in the early community is that of the Pentecost (Acts 2:4). Those who received the gift of the spirit claimed power and insight to speak the word of God in building up the Church, in encouraging and consoling the members of the early communities. Paul describes prophecy as one of the gifts of the Spirit manifest in the churches (Romans 12:6; I Corinthians 12:10). Acts 2:17,18 recalls the prophecy of Joel about the effect of the Spirit in the life of the community.[36]

The use of the doctrine of the Holy Spirit is closely related to prophecy in the early communities according to Ruth E. Bowlin who finds the interpretation of the Holy Spirit as a source of power and validity for Christian discipleship to be the work of the prophets.[37] The interpretation of Scripture became one of the controversial activities of early Christians as the ecstatic tenor of prophecy increased in the early Church. This resulted in the stipulations in the New Testament concerning the judgment of teachers and false prophets by the results of their teaching and the character of their lives. The Letter to the Ephesians 2:30 gives us the image of the household of God "built on the foundation of the apostles and prophets, Christ Jesus himself being the cornerstone. . ." A word of caution indicating the problems associated with the spirit of prophecy is found in I John 4:1.

Beloved, do not believe every spirit, but test the spirits to see whether they are of God; for many false prophets have gone out into the world. (I John 4:1)

Paul counsels the spirits of the prophets to be subject to the other prophets (I Corinthians 14:32) and restricts speaking in tongues as a sign of the prophetic spirit to that which is for the edification of the whole community (I Corinthians 14:1-4).

> For one who speaks in a tongue speaks not to men but to God;
> for no one understands him, but he utters mysteries in the Spirit.
> On the other hand, he who prophesies speaks to men for their
> upbuilding and encouragement and consolation. He who speaks
> in a tongue edifies himself, but he who prophesies edifies the
> church. (I Corinthians 14:1-4)

The swift decline of prophecy as a common activity in the Church
and the dying out of the public office of the prophet in the communities removed it as a major center of theological concern. Bowlin
cites the over-identification of prophecy with the delayed Parousia,
the return of a distant apocalyptic view which did not expect immediate
proclamation of divine mysteries in the present, the appearance of
canonical standards for Scriptural sources, and the growing authority
and influence of the office of bishop as teacher to be the reasons for
the failure of prophecy to survive the gnostic and Montanist crises.[38]
Lietzmann concurs with this view.

The Church prepared a three-fold defense against the pneumatic and gnostic danger. She fixed the sources of the normative
tradition in the Canon of Scripture, laid the foundations of
theological teaching in the Creed, and especially did she set the
ecclesiastical office of the bishop as a higher authority than that
due to the unbridled exercise of pneumatic gifts. Thus it came
about that, not merely books and doctrines, but living guardians,
faced living antagonists.[39]

The role of the prophet and its claims to power and authority was
rediscovered by these guardians as a defense of their task in building
up the body of Christ, defending the faith against the pagan world,
against the political concerns of empire, and even against decay within
the Church itself.

The priesthood of the early Church was associated with the image
of Jesus Christ as High Priest developed in Hebrews. The book of
Revelation identified the priesthood of the Church with the figure
of Christ in Rev. 1:4-6, 5:10 and 20:6. Those who shared in the resurrection were priests of God and Christ

> Grace to you and peace from him who is and who was and
> who is to come from the seven spirits who are before his throne,

100

and from Jesus Christ the faithful witness, the first born of the
dead, and the ruler of kings on earth.

To him who loves us and has freed us from our sins by his
blood and made us a kingdom, priests to his God and Father,
to him be glory and dominion for ever and ever. Amen. (Rev.
1:4-6)

The royal priesthood of Christ was extended to those who believe
through him.

But you are a chosen race, a royal priesthood, a holy nation,
God's own people, that you may declare the wonderful deeds
of him who called you out of darkness into his marvelous light.
(I Peter 2:4-5)[40]

On the basis of this survey of sources of the three-fold office in
the Old Testament, intertestamental literature, and the New Testament,
we hold that in the earliest strata of the biblical records of the institutions of priesthood, prophecy, and kingship in Israel, the offices
or religious-political structures represented by these offices were
already interrelated and regarded as having divine sanction for
mediating the relationship of Yahweh to the elect people Israel. The
conflicts between priest, king and prophet which were recorded in
some of the Old Testament narratives reflected the historical opposition of these institutions and their traditions. The use of the offices
together as a symbolic unit began to emerge following the exile when
the circumstances which had supported the rival claims of the several
offices for leadership had passed from memory. The offices could
be used to characterize Israel's hope for the future. The Old Testament reflects a stylization of Israel's heritage in the royal theologies
associated with the Davidic and Solomonic monarchies, in the distinctive interest in the Temple and Priesthood in the exilic and post-exilic
periods, and in the continuing interest in prophecy. These emphases
in the literature of the Old Testament reflected the importance of the
offices as part of the cultural heritage of Israel. The offices were
available to later stages in the Judeo-Christian tradition to serve as
symbols representing the ancient traditions. The use of these symbols could then represent a continuing *Heilsgeschichte*. When the
Christian community accepted the identity of being new heirs in

Christ, the inheritance included the use of the Old Testament categories, among them, prophet, priest and king. These institutions emerged as symbols in terms of which God's relationship to the new Israel was expressed. The presentation of Jesus as the Christ involved, in part, the proclamation of his fulfillment of the offices of prophet, priest, and king which had come to be symbolic of the old Law.

Prophet, Priest, and King in the Ancient and Medieval Church

The interpretation and application of the offices of prophet, priest, and king in the ancient and medieval Church was quite varied. We have found a variety of instances in which the Church has drawn upon the tradition of these offices to express the continuing presence of Christ. The effect of these images is at times like leaven in measures of meal, hidden, implicit, and presupposed, giving life to the expression of the faith. In this section we will present a series of references which demonstrate the use of the collection of titles prophet, priest, and king.

Justin Martyr (d. ca. 165 A.D.) wrote, sometime after 153 A.D., *Dialogue with Trypho* as an apologia for Christianity against Jewish objections. In it he took occasion to group titles of Christ together to indicate the character of the work and the authority of Christ.

> For Christ is appointed King and Priest and Lord and Messenger and man and leader.

and

> Christ is King and Priest and Messenger and whatever else He holds or ought to hold.[41]

Tertullian (ca. 150-220 A.D.) writing in *An Answer to the Jews,* 198 A.D., developed at length an argument that was directed to establish the authority of Jesus Christ over the law of Moses by proclaiming Christ priest according to the order of Melchizedek (Genesis 14:18), distinct from priesthood defined by the Levitical codes, and not dependent on the commission of Moses (Deut. 18:15). At another point in his text Tertullian portrayed Christ in terms of two advents, one in humility as the suffering servant of prophecy and one in exaltation as Christ, clothed in glory as the Son of Man.[42] Following Tertullian it is not surprising to find Cyprian (200-258 A.D.) examining

102

Christ from a similar perspective in *Testimoniorum contra Judeos.*
MSL, 4, 675-780.[43] Novatian (d. 257) argued for the unity of the
witness of the Old and New Testaments to the one and the same Jesus
Christ who was raised up as a prophet (Deut. 18:15), given as Chief
and Commander of Nations (Isaiah 55:4-5), and was a possessor of
righteousness as the son of the king possesses his father's authority
(Psalms 72:1), *De Trinitate*, IX, *MSL*, 3, 900-901.[44]

No definite date or authorship can be fixed for the *Constitution
of the Holy Apostles* beyond locating it in the late third or early fourth
century, but the image of Christ which appears in the text is that of
head and prototype of priests, kings and prophets.

> Him did Moses see in the bush; concerning Him did he speak
> in Deuteronomy, "A Prophet will the Lord your God raise up
> unto thee out of your brethren like unto me. . ."
>
> Him Samuel knew as the "Anointed of God" and thence nam-
> ed the priests and the kings the anointed. . . Ezekiel also, and
> the following prophets, affirm everywhere that He is the Christ,
> the Lord, the King, the Judge, the Lawgiver, the Angel of the
> Father, the only-begotten God.[45]

Eusebius of Caesarea, writing about 323 A.D. in his *Ecclesiastical
History*, I, 3 provided one of the strongest passages linking the offices of Christ in the close association that characterized the biblical
setting of the Messiah figure. The role of the priest-king which was
present in most other passages which develop the Melchizedek motif
was complemented here by the office of prophet.

> We have also received the tradition that some of the prophets
> themselves had by anointing already become Christs in type,
> seeing that they all refer to the Christ, the divine and heavenly
> Logos, of the world the only High Priest, of all creation the on-
> ly king, of the prophets the only archprophet of the Father.[46]

The holy chrism as a sign of divine authority and the title of Christ
as the *Anointed one* seized many writers' attention as the roles of
priest and king in the Melchizedek tradition and the religious interpretation of the life of Jesus as the Christ were compared in the early
church. The relationship of these offices to Jesus was involved in the
problem of understanding the Person of Christ. We can see in the

phrases of Cyril of Jerusalem (d. 386), a *homoiousian,* then an orthodox Nicene, the evidence of creedal language, joining two offices, like natures, in the unity of one person.

> Adding the name of "Christ" that it might represent the kingly and priestly authority through two select men, joined in the one future Jesus Christ.[47]

Hilary of Poitiers (d. 367) also developed the implications of chrism and charisma in respect to the offices of king and priest and added the notion of purity or righteousness, a sign of the prophet.

> What God conferred on those who by the anointing of oil were consecrated as kings and priests, this the Holy Spirit conferred on the man Christ, adding moreover a purification.[48]

Ambrose of Milan (339-397 A.D.) found the offices of prophet and priest involved in his own work as the servant of God. He interpreted his struggle with the Emperor Theodosius over the control of a basilica as an occasion on which he shared the prophetic heritage of Elijah and defended the place of Christ as judge of the emperor, subordinating the wishes of the palace to the faith of the Church and the authority of the earthly emperor to that of the divine king.[49]

Chrysostom (d. 407) made an explicit statement of the threefold office.

> . . . also because Christ was to have three dignities: King, Prophet, Priest; but Abraham was prophet and priest . . . David was king and prophet, but not priest. Thus He is expressly called the son of both, that the three-fold dignity of His forefathers might be recognized by hereditary right in Christ.[50]

Augustine (d. 430) found that the act of Christ's self-offering as priest and sacrifice was also a royal act. The performance of symbolic actions in one's own life which was typical of prophetic behavior (associated with Isaiah, Ezekiel and Hosea), was also characteristic of the priest and king as cultic types.

> For he was anointed as king (I Kings 16:13), and then only king and priest were anointed; in that time these two persons were anointed. In two persons was prefigured the one future king

and priest. However, not only had He been anointed our Head, but we ourselves have been anointed His body. Moreover, He is king because He rules and leads us; He is priest because He intercedes for us (Romans 8:24). Indeed, he alone stood forth as such a priest that he could himself be the sacrifice also. Therefore, there is an unction for all Christians.[51]

The offices and the anointment are extended to Christians in the liturgical life of the community.

The King fought for us, the priest offered Himself for us. Inasmuch as He fought for us, it was as though He were conquered, but He actually did conquer. For He was crucified, and on the cross to which He was nailed He slew the devil; therefore He is our king. But how is He priest? Because He offered Himself for us.[52]

Petrus Chrysologus (d. 450) made use of the threefold office as an image of the historical process of salvation converging in the Person of Jesus Christ.

He was called "Christ" by anointment, and "Jesus" by name because He poured Himself forth on those anointed with the full plenitude of the Spirit of divinity which in former times had been gathered together through kings, prophets. and priests, into one person, this king of kings, priest of priests, prophet of prophets.[53]

What we have found in the ancient Church is a variety of uses of the offices as interpretation of aspects of the redemptive work of Christ. In recognizing that their application is not consistent, we do not support the conclusion which Ritschl drew that the doctrine is unstable and invalid. We find the doctrine is legitimately part of the Christian tradition because it does have so many forms early in the history of Christian thought.

In the medieval Church, Alcuin (d. 804), whose contribution to the development of learning in the Frankish kingdom under Charlemagne would bear fruit in the prophetic role of the universities, presented Christ as Saviour, Priest and King.

Indeed He whom He anointed was called Christ, that is anointed. God is in man by the oil of gladness, that is, by the anointing of the Holy Spirit, in an everlasting priest and king, in order that He save Christians who are called by His name from their sins in that He is their Saviour, in order that He might reconcile them with God the Father in that He is their Priest and that He might gather them into His everlasting kingdom in that He is their King.[54]

The supremacy of Christ over kings and priests, and recognition of the anointed status of both offices, enjoying the sign of divine favor, were important elements for liturgical kingship in medieval political theory. Ernst H. Kantorowicz noted that the royal anointments were recovered during the seventh and eighth centuries A.D. The imperial title *Pontifex Maximus* was joined with the Melchizedek motif in which the liturgical symbols of the Kingdom of God were implied. The tradition of the pagan empire and the spiritual kingdom was intermingled in the *rex et sacerdos* ideal until Roman and Canon law were refined to produce a legal formulation of the relationships between Emperor and Pope, Church and State, Bishop and King.[55] Both political and religious history attest to the fact that there was no single solution but that the struggle to define the relationships persisted throughout the medieval period and into the Reformation and Renaissance.

Albertus Magnus (d. 1280) based the witness to the uniqueness of the power and authority of Christ on Simon Peter's confession in Matthew 16:16, "You are the Christ, the Son of the living God." The anointment of Christ was of a higher order than that of the priests and kings of Israel.

He was anointed [Christ] moreover as a king that He might establish a new law, and as a priest that He might minister a new holiness.

and

However, kings and priests were anointed. But Christ is king and priest according to the order of Melchizedek, who was king and priest.[56]

In Thomas Aquinas' (d. 1274) *Summa Theologica* the offices received separate consideration as well as being grouped in a triad.

106

Now Christ before His passion touched our state inasmuch as He was not merely a *comprehensor* but a *wayfarer.* Hence it was prophetical in Him to know and announce what was beyond the knowledge of other wayfarers: and for this reason he is called a prophet. (*Summa Theologica*, III, 7,8)

The office proper to a priest is to be a mediator between God and the people: to wit, inasmuch as He bestows Divine things on the people, wherefore *sacerdos.* .., and again, forasmuch as He offers up the peoples' prayers to God, and, in a manner, makes satisfaction to God for their sins; wherefore the Apostle says (Hebrews 5:1) *Every high-priest taken from among men is ordained for men in the things that appertain to God, that he may offer up gifts and sacrifices for sins.* Now this is most fitting that Christ should be a priest. (*Summa Theologica.* III, 22, 1)

By proclaiming Christ King, the Magi foreshadowed the constancy of the Gentiles in confessing Christ even until death. Whence Chrysostom says (Hom. XI in Matth.) that while they thought of the King who was to come, the Magi feared not the king who was actually present. They had not yet seen Christ, and they were already prepared to die for Him. (*Summa Theologica*, III, 36, 8)

The three offices are drawn together in the image of the fount of grace.

As stated above. . .other men have this or that grace bestowed on this or that one, but Christ, as being Head of all, has the perfection of all graces. Wherefore, as to others, one is a *lawgiver*, another is a *priest*, another is a *king*; but all these concur in Christ as the fount of all grace. (*Summa Theologica*, III, 22, 1)[57]

Thomas knows of the tradition of the *munus triplex* in exegesis of the name of Christ. In *Catena Aurea* he lists the interpretations of the name of "Christ" in association with the offices in dealing with Matthew 1:1. He associates the threefold usage with Chrysostom and the references to priest and king with Rabanus and Augustine.[58]

As an organizing principle for the balance of powers, spiritual, temporal, and intellectual, the threefold office was recovered as an idealized model for socio-political thought with implications for the prophetic role as the pattern for the universities. The emperor and pope,

107

king and bishop, magistrate and priest were all sensitive in the middle ages to the biblical warrants for the source of their authority in the offices of Christ as King and High-Priest. Alexander of Roes writing in 1281 and 1289 saw the Christian commonwealth in terms of several analogies. A trinity of soul, body and mind on the individual level was related to society at large as administered by the priest, the king, and the prophet as the teacher, *doctor ecclesiae*. Alexander correlated the three offices with the persons of the Trinity and three power centers in Christendom.

For Father, Son, and Holy Spirit, one God, has so arranged it that *sacerdotium, regnum* and *studium* should constitute one Christian society (*ecclesia*). Since, then, the faith of Christ is ruled by these three principles, the clergy, magistracy, and scholarship—the Papacy in Italy maintaining the faith, and royalty in Germany securing the protection of the same, and scholarship in France so teaching that faith may be sustained—it is clear that the commonwealth of the Christian faith has here in these three provinces its principal supports.

If [co-ordinated] in these three—namely, the *sacerdotium*, the *imperium*, and the *studium*—then the Christian body politic and ecclesiastical (*sancta ecclesia catholica*) is spiritually vitalized, enlarged, and guided as is the individual by the integration of his three component parts: soul, body, and mind.[59]

Our survey of evidence of the origin of the threefold office of Christ as prophet, priest and king has found that the three offices refer to authentic biblical sources in the Old Testament for the expression of the action of God in the history of his people for their salvation. The offices were employed in a similar way in the intertestamental literature and began to be linked with historical persons as bearers of the offices in one person as a sign of divine election. The offices received further treatment in the New Testament as writers expressed the way in which God's actions were manifest to his people in the midst of history by means of prophecy, priesthood, and kingship, and how, for the Christian, these institutions find unique expressions in the person and work of Jesus Christ. Ancient and medieval Christian writers, from the apologists to the philosopher-theologians of the thirteenth century accepted the portrayal of Christ as prophet, priest, and king as part of the biblical witness of Jesus of Nazareth as the Christ. The prophetic office was seen to have no less ancient rootage as a source for typology by the Christian community than kingship or priesthood, as they are all present in the Old Testament. The ascription of the full threefold title to Moses and John Hyrcanus was evidence of the convergence of the three offices into a unit prior to the Christian traditions in Eusebius. The consideration of the work of Christ from the perspective of these offices is part of the witness of the New Testament itself. The continuity of these categories with the Old Testament in the presentation of the full identity of Jesus Christ with the promise of the Kingdom of God is one of the elements of their authority for the early Christian community.

We do acknowledge that the prophetic office has not been as consistently important as have the offices of king and priest in the traditions of Western Christian thought. The offices of king and priest have been employed in the definition and defense of the imperial and papal authority in the interaction of Church and State. However, a fuller treatment of the development of the prophetic office in teaching, preserving the texts of the word of God, and speaking in word and actions about the righteousness of the Christian life in the ancient and medieval Church is needed. Consideration of the role of monasticism as critic of the emperor and the general state of the clergy, as a source of missionary activity and as a model for university life, may reveal the place of the prophetic office in this period. Alexander of Roes could identify the tradition of the prophetic office with the University and place the concept of a succession of doctors of the Church parallel to the notions of apostolic priesthood and divine-right kingship. The leaders of the Reformation were to find their authority for criticism of the Church in the prophetic office. Our limited objective in respect to the threefold office is accomplished by demonstrating its presence in the literature of Christian teaching and indicating its embodiment in the institutions of Christendom prior to the Reformation.

The Reformation

In the Reformation period, discussion of the offices of Christ as prophet, priest and king was employed to designate the benefits of salvation for the Christian as he participates by faith in the work of Christ for the redemption of mankind. The character of the work of Christ was expressed through the offices. The representation of the offices of Christ as part of the divine sanction for the papal and imperial offices was not important for those who separated from the Roman Church as a religious institution or from the Holy Roman Empire as the sole legitimate secular rule. In the Reformation there was renewed interest in the offices of Christ, but the emphasis was on the way in which the benefits of the offices of Christ pass to the believer apart from the sacramental structure of the Roman Catholic Church and the political framework of the Empire in obedience to the Church. The motifs of prophecy, priesthood, and kingship were present in the Reformation tracts (1520) of Martin Luther and were also mentioned in the writings of Osiander (1530) and of Bucer (1536). The fullest development of the offices was presented by John Calvin in the *Institutes of the Christian Religion* (1559). It was Calvin's treatment of the threefold office that Ritschl examined as the most developed form of the *munus triplex* in Reformation theology. We shall begin with Luther and the other reformers and then move to an account of the work of Christ as it appears in Calvin's thought.

Luther and the Royal Priesthood

In describing Luther's evaluation of the offices of Christ as king and priest in relation to the medieval usage which correlated the offices of pope and emperor with the images of priest and king, we find the Reformation emphasis on justification by faith and anti-Roman polemic colored the presentation. In *Freedom of a Christian* (1520) Luther spoke of the grace provided by Christ for the inner man as a birthright which follows from the Old Testament covenant, and developed the content of the notion of grace in terms of the offices of priest and king.

The birthright was highly prized for it involved a twofold honor, that of priesthood and that of kingship. The first-born brother was priest and Lord over all the others and a type of Christ, the true and only first-born of God the Father and the Virgin Mary and true king and priest, but not after the fashion of flesh and the world, for his kingdom is not of this world (John 18:36).[60]

110

The true kingdom of Christ was distinguished from flesh and the world. The effect of this distinction was to sever the authority of Christ's kingship and priesthood from the historic institution of the Roman Church and to express an insight into the character of the work of Christ by contrasting his priesthood with that of the tradition represented by Aaron. The parallel was, for Luther, the claim of the papacy to apostolic (quasi-Aaronic) succession as the basis of its authority and the claims of the Protestant clergy to a ministry of the Word rooted in the priesthood of all believers.[61] The immediate relationship to Christ as the Mediator with the Father for the individual Christian could replace the Roman sacramental structure as an effective source of grace for the reformers. In this situation the saving work of Christ was brought closer to the daily life of the Christian and Christ himself was the effective king and priest.

He reigns in heavenly and spiritual things and consecrates them—things such as righteousness, truth, wisdom, peace, salvation, etc. This does not mean that all things on earth or in hell are not also subject to him—otherwise how could he protect and save us from them?—but that his kingdom consists of neither of them. Nor does his priesthood consist in the outer splendor of robes and postures like those of the human priesthood of Aaron and our present day church; but it consists of spiritual things through which he by an invisible service intercedes for us in heaven before God, there offers himself as a sacrifice; and does all things a priest should do, as Paul describes him under the type of Melchizedek in the Epistle to the Hebrews (Hebrews 6-7). Nor does he only pray and intercede for us but he teaches us inwardly through the living instruction of his Spirit, thus performing the two real functions of a priest, of which the prayers and the preaching of human priests are visible types.[62]

In his discussion of the priestly office Luther mentioned the intercessory role of the high priest described in the Epistle to the Hebrews *but also extended the office to include the preaching and teaching of the word of God by means of the Holy Spirit.* These are functions associated with the prophetic office. This extension suggests that the complex of ideas associated with the work of Christ and expressed in the three-fold office is concentrated in Luther's consideration of the priestly office. In elaborating the work of the priestly office, Luther includes the function of prophetic teaching.[63] With this in mind we cannot maintain a clear distinction in Luther's interpretation of the work of Christ between the twofold office and the three-fold office. Rather, we *regard the formulations "priest and king" and "prophet, priest and king" as related forms developed from the same content, the person and life-work of Christ expressed in the concepts of prophecy, priesthood and kingship as they appear in the Old and New Testaments.*

The way in which the offices of Christ are shared with believers began for Luther with the notion of the marriage of Christ and the believer and the common property of their union. The model was the community property of a bride and groom.

> Thus the believing soul by means of the pledge of its faith is free in Christ, its bridegroom, free from all sins, secure against death and hell, and is endowed with the eternal righteousness, life, and salvation of Christ its bridegroom.[64]

> Now just as Christ by his birthright obtained these two prerogatives, so he imparts them to and shares them with everyone who believes in him according to the law of the above mentioned marriage, according to which the wife owns whatever belongs to the husband. Hence all of is who believe in Christ, as I Peter 2:9 says: "You are a chosen race, God's own people, a royal priesthood, a priestly kingdom, that you may declare the wonderful deeds of him who called you out of darkness into his marvelous light."[65]

Osiander and Bucer

Andreas Osiander (1498-1552) began his discussion of the offices of Christ by relating them to the exegesis of the name of Christ as the *anointed*. Osiander refers to the association of the offices with the practice of anointment described in the Old Testament and finds that this is adequate warrant for his interpretation.

> Moreover we must understand this of His office that He is Christ, that is Master, King, and High Priest. For a Christ means anointed, and only prophets, kings and priests were anointed,

so one sees that all three offices apply to Him: the prophetic office, for He only is our teacher and master (Matthew 23:8), the kingly authority, for He rules forever in the house of Jacob (Luke 1:32), and the priestly office, for He is a priest forever according to the order of Melchizedek (Psalm 110:1). That is now His office, that He may be our wisdom, righteousness, sanctification and redemption as Paul testifies (I Corinthians 1:30).[66]

When Osiander considered the name of Christ as the sign of the anointed offices, he was basing his interpretation on what he considered to be good scriptural evidence. He cited the New Testament in his exposition to show how the person and work of Christ, as they were presented in the Gospels, demonstrated the fulfillment of these offices. The sole Old Testament allusion to Melchizedek is clearly taken in the same sense as Hebrews 7:17.

Martin Bucer (1491-1551) followed the same emphasis on the relation of the offices to the anointment which Osiander indicated.

As once kings, priests and prophets were anointed in order that they might enter upon their several offices, so (as the anointed) Christ is king of kings, high priest, and head of the priests and head of the prophets.[67]

Calvin, the *Munus Triplex*, and the Work of Christ

The second book of the *Institutes of the Christian Religion* (1559 edition) begins Calvin's discussion of the knowledge of God the Redeemer in Christ.[68] The opening chapters of the book recall the fall of Adam and the effect of his fall on the entire human race, while the closing chapters tell of the work of Christ and his obedience which restores men to salvation. The role of Christ as Mediator was mentioned in the beginning of the *Institutes* (I,ii,1) where Christ was described as coming forward to reconcile God to men in the midst of the ruin of mankind. The office of Christ as Mediator comes up for discussion in the second book under consideration of the person and work of Christ. In Chapters XV-XVII the work of Christ is discussed according to the offices of prophet, priest, and king in which the Redeemer fulfilled his function, and God's grace and salvation were secured through the death and resurrection of Christ. Calvin's discussion of the work of Christ in the *Institutes* (II,xv-xvii) advances on three levels. The work of Christ is considered first as the unique activity of Christ alone, appropriate to his Person as the Mediator chosen by the Father. The work of Christ is next related to the supreme mercy of God. As the description of the work of Christ proceeds, we see the task of the Mediator finally from the perspective of the benefits which he makes available to men. In Calvin's description of the offices of Christ each of these levels receives attention.

The distinctive feature of Chapter XV is the statement of the threefold office of Christ as prophet, priest and king. These three functions describe the relationships in terms of which the office of the Mediator was fulfilled by Christ. Calvin's avowed source for the threefold office was interpretation of the name of Christ as it was present in Scripture and Creed. He warns against the mere profession of the name of Christ and its use by heretics as a vain pretense. It is in order to correct a superficial understanding of the work of Christ that Calvin wrote to provide a "firm basis for salvation in Christ and this [salvation] rest in him, that this principle must be laid down: the office enjoined upon Christ by the Father consists of three parts (II,xv,1)." The title "Christ denoted these three offices by referring to the Old Testament custom of anointing prophets, priests, and kings with holy oil. Calvin refers to his demonstration of the validity of applying the name Messiah to Christ because of his kingship (II,vi,3), and considers in addition the offices of prophet and priest. The anointment of prophets is supported by reference to Isaiah 61:1-2, which was quoted in Luke 4:18, rather than by the tradition of the anointment of Elisha in I Kings 19:16. In doing this Calvin avoids the disputed tradition associated with the reference in Kings.[69] Resting his case with Isaiah, Calvin explains that the task of the prophets was to provide useful doctrine sufficient for salvation, to keep alive the expectation of the full light of understanding with the coming of the Messiah, and to support the Church in its waiting (II,xv,1). The work of Christ as a prophet was to be herald and witness of the Father's grace. His own anointment and prophetic work were distinct were distinct from those of the other teachers (*doctoribus*), for in addition to Christ's carrying out of the office of teaching, ". . . he received anointing, not only for himself that he might carry out the office of teaching, but for his whole body that the power of the Spirit might be present in

the continued preaching of the gospel (II,xv,2)."[70] The teaching of
Christ is presented by Calvin as the perfect doctrine (*perfectione doc-
trinae*) that brought an end to all prophecies. As a prophet Christ
bears the mantle of the Holy Spirit and teaches the sum of perfect
doctrine. This will be an authority and power given to Christ's followers as a benefit of his ministry according to the prophecy in Joel
2:28, which Calvin recalled, blending together Old and New Testament material following the lead of Acts 2:14-39, in the presentation
of Christ's prophetic office. The tradition of prophecy in the Old Testament was seen to refer directly to the events of the New Testament;
the expectation of the fulfillment of the office of prophecy that is
expressed in Daniel 9:24 was interpreted as an expectation of the coming of Jesus. Symbolic and historical events are linked together in
an interpretation of the salvation of God in Christ. Calvin saw Christ
coming as the greatest prophet, fulfilling the office as it was known
in the Old Testament and bringing the further message that is found
to be manifest in the New Testament, the message of his own person.

Following the prophetic office comes the consideration of kingship
(II,xv,3), which, Calvin warns us from the start, is spiritual in nature,
giving it efficacy for salvation and eternal validity. This office will
in due course be shared by the people of Christ. Just as history had
witnessed the end of prophecy in Israel in preparation for the coming of Christ, so also early kingship in Israel ended, contrasting with
the completeness of Christ's authority as eternal protector and de-
fender of the Church. The eternal authority of Christ (Isaiah 11:2,
Psalm 110) stood for Calvin as the promise of immortality to the Christian and consolation for the harsh and wretched character of life in
the everyday world. Christ was then properly prophet and king in
his own person as the truth and the authority of God, and the sup-
plier of truth and immortality to his people. The result of this relationship was that the mercy of God for the salvation of men in Christ
was accomplished. The benefits of the royal office, shared as fruits
of the Spirit, were "victory over the devil, the world and every kind
of harmful thing."

Thus it is that we may pass through this life with its misery,
hunger, cold, contempt, reproaches, and other troubles—content
with this one thing: that our King will never leave us destitute,

but will provide for our needs until, our warfare ended, we are called to triumph. Such is the nature of his rule, that he shares with us all that he has received from the Father. Now he arms and equips us with his power, adorns us with his beauty and magnificence, enriches us with his wealth. These benefits, then, give us the most fruitful occasion to glory, and also provide us with confidence to struggle fearlessly against the devil, sin and death. Finally clothed with his righteousness, we can valiantly rise above all the world's reproaches; and just as he himself freely lavishes his gifts upon us, so may we, in return bring forth fruit to his glory (II,xv,4).

The anointment of the spiritual king was a spiritual anointment in which the visible symbol of Christ's anointment as king was the presence of the Holy Spirit in the form of a dove at his baptism (Luke 3:22, John 1:32). The oil or unguents of earthly anointment were rejected as inappropriate by Calvin, if not by Jesus (Luke 7:36-50). The reign of Christ was the triumph of the Christians over sin and death and was the result of the mercy of God. Christ serves as king and pastor until the final act of his reign, the Last Judgment (*ultimo iudicio*); in doing so, he sustains and protects the godly while bearing the rod to strike down those who oppose him. The reference to the reign of Christ is not purely eschatological. The language which Calvin uses to describe the reign of Christ includes the idea that he helps man in his present worldly needs. The reign of Christ is finally bounded by the notion of the further reign of God which Calvin finds mentioned in I Corinthians 15:24. Calvin finds that the images of the reign of Christ and the reign of God do not present contradictory views of the eternity of Christ's kingship but rather they recognize the final authority of God behind the actions of Christ as king and pastor (II,xv,5).

In the priestly office Christ functions as a sacrifice for the expiation of God's curse against disobedient and sinful men. Christ is the intercessor through whose pleading men are restored to God's favor. The scriptural basis of the office and its content come from the Letter to Hebrews which Calvin summarized: "The priestly office belongs to Christ alone because by the sacrifice of his death he blotted out our own guilt and made satisfaction for our sins (Hebrews 9:22)."

Calvin said that "God undoubtedly willed...to ordain" the point on which our salvation turned. For Calvin this was the notion that without Christ as our high priest, to wash away our sins, to sanctify and obtain grace for us, our prayers have no access to God because of our uncleanness. Christ was both priest and sacrifice to God, even as he alone was worthy to *be* the sacrifice (II,xv,6). The benefits of priesthood and sacrifice were also communicated to the followers of Christ as they shared in the powers of the office in spite of their shortcomings.

> For we who are defiled in ourselves, yet are priests in him, offer ourselves and our all to God, and freely enter the heavenly sanctuary that the sacrifices of prayers and praise that we bring may be acceptable and sweet smelling before God...For we, imbued with his holiness in so far as he has consecrated us to the Father with himself, although we would otherwise be loathsome to him, please him as pure and clean—and even as holy (II,xv,6).

Calvin found in the designation of Christ as the anointed of God an occasion for understanding the gifts and authority of Christ in the threefold office of prophet, priest, and king. The individual offices give content to the notion of how God is known through Christ. Pure doctrine, expectation of the Messiah, power over the devil, sin and death, forgiveness of sins, and acceptability before God are all gifts of the work of Christ, received by him in the authority of his offices and shared by the elect in Christ.

Analysis of the name "Christ" for Calvin required the principle of the threefold office in Chapter XV, Book II of the *Institutes* in order to insure proper use and understanding of the relationship of the believer to the work of Jesus Christ. In the sixteenth chapter, Calvin continues his examination of Christ's work and name by focusing in particular on the death of Christ and his identity as Saviour. Calvin points to the interpretation of the name "Jesus" as meaning "Saviour," and then follows the text of the Apostles' Creed in exposition of his understanding of Christ's atonement. His presentation of the knowledge of God as Redeemer in Christ in Book II of the *Institutes* began with an examination of the Biblical witness in the Old Testament (II, i- viii), shifted to a consideration of the New Testament witness (II, ix-xi), and then followed the Christological themes of the

Nicene and Apostles' Creeds (II, xii-xvi), concluding with a defense of his position against Socinian and scholastic critics (II, xvii). In his treatment of the name "Jesus Christ," Calvin is referring directly from Creed to Scripture, trying to keep his dogmatic development firmly based in the Biblical witness and attached to the traditional teaching in the Creeds, which he sees to be at the heart of the Christian faith. The development in Chapter XVI is for Calvin the complement of Chapter XV, presenting the explicit description of how the work of the offices has been accomplished by Christ as Saviour. However, laying upon Christ the office of Redeemer and Saviour is still not enough for perfect redemption. The problem is to keep men from turning away from Christ even momentarily and jeopardizing their salvation. Calvin intends that the study of how salvation is won should give a stable support for faith just as the understanding of the threefold office aims at preventing vain use of the name of Christ. The superficial use of biblical images in support of spurious ritual is condemned, and an attempt is made to control the meaning of theological language by placing it in a larger context. For Calvin the controlling notion is the ultimate success of God in the salvation of his elect.

But here we must earnestly ponder how he accomplishes salvation for us. This we must do not only to be persuaded that he is its author, but to gain a sufficient and stable support for our faith, rejecting whatever could draw us away in one direction or another (II,xvi,1).

The danger is that men may underestimate the benefit of liberation. For this reason Calvin sees it fitting that the expressions in Scripture speak of God as man's enemy and of men as being under a curse because of their iniquity, in order to dramatize the predicament of man without Christ.

To sum up: since our hearts cannot, in God's mercy, either seize upon life ardently enough or accept it with the gratefulness we owe, unless our minds are first struck and overwhelmed by fear of God's wrath and by dread of eternal death, we are taught by Scripture to perceive that apart from Christ, God is, so to speak, hostile to us, and his hand is armed for our destruction;

to embrace his benevolence and fatherly love in Christ alone (Il,xvi,2).

This description of life apart from Christ was not just a psychological image in order to elicit more effective response. It was for Calvin based on Scripture and "not said falsely," but it was accomodated to man's sinful state, that God is righteous, man is unrighteous. In this context, Calvin viewed God's anger against man as just.

With regard to our corrupt nature and the wicked life that follows it, all of us surely displease God, are guilty in his sight and are born to the damnation of hell (Il,xvi,3).

Yet God "wills not to lose what is his in us, out of his own kindness he still finds something to love." This brought about a paradoxical situation in which God hated man's unrighteousness and still loves man as his creature. The significance of this paradox was not that God contradicted himself. His unity for Calvin was beyond the limits of human intuition, either of God's wrath or his mercy. The contradiction and disagreement were within man, which God acted in Christ to resolve.

Since there is a perpetual and irreconcilable disagreement between righteousness and unrighteousness so long as we remain sinners he cannot receive us completely. Therefore, to take away all cause for enmity and to reconcile us utterly to himself, he wipes out all evil in us by the expiation set forth in the death of Christ; that we, who were previously unclean and impure, may show ourselves righteous and holy in his sight. Therefore, by his love God the Father goes before and anticipates our reconciliation in Christ... But until Christ succors us by his death, the unrighteousness that deserves God's indignation remains in us, and is accursed and condemned before him. Hence we can be fully and firmly joined with God only when Christ joins us with him (Il,xvi,3).

The exact means by which Christ abolished sin, banished the separation of man and God, and gave to men the righteousness which was able to render men acceptable to God was "by the whole course of his obedience." The account of Christ's obedience was given in the Scriptures. For a concise statement of the content of the Scripture

Calvin went to the Apostles' Creed. The account of the work of Christ mentioned in the second article of the creed served as the framework for the development of the rest of Chapter XVI, dealing with the necessary elements of the obedience of Christ required by God for the full and complete salvation of mankind.

> ...the noteworthy point about the Creed is this: we have in it a summary of our faith, full and complete in all details; and containing nothing in it except what has been derived from the pure word of God...(II, xvi, 8).

In following the account in the Creed, that Christ suffered under Pontius Pilate, Calvin read this not just as death, but a death suffered in condemnation and guilt as payment for the sins of the world. The mode of death is important for the completion of salvation. The cross is important as the means of death. God's curse directed at the unrighteous is lifted from man and laid upon Christ in the detail of the symbol. The Scriptures gave the conditions of God's law (Deuteronomy 21:23, Isaiah 53:10) which must be met for worthy sacrifice. Men's assurance of the certainty of their salvation lies in the completeness with which Christ filled these conditions. Therefore Christ was sacrificed.

> For we could not believe with assurance that Christ is our redemption, ransom, and propitiation, unless he had been a sacrificial victim. Blood is accordingly mentioned wherever Scripture discusses the mode of redemption (II,xvi,6).

In the death and burial of Christ men received liberation from death and mortification of the flesh. The destruction of the devil and with him the powers of sin and death was the first fruit of Christ's death according to Calvin's view. Just as the Christians participated in the victory and benefits of Christ in fulfilling the offices of prophet, priest, and king, they shared in the death of Christ, dying with him and undergoing mortification of the flesh. This understanding of death as necessary and efficacious is offered by Calvin in order to aid Christians in answering those who regard Christ's death as useless and unfruitful. The descent of Christ into hell was included becasuse "it contains the useful and not-to be-despised mystery of a most important matter." Calvin said that the explanation given in God's word was at once holy, pious and of wonderful consolation.

The point is that the Creed sets forth what Christ suffered in the sight of men, and then appositely speaks of that invisible and incomprehensible judgment which he underwent in the sight of God in order that we might know not only that Christ's body was given as the price of our redemption, but that he paid a greater and more excellent price in suffering in his soul the terrible torments of a condemned and forsaken man (II,xvi,10).

The basis in Scripture to which Calvin turned to support this interpretation was the image of the suffering servant in Isaiah 53:5 and the cry of anguish in Matthew 27:46. The spiritual struggles of Christ were real for Calvin and do not threaten his appreciation of Christ's full divinity. To deny the reality of the spiritual struggle seemed to jeopardize the salvation of men's souls in their participation with Christ in his passion. The intimate correspondence between the varieties of human weakness, physical and spiritual, and the manifold works accomplished by Christ in the work of salvation lies behind the argument which Calvin presents in this section. "And surely, unless his soul shared in the punishment, he would have been the Redeemer of bodies alone (II, xvi,12)," and "We know that it was for this reason that his soul was troubled: to drive away fear and bring peace and repose to our souls (II,xvi,12)." The death of Christ paid the penalty in full and removed the curse which faced men. But Christ's death was not complete without the resurrection which triumphs over death. The death of Christ was a death seen within the context of the plan of salvation outlined in the substitutionary theory of atonement. The resurrection was the victory in terms of which Christ's death is said to be worthwhile.

Therefore, we divide the substance of our salvation between Christ's death and resurrection as follows: through his death, sin was wiped out and death extinguished; through his resurrection, righteousness was restored and life raised up, so that— thanks to the resurrection—his death manifested its power and efficacy in us...So let us remember that whenever mention is made of his death alone, we understand at the same time what belongs to his resurrection. Also the same synecdoche applies to the word *resurrection*: whenever it is mentioned separately from death...(II,xvi, 13).

121

The holistic character of the doctrine of salvation as Calvin understood it is apparent here. Just as Christ corresponded at once to the righteousness of God and the weaknesses of men for the work of salvation to be full and complete, so also, the power and effectiveness of each part of the total work was required for the full understanding and appreciation of God by men.

Calvin continues his description of the actions of Christ through the ascension. In heaven the authority of Christ's reign over heaven and earth is more immediate in its power. The reign of Christ is truly eternal for it has risen above time and beyond the limits of heaven and earth. The truly spiritual character of Christ's presence with his followers is possible because a spiritual union has replaced the relationship of physical presence which preceded the ascension. The limitations of wordly existence are placed under the dominion of Christ. His authority is secured at the right hand of God and is to be involved in the final judgment. The benefits of this heavenly reign of Christ are several. The hope of men for admission to heaven has been realized in part, for what Christ the Head possesses will come to the members of the body in due course. Christ the Mediator and Advocate is present with men before God as intercessor, insuring that grace and kindness await men instead of condemnation and destruction. The fullness of the power of God in Christ will be manifest and complete in the judgment of the living and the dead as the final act of Christ's reign. The spiritual authority which Calvin held is apparent to faith will then also demonstrate its authority visibly to everyone, living and dead, elect and reprobate. The future for the elect is secured in the fact that their judge is also their advocate and will defend and protect his people.

> No mean assurance, this—that we shall be brought before no other judgment seat than that of our Redeemer, to whom we must look for our salvation (II,xvi,18).

By means of following the outline of Christ's life in the Creed, Calvin advanced the portrayal of the drama of salvation through Christ's death and resurrection to a vision of the final act in which the redeemed sinners were to be presented to the Father. Calvin referred to his use of the Creed and its order for exposition of the life of Christ, acknowledging that there are disputes about its exact historical origin but affirming its authority as the testimony of the Spirit. This gave

Calvin a means of accepting those elements of the tradition and teaching of the Christian faith which he found to be in accord with the Scriptures and the Holy Spirit without yielding to the ecclesiastical authority of the Roman Church. At the same time, he avoids the risk of having no standard for interpretation of Scripture but the spirit which had stirred the radical response of some anabaptist communities. The authority of the Scriptures, sealed by the Holy Spirit, and the Apostles' Creed, as the summary of Scripture authenticated by the Spirit, are behind Calvin's teaching and support in his mind the interpretation which he gives to the work of Christ. To press further for justification of the basic content of the Creed beyond the testimony of the Spirit is to miss the point of its witness.

> We consider to be beyond controversy the only point that ought to concern us: that the whole history of our faith is summed up in it [the Creed] succinctly and in definite order, and that it contains nothing that is not vouched for by genuine testimonies of Scripture. This being understood, it is pointless to trouble oneself or quarrel with anyone over the author. Unless perchance, it is not enough for one to have the certain truth of the Holy Spirit, without at the same time knowing either by whose mouth it was spoken or by whose hand it was written (Il,xvi,18).

Calvin saw the actions of Christ to be the effective center of salvation. Christ was the content of Scripture and the heart of the Creed. All powers and gifts were in Christ. "Where the rich abundance of his blessings is understood and received in faith, distrust and uncertainty which might lead men away from righteousness are dispelled (Il,xvi,19)."

In Chapter XVII Calvin turned to consider Christ's work in respect to God's grace, denying the objection that Christ's merit is opposed to God's grace. The result of Christ's work was to merit God's grace and salvation for men. The harmony of Christ's work and the will of God was as perfect as Christ's obedience. The merit which Christ earned in the course of his obedience was real and effective for salvation. The value of the Mediator lay with God himself who appointed Jesus Christ to that office. There was for Calvin no improper conflict between God's grace and Christ's merit. It is clear that the human righteousness, even of the man Jesus Christ, was not the source of salvation. When people were saved it was because Christ had fulfilled the divine intention and bestowed upon the undeserving the merit which his passion had acquired by God's grace. The reality of our human righteousness is not in itself, but in its dependence upon Christ's work.

> In discussing Christ's merit we do not consider the beginning of merit to be in him, but we go back to God's ordinance, the first cause. For God solely of his own good pleasure appointed him Mediator to obtain salvation for us. . . For this reason nothing hinders us from asserting that men are freely justified by God's mercy alone, and at the same time that Christ's merit, subordinate to God's mercy also intervenes in our behalf. . . To sum up: inasmuch as Christ's merit depends upon God's grace alone, which has obtained this manner of salvation for us, it is just as properly opposed to all human rightousness as God's grace is (II,xvii,1).

This was borne out for Calvin in Scripture as he construed it in dealing with the reconciliation of men with God in Christ in Chapters XV and XVI. The sacrifice and obedience of Christ merited grace for men from the Father. This was the significance of Romans 5 and Hebrews 9. The claim that the merit of Christ was achieved by Christ apart from the Father was stupid and curious to Calvin. The exaltation of Christ came in relation to his humiliation in obedience to God. Calvin completed his explanation of this by reference to Scripture, "It was necessary that the Christ should suffer. . .and so enter into the glory of the Father (Luke 24: 26)."

In Calvin's treatment of the work of Christ we have found that he has ordered his discussion by principles which he felt were required for understanding and for firm faith, by specific teachings from the Scriptures which he held to be the Word of God, by the summary of faith in the Apostles' Creed, and by replying to theological errors. Calvin's interest in the doctrine of atonement and the threefold office of Christ may be seen in the growth of the *Institutes* from 1536 to 1559.

According to McNeill, the fifteenth chapter of Book II is almost completely new material in the 1559 edition, containing only a few sentences that have been reworked from the 1539 edition of the *In-*

stitutes. The sixteenth chapter contained a great deal of older material dated from 1543, especially in the discussion of God's wrath against unrighteousness and the necessity of man's being struck and overwhelmed by fear in order to appreciate the greatness of the calamity from which he has been saved.[71] The discussion of the Creed in understanding how Christ fulfilled the function of the Redeemer contained material from the earliest strata of the *Institutes* which had been extensively reworked. New passages were added to answer the charges of Castellio on the matter of Christ's descent into hell, and in the seventeenth chapter against Lombard, Socinus and the schoolmen for disputing the merit of Christ.

The doctrine of the threefold office of Christ as prophet, king, and priest proved to be a suggestive one for later scholarship in the Reformed tradition as well as Protestantism generally.[72] In addition to the more self-conscious descendants of Calvin and Calvinism, the *munus triplex* has received treatment in Lutheran, Anglican, Orthodox and Roman Catholic theologians.[73]

Jean Bosc in *The Kingly Office of the Lord Jesus Christ* found sources of the threefold doctrine in Eusebius, Jerome, St. Augustine, and St. Thomas Aquinas. The origin of the doctrine with Calvin cannot be maintained. Bosc sought to define Calvin's distinctive use of the doctrine.

> What can be truly said, it seems to me, is that before Calvin the doctrine is always mutilated or at least not developed in all its fullness. It frequently happens that one of the three offices is neglected—generally that of the prophet. The place at which Calvin clearly breaks new ground is in making the three points of departure from which it is possible and necessary to consider the mediating work of Christ, and which when they have been fully explored, allow the work to be comprehended in its fullness.[74]

A more complete historical study of the doctrine was given by J. F. Jansen in *Calvin's Doctrine of the Work of Christ.*[75] Jansen placed the unity of the work of Christ in the unity of the person of Christ, "the work of Christ is a personal work, therefore it must be a unitary work."[76] Jansen traced the early development of the doctrine of the work of Christ according to two patterns of organization of the offices of Christ. One pattern dealt with the offices of priest and king as a twofold office, the other pattern included the prophetic office with the priestly and kingly, a threefold office. While the earliest listing of the offices together in Judeo-Christian literature which Jansen recognized is Jeremiah 32:32, it is clear that the reference was not applied to Christ or to the Messiah, but merely listed the holders of the offices together as being under the judgment of God. For Jansen, the earliest mention of the three offices together, with reference to Christ seems to be in Eusebius' *Ecclesiastical History.*[77]

In examining the discussion of the work of Christ and the interpretation of the messianic unction in the development of Calvin's treatment of the offices, Jansen found that only the king and priest were treated in the *Institutes* in 1536 and in *Instruction in Faith* in 1537.

We also believe that He is Christ, that is filled with all the gifts of the Holy Spirit. These are spoken of as oil because without them we languish dry and barren. And we believe that the Spirit rested upon Him in such a way that it shed itself completely in Him, and that we, who through faith are His co-heirs and partners, receive all things from His fullness. Accordingly, we believe that by this anointing He was appointed king by the Father to subdue unto himself all power in heaven and in earth that we might be kings in Him, having power over the devil, sin, death, and hell. Again we believe that He was appointed priest to placate and conciliate the Father for us, that in Him we might be priests offering prayers to the Father, thanksgivings, ourselves, and all we have, through His intercession and mediation. (Calvin *Opera* I. p. 68, *Institutes* [1536])

The title *Christ* signifies that through unction he has been fully endowed with all the graces of the Holy Spirit. These graces are called oil in Scripture, and rightly so, because without them we fall as dry and barren (branches).

Now, through such an unction the Father has constituted him King in order that he subject unto himself all power on heaven and on earth, to the end that we too may become kings in him, having dominion over the devil, sin, death, and hell. Secondly, God has constituted him Priest in order to satisfy the Father for us and to reconcile him through his sacrifice, to the end that in him we too might become priests, offering to the Father prayers, thanksgivings, ourselves, and all things of ours, having him as our intercessor and mediator. (*Instruction in Faith*, Chapter 20, 2)

In the edition of 1539, the *Institutes* show the office of prophet appearing in the interpretation of *Christ*.

The name Christ is added, which, though not inappropriately attributed to others, is none the less His by particular right. For the Lord anoints all on whom He sheds the grace of His Spirit, and there is no one faithful, nor has there been any, whom He did not fill with His unction. Therefore it is accomplished that all the faithful were anointed. The prophets have their own unction also and the kings have it, and the priests, not in the manner of ceremony but spiritually. Thus it is agreed that a king also who bears the image of the divine majesty on earth, is similarly endowed and equipped. Therefore the oil whereby prophets as well as priests and kings were consecrated was not a useless symbol but a sacrament of His true and unique anointing. . . Moreover, in this anointing He was established as king by the Father to bring into subjection to Himself all power in heaven and earth, and the second Psalm teaches (v.6): and He was consecrated as priest to perform the function of intercession with the Father. (Calvin *Opera* I, pp. 513, 515, *Institutes*)

In the Geneva Catechism of 1542 (French) and 1545 (Latin) the change in the description of the title was also apparent. "By this title is clearly declared His office. He was anointed by the heavenly Father to be ordained as King, Priest or Sacrifice, and Prophet."[78] The 1559 edition of the *Institutes* contained a whole chapter (II, xv) in which the threefold office was stated and the individual offices described. The material from the older editions continued in the further description of the work of Christ and the exposition of the second article of the Creed with which the corresponding section began in the *Institutes* in 1536. Jansen argued that Calvin moved from the twofold office to the threefold office in the exposition of the work of Christ because of his occupation with the organic unity of the presentation of the doctrine and with concern to clarify the status of ministerial authority in the Reformed Church.

127

One reason doubtless lies in the conceptual character of Calvin's thought that seeks in any problem a principle of unity. Here the problem is to relate the revelatory character of Christ's work to his kingly and priestly functions. Calvin seeks to express this in the formula of the three offices. It is precisely this sense of wholeness that commended the formula to later writers ...also Calvin is anxious to find an adequate biblical foundation for the Church's ministry that will preserve the principle of the priesthood of all believers while safeguarding the ministerial order against a Roman denial of its autheticity and an Anabaptist repudiation of Church orders.[79]

It was Jansen's contention that the doctrine of the threefold office as stated in 1559 did not reflect Calvin's real intention in teaching about the work of Christ. This contention was based on the fact that earlier editions of the *Institutes* (1536 and 1539) did not employ the full threefold office but only mentioned priest and king. Jansen found that this conclusion was supported by the fact that the doctrine of the threefold office did not appear in the *Commentaries* where Calvin was closest to the Scriptural texts. Finally, Jansen found no use of the threefold office by Calvin in the *Institutes* of 1559 after his introduction of it in Book II, Chapter XV. Jansen maintained that the twofold office of Christ as King and Priest was the most accurate formulation of Calvin's thought on the work of Christ.

Our study of the materials in Chapters XV and XVI of Book II of the *Institutes* of 1559 showed Calvin concentrating on the significance of the name *Jesus Christ* and its relationship to the work of Christ for salvation. In the *Institutes* (1536), *Instruction in Faith* (1537), *Institutes* (1539), and the *Geneva Catechism* (1545), Calvin was concerned with the relationship between the work of Christ, the name of Christ and understanding the Apostles' Creed. It was in continuity with this concern that Chapter XV appeared in 1559, not as a departure from it. Bucer employed the threefold formula in 1536 at a time when his influence on Calvin was great, and McNeill cites Benoit (*Institution* II, 267, n. 8) as suggesting that Calvin may have borrowed the usage.[80] We also found it in Osiander in 1530. We have shown that the threefold formula was present in Roman Catholic and Protestant dogmatics and biblical interpretation well before Calvin, and that even Luther, in *Christian Freedom*, Jansen's *locus classicus* for the twofold office, included "teaching through the living instruction of his Spirit," a prophetic motif, in his notion of the priesthood. Consideration of the prophetic office as a part of the nature of the Church and as characteristic of the work of Christ did appear in Calvin's thought outside of the *Institutes* of 1559. It was present in his letters, tracts, and commentaries. In the letter "On Shunning the Unlawful Rites of the Ungodly," (1537) Calvin referred to the prophetic office as valid authority for criticism of corruption in the existing Church.[81] He mentioned "the Church built on the foundation of apostles and prophets (Ephesians 2:20)" and the "testimony of the prophets to the renewal of the Church" in his *Reply to Cardinal Sadoleto* (1539).[82] Referring the Cardinal to the statements of the Geneva Catechism for further exposition, Calvin acknowledged that the office of prophet was the standard for measuring the fidelity to Christ and the purity of the preaching of all Christian teachers, even the Pope. In his earliest commentary, *Commentary on Romans* (1540) in the section on 12:6, Calvin says:

There are those who consider that by prophecy is meant the gift of predicting which prevailed at the commencement of the gospel in the Church; as the Lord then designed in every way to commend the dignity and the excellency of his Church; and they think that what is added, *according to the analogy of faith*, is to be applied to all the clauses. But I prefer to follow those who extend this word wider even to the peculiar gift of revelation, by which any one skillfully and wisely performed the office of an interpreter in explaining the will of God. Hence prophecy at this day in the Christian Church is hardly anything else than the right understanding of the Scripture, and the peculiar faculty of explaining it, in as much as all the ancient prophecies and all the oracles of God have been completed in Christ and in his gospel.[83]

Finally, in the *Geneva Catechism* of 1545, the exposition of the Apostles' Creed shows that Calvin regards the prophetic office as part of the work of Christ, involved in the exegesis of "Christ" as related to anointing, and as part of the over-all witness of Scripture in attributing the three offices to Christ as Mediator.

M. Let us now come to the second part.
S. It is that we believe "in Jesus Christ his only Son our Lord."
M. What does it chiefly comprehend?
S. That the Son of God is our Saviour, and at the same time explains the method by which he has redeemed us from death and purchased life.
M. What is the meaning of the name Jesus which you give to him?
S. It has the same meaning as the Greek word *soter*. The Latins have no proper name by which its force may be well expressed. Hence the term Saviour (Salvator) was commonly received. Moreover, the angel gave this appellation to the Son of God, by the order of God himself. (Matt. 1:21)
M. Is this more than if men had given it?
S. Certainly. For since God wills that he be called so, he must absolutely be so.
M. *What next, is the force of the name Christ?*
S. *By this epithet, his office is still better expressed—for it signifies that he was anointed by the Father to be a King, Priest, and Prophet.*
M. *How do you know that?*
S. *First, Because Scripture applies anointing to these three uses; secondly, Because it often attributes the three things which we have mentioned to Christ.*
M. But with what kind of oil was he anointed?
S. Not with visible oil as was used in consecrating ancient kings, priests, and prophets, but one more excellent, namely, the grace of the Holy Spirit, which is the thing meant by that outward anointing.
M. But what is the nature of this kingdom of his which you mention?
S. Spiritual, contained in the word and Spirit of God, which carry with them righteousness and life.
M. What of the priesthood?
S. It is the office and prerogative of appearing in the presence of God to obtain grace, and of appeasing his wrath by the offering of a sacrifice which is acceptable to him.

M. In what sense do you call Christ a Prophet?

S. Because on coming into the world he declared himself an ambassador to men, and an interpreter, and that for the purpose of putting an end to all revelations and prophecies by giving a full exposition of his Father's will.

M. But do you derive any benefit from this?

S. Nay, all these things have no end but our good. For the Father hath bestowed them on Christ that he may communicate them to us, and all of us thus receive out of his fullness.

M. State this to me somewhat more fully.

S. He was filled with the Holy Spirit, and loaded with a perfect abundance of all his gifts, that he may impart them to us.—that is, to each according to the measure which the Father knows to be suited to us. Thus from him, as the only fountain, we draw whatever spiritual blessings we possess.

M. What does his kingdom bestow upon us?

S. By means of it, obtaining liberty of conscience to live piously and holily, and being provided with his spiritual riches, we are also armed with power sufficient to overcome the perpetual enemies of our souls—sin, the world, the devil, and the flesh.

M. To what is the office of priest conducive?

S. First, by means of it he is the mediator who reconciles us to the Father, so that we too can come with boldness into his presence, and offer him the sacrifice of ourselves, and our all. In this way he makes us, as it were, his colleagues in the priesthood.

M. *There is still prophecy.*

S. *As it is an office of teaching bestowed on the Son of God in regard to his own servants, the end is that he may enlighten them by the true knowledge of the Father, instruct them in truth and make them household disciples of God.*

M. *All that you have said then comes to this that the name of Christ comprehends three offices which the Father hath bestowed on the Son, that he may transfuse the virtue and fruit of them into his people?*

S. *It is so.*[84]

131

T. H. L. Parker noted the place of the creeds and the influence of patristic thought in Calvin's work.

... study of the Fathers and Creeds, lasting throughout his life showed him two things: that the Creeds were true expositions and arrangements of the teaching of the Scriptures; and that the orthodox doctrine of the Trinity said precisely what he himself wanted to say. The result is that in succeeding editions of the *Institutes* new quotations from the Fathers are being continually added; and the form of the book approximates to the Apostle's Creed until finally it becomes an exposition of it.[85]

Given the exposition of the threefold office in the *Geneva Catechism* in 1545, the revision of the *Institutes* in 1559 is an example of Calvin's use of the threefold formula as a dogmatic formula. The discussion of the threefold office provides both form and content for Calvin's discussion of the work of Christ. Jansen's suggestion that the shift from a twofold to a threefold formula in the later editions of the *Institutes* was a change away from the real position of Calvin is peculiar. This reverses the usual process of correction. Changes in subsequent editions of the text by the original author should be expected to reflect his intention more closely, rather than be read as contrary to his basic intention. In this case, Calvin was not cancelling his former position but expanding it. Calvin's interest in the prophetic office is related to his concern for the role of the ministry in the reform of the Christian Church but we must disagree that there is the difference between the twofold office of Christ as King and Priest and the threefold office of Christ as Prophet, Priest and King, or the direct concern with defending reformed clergy which Jansen implies. Calvin had an inclusive view of the meaning of the name Jesus Christ and after the explicit development which he gives in the *Catechism* and the *Institutes* it is clear that the *munus triplex* is in line with his intentions.

In his *Commentary on a Harmony of the Evangelists* (1563) Calvin referred to the common end of the various offices in the notion of the Redeemer.[86] It was under this notion that he considered the threefold office to be an exposition of the meaning of the work of Christ. E. David Willis in *Calvin's Catholic Christology* points to the unity that controls the whole figure in Calvin's application of it.

The triplex munus scheme is not a vehicle to help Calvin delineate three different functions of Christ; it sets forth three aspects of the ministry of the one redeeming Mediator. And the central fact about that office...is the obedience of the one who is the subject and the active executor of these functions.[87]

The balance of the *Institutes* (1559) deals with receiving the grace of Christ in faith as the work of the Holy Spirit in the Christian life and with the character of the Church and State in keeping with the intention of God for the salvation of men. Calvin is not restricted to the notion of the *munus triplex* as the only dogmatic category or exegetical formula and moves on with the insight that the fullness of the activity of God is revealed in the process of salvation.

Setting exegetical evidence from the *Commentaries* up against the dogmatic structure of the *Institutes*, Book II, Chapter XV, as Jansen did, forced an interpretation of Calvin that appeared to set his exegesis against his doctrine, holding Calvin to be properly biblical in spite of his dogmatic writing. This aspect of Jansen's approach was not fair to the sense of unity in doctrine and Scripture which Calvin demonstrated in his determination to see doctrine and creed derived from the Scriptures and validated by the Holy Spirit.

Besides exegetical traditions associated with the title *Christ*, different theories of atonement are involved in the description of the work of Christ in relation to the offices of prophet, priest, and king. J. T. McNeill noted that Calvin adhered to the substitutionary doctrine of atonement following Anselm.[88] It is the emphasis on substitutionary atonement more than any other which is foreign to Ritschl's orientation and makes Calvin's attempts to express in detail the benefits of the offices of Christ for the individual Christian of little or no value for Ritschl. We have seen that Ritschl objected to the ethical relationship between man and God presupposed in the substitutionary model. Ritschl ruled out the possibility of certainty in accepting the metaphysical perspective entailed in the substitutionary atonement theory. T.F. Torrance in *The School of Faith* found three conceptions of redemption converged in the work of the Mediator in the course of examining the threefold office.[89] The three were: *dramatic*—in which redemption is by the hand of God in sheer grace, lifting man out of evil, judgment and death, through the holiness of Christ and his obedience on the cross; *cultic forensic*—in which redemption is by means of an expiating sacrifice for sin according to laws of guilt and obligation, through Christ as priest and sacrifice removing the barrier of guilt dividing God and man; and *incarnational and ontological*—in which redemption is achieved by Christ as a kinsman bound by blood ties, covenant, or pure love, acquitting men and redeeming them by their connection to Himself. Torrance saw that these basic views of redemption overlapped in descriptions of atonement. In turn the views of atonement corresponded to different aspects of the three offices, mixing the elements of the individual figures of prophet, priest and king in their expression of the relationship between the redeemed and the Redeemer. Torrance went on to suggest how heretical positions in doctrine developed from concentrating on one aspect of atonement to the exclusion of others. In so doing the heretical positions divided the offices of Christ and judged the adequacy of each individual office from the distinctive perspective of another office. Van Buren was close to such an exclusion when he presented Calvin from the perspective of the *substitutionary—cultic forensic* viewpoint in his description of the three areas of Christ's work as "His incarnation, His early life and His death."[90]

Ritschl's acceptance of the ontological and incarnational notions of atonement had been conditional on his supplying his own restrictions to the terms, one of which involved removing the very Anselmic notion of atonement that was basic to understanding Calvin. Calvin stressed that to speak of redemption by the death of Christ was synecdoche and that the resurrection was not to be separated from it in appreciating the work of Christ. The sacrifice of the priest was not complete without the triumphal reign of the resurrected king, and the fullest understanding of salvation is the aim of the teaching of the true prophet. Although Calvin did teach the substitution theory of atonement, he did adopt other motifs as well, and Ritschl's criticism of Calvin does not distinguish the flexibility of the threefold office in Calvin's application of it from Ritschl's own intuition of its correct form.

Our evaluation of the doctrine of the threefold office of Christ for Calvin and the Reformation traditions associated with him is that the *munus triplex* was a didactic formula, received in the earliest traditions of the Church, associated with the major themes of biblical theology about the work of Christ, and capable of being illuminated by the Holy Spirit in order to communicate a proper understanding of the work of Christ. The *munus triplex* related the Old Testament motifs of prophetic teaching and witness, messianic kingship, and ritual observance of the covenant law which characterized the Israelite community at its best, to the unique fulfillment of these themes by the life, death, and resurrection of Jesus Christ. The benefits and powers of the offices that come from the Holy Spirit were realized by Christ and were shared with his people, uniting the past history of God's dealing with his people Israel to the future hope of the followers of Christ.

As Calvin described the work of Christ in terms of the *munus triplex*, he sought to present a teaching that was faithful to the Scriptures, and which presented a rational development of the understanding of Christ which would invite agreement and demonstrate the abundance of Christ's work in obedience to God and for the sake of His people. The *munus triplex* commended itself to this task.

In the section of the *Institutes* with which we have dealt, Calvin was close to the heart of the catholic faith.[91] Extensive polemic was not found, and the pastoral concern for the trembling consciences of the faithful was expressed, seeking to inform and strengthen them in their faith by presenting them with the most precious and efficacious gift—knowledge of God the Redeemer at work in Jesus Christ on their behalf.

On the basis of this survey of the place of the *munus triplex* in the history of Christian thought through the Reformation, we are now in a position to examine in the next chapter the validity of Ritschl's criticism of the *munus triplex* and to consider the value of this own Christology as a re-formulation of the *munus triplex*.

NOTES CHAPTER III

[1] Justin Martyr, *Apologia prima pro Christianis,* 44-87 in Migne, *Patrologiae Series Graeca* (Paris: 1857-66), 6, 327-440. The Migne *Patrologiae Cursus Completus* hereafter cited as *MSG* or *MSL.* English translation for Justin Martyr, T. B. Falls in *Saint Justin Martyr* (Washington: Catholic University Press, 1965).

[2] John Bright, *A History of Israel* (Philadelphia: Westminster Press, 1959), pp. 159-160.

[3] Sigmund Mowinckel, *He That Cometh* (New York: Abingdon Press, 1954), p. 21.

[4] S. H. Hooke, "Genesis," *Peake's Commentary on the Bible* (rev. ed.; London: Nelson, 1962), p. 190.

[5] Mowinckel, *He That Cometh,* p. 59.

[6] B. D. Napier, "Prophets," *Interpreter's Dictionary of the Bible* (New York: Abingdon Press, 1962), pp. 896-919; pp. 907-910.

[7] I Kings 21: 1-29.

[8] Discussion of the relationship between strata in Samuel is found in Sellin-Fohrer, *Introduction to the Old Testament* (New York: Abingdon Press, 1968), pp. 217ff. and in the commentary by W. F. Stinnesring to I and II Samuel in *The Oxford Annotated Bible,* ed. by H. G. May and B. M. Metzger (New York: Oxford University Press, 1962), pp. 330-412.

[9] The literature on sacred kingship includes Sigmund Mowinckel, *He That Cometh,* pp. 21-95, on the history of kingship of the Ancient Near East and Israel, and pp. 91-186 on the ideal king in Jewish eschatology. Other sources are I. Engell, *Studies in Divine Kingship in the Ancient Near East* (Uppsala, 1943); H. Frankfort, *Kingship and the Gods* (Chicago: University of Chicago Press, 1948) and S. H. Hooke, ed., *Myth and Ritual* (London: Oxford University Press, 1933). A more recent source is Helmer Ringgren, *Israelite Religion* (Philadelphia: Fortress Press, 1965), p. 59.

[10] Mowinckel, *He That Cometh.* p. 66.

[11] *Ibid.,* p. 89.

[12] *Ibid.,* p. 92.

[13] James Muilenburg, "Old Testament Prophecy," *Peake's Commentary on the Bible* (rev. ed.; London: Nelson, 1962), p. 476.

[14] G. Ernest Wright and Reginald Fuller, *The Book of the Acts of God* (New York: Anchor Doubleday, 1960), pp. 150-156.

[15] Joel 2:28-29; Zech. 13:4-6; Mal. 4:5-6; Test. Levi 8:14; Test. Benj. 9:2.

[16] Oscar Cullmann, "The Eschatological Prophet in Judaism," in *Christology of the New Testament* (Philadelphia: Westminster Press, 1959), p. 22. "We may describe the function of the Prophet as follows: He preaches, reveals the final mysteries, and above all restores revelation as God had given it in the law of Moses. But he does not simply preach as did the earlier prophets; his proclamation announces the end of this age. His call to repentence is God's very last offer. Thus his coming and his preaching as such constitute an eschatological act which is part of the drama of the end. Although by its very nature the principal function of the Prophet is to reveal the will of God, his function is also to establish the tribes of Israel (Eccles. 48:10). The task of Elijah *redivivus* is to overcome the world powers and to redeem Israel. He has to battle with the Antichrist."

[17] Raymond Abba, "Priests and Levites," *Interpreter's Dictionary of the Bible,* III (New York: Abingdon, 1964), 876-889.

[18] *Ibid.*, p. 881.

[19] Massey U. Shepherd, Jr., "Priests in the New Testament," *Interpreter's Dictionary of the Bible,* III (New York: Abingdon, 1964), 889-891.

[20] *Testament of Levi* 8:14. English translation in R. H. Charles, *Apocrypha and Pseudeoigrapha of the Old Testament* (London: Oxford University Press, 1913). Cited in Franklin W. Young, "Jesus the Prophet: A Reexamination," *Journal of Biblical Literature,* LXVIII (1949), 285-299, and George H. Williams, *Wilderness and Paradise in Christian Thought* (New York: Harper & Row, 1962), p. 188.

[21] Flavius Josephus, *Bellum Judaicae,* I, ii, 8. English translation, Traill (London: Routledge, 1851).

[22] Young, "Jesus the Prophet: A Reexamination," pp. 285-299. See note 19 above.

[23] Frank M. Cross, Jr., *The Ancient Library of Qumran* (New York: Anchor Doubleday, 1961), p. 112.

[24] Philo Judaeus, *De Vita Moses,* II, i, 3. English translation, C. D. Yonge (London: Bohn, 1855), III, 89-136.

[25] Cf. Muilenburg, "Old Testament Prophecy," p. 141, note 2 above.

[26] Ruth E Bowlin, "The Christian Prophets in the New Testament" (unpublished Ph.D. dissertation, Vanderbilt University, 1958), pp. 114-115. "The most important point for this study is the fact that in Judaism from about 200 B.C. to the Christian era hopes for the revival of prophecy centered in the prophet who had been promised. This prophet, traditionally identified as Elijah, would immediately precede the Messiah, who, bearing the Holy Spirit would be a prophet himself."

[27] Cf. Young, "Jesus the Prophet: A Reexamination," pp. 285-299. Young recalls Josephus' reports of the execution of false prophets.

[28] Felix Gils, *Jésus Prophète* (Louvain: Publications Universitaire, 1957), p. 3.

[29] Massey U. Shepherd, Jr., "Prophet in the New Testament," *Interpreter's Dictionary of the Bible* (New York: Abingdon, 1964), pp. 919-920.

[30] Gils, *Jésus Prophète*, pp. 25-43. "Especially in the interpretation of Luke 13:30 'for it cannot be that a prophet should perish away from Jerusalem.'"

[31] Cf. Paul E. Davies, "Jesus and the Role of the Prophet," *Journal of Biblical Literature*, LX (1945), 241-254 and H. McKeating, "The Prophet Jesus," *Expository Times*, LXXIII (1961), 4, 50ff.

[32] Gils, *Jésus Prophète* pp. 45-46. "Nous verrons plus loin que, d'après les evangelistes, Jésus a réelement fait de nombreuses prédictions et qu'il a accompli des miracles et particulièrement des gestes symboliques, prophéties en action. Nous ne pouvons donc pas douter qu'ils reconnaissaient au Christ le caractére prophétique... Avec d'autres auteurs nous penson donc que ce titre de prophète doit etre regarde comme un des plus anciens, sinon le plus ancien, attribué au Christ durant sa vie publique... [Mais] il etait destiné à tomber rapidement dans l'oubli parce que inapte à exprimer la réalité plus riche decouverte en Jésus."

[33] Cf. John 17:1-8. This text is identified by tradition as the high priestly prayer of Christ. See R. H. Fuller, *A Critical Introduction to the New Testament* (London: Duckworth, 1966), p. 173.

[34] The references to Jesus as the high priest and to the Christian community as a priestly nation carry forward the use of Exodus 19, Cf. *supra* n. 16, 18.

[35] Vincent Taylor, *The Names of Jesus* (New York: St. Martin's Press, 1953). Cullman, *The Christology of the New Testament,* approaches Christology as the interpretation of the titles of Christ, p. 315. Cf. Norman Perrin, *The Kingdom of God in the Teaching of Jesus* (Philadelphia: Westminster Press, 1963), pp. 107-109; 148-157. Reginald H. Fuller, *Foundations of New Testament Christology* (New York: Scribner, 1965).

[36] Cf. Paul in Romans 8:9-17. The notion of spirit binds the Christian, Christ and God in opposition to the spirit of the world, flesh, or the wisdom of men. The important relation is that between the spirit of Christ and the Christian which is the source of the power of Christ. Paul generally is conscious of the possession of the spirit of Christ but he is not employing the titles of Christ as strongly related to prophet, priest, and king.

[37] Bowlin, "The Christian Prophets in the New Testament," p. 115.

[38] *Ibid.*, p. 225.

McCulloh

³⁹Hans Lietzmann, *A History of the Early Church,* II (New York: Meridian Press, 1963), 57.

⁴⁰See pp. 145-146, 155 above.

⁴¹Justin Martyr, *Dialogus cum Tryphone Judaeo* in *MSG,.* 6, 547, 682 and cited in Jansen, *Calvin's Doctrine of the Work of Christ,* p. 26. In reviewing the documentation of the *munus triplex* in the ancient, medieval, and reformation periods I began with Jansen's collection of texts. I found in surveying the biblical and extra-canonical material that a fuller presentation of the importance of the offices for the biblical literature was in order. I found Jansen's account of the separation in the two traditions of exegesis in the treatment of the messianic title did not express the full range of use of the *munus triplex* in the tradition of Christian thought. In my presentation I have given more extensive documentation of the importance of the offices in the Old Testament, the intertestamental literature, and the New Testament. I combined the material from Jansen in the ancient and medieval period, adding passages from Tertullian, Cyprian, Novatian, the Apostolic Constitution, Ambrose and Alexander of Roes some of which I found in the Migne collection and some of which were suggested by Professor Williams. I am indebted to Professor McNeil for his suggestion of the text from Bucer in the Reformation period.

⁴²Tertullian, *Adversus Judaeas* in Migne *Patrologiae Series Latinorum (MSL),* 2, 600, 640. English translation, Cox, *Ante Nicene Fathers,* V.

⁴³Cyprian, *Testimoniorum contra Judeos, MSL,* 4, 675-780.

⁴⁴Novatian, *De Trinitate,* IX, *MSL,* 3, 900-901.

⁴⁵*Constitutions of the Holy Apostles,* V, 3, 20. English translation in *Ante Nicene Fathers,* VII.

⁴⁶Eusebius of Caesarea, *Ecclesiasticae Historiae,* I, 3, in *MSG,* 67-76. English translation *Ecclesiastical History,* Loeb ed. (Cambridge: Harvard University Press, 1959), p. 32.

⁴⁷Cyril of Jerusalem, *Catechesis,* X, ii, *MSG,* 33, 676, cited in Iansen, *Calvin's Doctrine of the Work of Christ,* p. 27.

⁴⁸Hllary of Poitiers, cited by Thomas Aquinas in *Catena Aurea,* Matthew 1:1, ed. by J. H. Newman, I (Oxford: Oxford University Press, 1841-45), 10.

⁴⁹Ambrose of Milan, *De Nabuthe Jezraelita,* I, ix, 45; *Sermo contra Auxetium,* xvii, xxxi, xxxv; *De mysteriis,* v, 26, ix, 52; *Epistola,* xx, xl, xli; *De fide,* ii, iii, v. *MSL,* 14-17. Cited by George H. Williams, Selected Texts in Church History 183, Harvard University, 1964 (Mimeographed).

⁵⁰St. John Chrysostom, cited in Thomas, *Catena Aurea,* Matthew 1:1, I, 11.

[51] St. Augustine, *Enarratio in Ps.* 26:2 in *MSL*, 36, 199 cited in Jansen, *Calvin's Doctrine of the Work of Christ,* p. 28.

[52] St. Augustine, *Epistola Ioannis ad Parthos,* III, 2. *MSL,* 35, 2000, and cited in Jansen, *Calvin's Doctrine of the Work of Christ,* p. 28.

[53] Petrus Chrysologus, *Sermo lix, MSL,* 52, 363 and cited in Jansen, *Calvin's Doctrine of the Work of Christ,* p. 31.

[54] Alcuin, *Interpretationes nominum Hebraicorum progenitorum Domini nostri Jesu Christi, MSL, 100, 728,* and cited in Jansen, *Calvin's Doctrine of the Work of Christ,* p. 28.

[55] Ernst H Kantorowicz, "Mysteries of State," *The Harvard Theological Review,* LVIII (1955), 65-91, esp. pp. 72-74; and R. W. Southern, *The Making of the Middle Ages* (New Haven: Yale University Press, 1953), p. 93.

[56] Albertus Magnus, *Opera Omnia* (Paris: no publisher given, 1890), XX, 637; XXII, 207 and cited in Jansen, *Calvin's Doctrine of the Work of Christ,* p. 29. Peter Lombard does mention the work of Christ as king and prophet in his *Book of Sentences,* III, 798-799, 830, and 856 but he does not make use of the threefold office as the main vehicle for his discussion. His concern is rather to examine the role of the Incarnate Word as the bearer of divine attributes drawn from philosophical categories rather than the biblical categories of sovereignty, Fatherhood or authority.

[57] St. Thomas Aquinas, *Summa Theologica,* III. English translation by Fathers of the English Dominican Province (New York: Benziger Bros., 1917). The *lawgiver* is consistent with the notion of prophet as reeve, announcing the terms and interpretation of the law. Cf. pp. 141-144 above.

[58] St. Thomas Aquinas, *Catena Aurea* (Rome: Auguste Taurinorum, 1888), p. 2.

[59] Alexander of Roes, *"Memoriale de prerogativa Romani imperii,"* and *"Notice seculi"* ed. by George H. Williams, in Selected Texts Church History 183, Harvard University (1964) (Mimeographed). Professor Williams develops the theme of the prophet as *doctor ecclesiae* in *Wilderness and Paradise in Christian Thought* (New York: Harper & Row, 1962), pp. 157, 171-173. Thomas Cranmer made a suggestion that the Universities might mediate the controversy between Henry VIII and the Pope. On the contemporary scene, concern for having an educated laity participate in the decision making process in the Church has been expressed in both Roman Catholic and Protestant circles. Evaluation of the ancient and medieval materials on the *munus triplex* can be found in Ernesti, Krauss, Jansen and in Wolfhart Pannenberg, *Jesus—God and Man* (London: SCM Press, 1968). Appreciation of the place of *munus triplex* in Christian thought prior to the Reformation can be found in R. W. Southern, *The Making of the Middle Ages;* Walter Ullmann, *A History of Political Thought in the Middle Ages* (Baltimore: Pelican, 1965); and in Paul Dabin, *Le sacerdoce royal des fidèles dans les livres saints* (Paris: Librarie Baudard et Gay, 1941), and *Le Sacerdoce des fidèles dans la tradition ancienne et moderne* (Paris: De Brouwer, 1950). A recent positive exposition of the *munus triplex* is by H. H. Farmer, *The Word of Reconciliation* (New York: Abingdon, 1966).

[60] Martin Luther, *Von der Freiheit eines Christenmenschen,* 1520 (Weimarer Ausgabe), W. A. 7.56.15-34. English translation by W. A. Lambert and H. J. Grimm in *Martin Luther: Selections from His Writings,* ed. by J. Dillenberger (New York: Anchor Doubleday, 1961), p. 62. Passages from Luther will cite the Weimar edition and the source of the translation.

[61] *Ibid.*

[62] W. A. 7.56.35-57.2. English translation, Dillenberger, pp. 62-63.

[63] Jansen notes Luther's interpretation of the priestly function as one which includes teaching and rejects those scholars who have found some basis for regarding Luther as an exponent of the *munus triplex.* Cf. Jansen, *Calvin's Doctrine of the Work of Christ,* p. 34, n. 1; B. A. Gerrish, "Priesthood and Ministry in the Theology of Luther," *Church History,* XXXIV, No. 4 (December, 1965), 404-422; and my n. 40 above. The task of proclaiming the word of God is the task of the prophet in the Old Testament.

[64] W. A. 7.55.17-20; English translation, Dillenberger, p. 61.

[65] W. A. 7.56.35-57.2. English translation, Dillenberger, p. 63. An interesting warning from Luther follows this passage which speaks to those who may attempt to establish the historical Jesus as the only basis of a post-Christian faith. W. A. 7.58.31-59; English translation, Dillenberger, pp. 65-66. "I believe that it has now become clear that it is not enough or in any sense Christian to preach the works, life and words of Christ as historical facts, as if the knowledge of these would suffice for the conduct of life; yet this is the fashion among those who must today be regarded as our best preachers... Rather ought Christ to be preached to the end that faith in him may be established that he may not only be Christ, but be Christ for you and me, and that what is said of him and is denoted in his name may be effectual in us. Such faith is produced and preserved in us by preaching why Christ came, what he brought and bestowed, what benefit it is to us to accept him. This is done when that Christian liberty which he bestows is rightly taught and we are told in what way we Christians are all kings and priests and therefore lords of all and may firmly believe that whatever we have done is pleasing and acceptable in the sight of God..."

[66] Andreas Osiander, *Schirmschrift zum Augburger Reichstag,* 1530, cited in *Quellen und Forschungen zur Geschichte des Augburgischer Glaubensbekenntisses* I/1 (Berlin, n.p., 1911), p. 302 and cited in Jansen, p. 37. This may be the earliest explicit use of the *munus triplex* by a Reformation writer.

[67] Martin Bucer, *In sacra quator evanglia enarrationes,* p. 606, cited in George H. Williams, *Wilderness and Paradise in Christian Thought* and Jansen, *Calvin's Doctrine of the Work of Christ.* Jansen also records Melanchthon, Bullinger, and Zwingli discussing the priestly and kingly offices of Christ. Further development of the *munus triplex* can be followed in John W. Beardslee, III, *Reformed Dogmatics* (New York: Oxford University Press, 1965).

141

[68] John Calvin, *Institutio Religonis Christianae, Corpus Reformatorum (CR),* Vol. 29-30 (Brunsvigae: Schwetschke, 1863). English translation ed. by John T. McNeill, *Calvin: Institutes of the Christian Religion* (Philadelphia: Westminster Press, 1960).

[69] Cf. n. 8 above.

[70] Cf. Jansen, *Calvin's Doctrine of the Work of Christ,* pp. 45-51.

[71] McNeill, *Calvin: Institutes of the Christian Religion,* pp. 494-534.

[72] Jansen sees a clear distinction between the work of Christ presented in a twofold office and the presentation of the threefold office, preferring the former. Franks and Dabin, from a broader perspective, recognize the validity of the threefold office as a motif in Christology independent of its development in Calvin's thought. R. H. Franks, *A History of the Doctrine of the Work of Christ* (London: Hodden and Stoughton, 1918) and Paul Dabin, *Le sacerdoce royal des fidèles dans les livres saints* (Paris: Librarie Blaudard et Gay, 1941).

[73] Wilhelm Niesel, *The Theology of Calvin* (Philadelphia: Westminster Press, 1956), p. 120. "Calvin in the *Institutes* added to his teaching about the person of Christ a special section on the work of Christ in Chapters 15-17 at the close of the second book. As we do not propose to give an account of all the doctrines of Calvin but rather to investigate the tendency of his teachings as a whole, it will be preferable to omit any consideration of this section. For what he has to say about the Work of Christ has inevitably been implied in his chapter on the Person of Christ." E. A. Dowey, Jr., *The Knowledge of God in Calvin's Theology* (New York: Columbia University Press, 1952), pp. 148ff.; T. H. L. Parker, *Calvin's Doctrine of the Knowledge of God* (Grand Rapids: Eerdmans, 1959), p. 78.

[74] Jean Bosc, *The Kingly Office of the Lord Jesus Christ* (Edinburgh: Oliver and Boyd, 1959), pp. 6, 15.

[75] Jansen, *Calvin's Doctrine of the Work of Christ.*

[76] *Ibid.,* p. 52.

[77] Eusebius of Caesarea, *Ecclesiasticae Historiae,* 1, 3.

[78] John Calvin, *Calvin: Theological Treatises,* ed. by J. K. S. Reid (Philadelphia: Westminster Press, 1954), p. 94. Cited in Jansen, *Calvin's Doctrine of the Work of Christ.*

[79] Jansen, *Calvin's Doctrine of the Work of Christ.* p. 45.

[80] McNeill, *Calvin: Institutes of the Christian Religion,* p. 495, n. 7. "Benoit suggests that Calvin may have borrowed the idea from this statement of Bucer (Benoit, *Institution* II, 267, n. 8)."

[81] John Calvin, *De fugiendis impiorum illicitis sacris, CR.* 33.239-78. English translation by H. Beveridge, *Calvin, Tracts Relating to the Reformation* (Edinburgh: Calvin Translation Society, 1844), III, 400-411.

[82] John Calvin, *Responsi ad Sadoleti Epistolam, CR.* 33. 385-416, esp. pp. 404-405. English translation by Beveridge, I, 35-36, 52. "Let your Pontiff, then, boast as he may of the succession of Peter: even should he make good his title to it, he will establish nothing more than that obedience is due to him from the Christian people, so long as he himself maintains his fidelity to Christ, and deviates not from the purity of the Gospel. For the Church of the faithful does not force you into any other order than that in which the Lord wished you to stand, when it tests you by that rule by which all your power is defined—the order, I say, which the Lord himself instituted among the faithful, viz. that a Prophet holding the place of teacher should be judged by the congregation (*consessu*), I Corinthians 14:29. Whoever exempts himself from this must first expunge his name from the list of Prophets."

[83] John Calvin, *Commentarius in Epistolam Paul ad Romanos,* CR.77.23-39. English translation by John Owen, *Calvin's Commentaries* (Edinburgh: Calvin Translation Society, 1849), p. 460.

[84] John Calvin, *Catechismus Genevensis, CR.* 34.17-24. English translation by J. K. S. Reid, *Calvin: Theological Treatises,* pp. 88-139. Emphasis mine.

[85] Parker, *Calvin's Doctrine of the Knowledge of God,* p. 62.

[86] John Calvin, *L'Harmonie des Trois Evangelistes, CR.* 74.223-48. English translation by Beveridge, *Commentary on a Harmony of the Evangelists, Matthew. Mark. Luke,* I (Edinburgh: Calvin Translation Society, 1845), 92-93 on Matthew 1:16. "Jesus, who is called Christ. By the sir-name *Christ, Anointed,* Matthew points out his office to inform the readers that this was not a private person, but one divinely anointed to perform the office of Redeemer. What that anointing was, and to what it referred, I shall not now illustrate at great length. As to the word itself, it is only necessary to say that, after the royal authority was abolished, it began to be applied exclusively to Him, from whom they were taught to expect a full recovery of the lost salvation. . . but that the fearful desolation. . . might not throw the minds of the godly into despair, it pleased God to appropriate the name of Messiah, Anointed to the Redeemer alone. ."

[87] The unity and positive character of the threefold office in Calvin's thought is upheld by E. David Willis, *Calvin's Catholic Christology* (Leiden: E. J. Brill, 1966), pp. 86-90, and by Klauspeter Blaser, *Calvins Lehre von den drei Amtern Christi, Theologische Studien,* CV, 1-51.

[88] McNeill, *Calvin: Institutes of the Christian Religion,* p. 505, note 5. "E. Brunner has justly stressed Calvin's adherence to the substitutionary doctrine of Anselm." One might more properly speak of Anselm's theory as that of objective satisfaction resting on supererogatory merit.

[89] T. F. Torrance, *The School of Faith* (London: James Clarke, 1959), p. lxxxvii.

[90] Paul Van Buren, *Christ in Our Place* (Edinburgh: Oliver and Boyd, 1957), p. 28.

[91] Interest in the *munus triplex* continues in the Roman Catholic tradition in the formal reliance on Thomas Aquinas' *Summa Theologica* as a standard of doctrine and in the less formal catechetical teaching following the Council of Trent. *Cathechism of the Council of Trent for Parish Priests,* English translation by J. A. McHugh and C. J. Callan (London: B. Herder, 1934), pp. 35-36. Part I. Art. II, *Christ.* "To the name *Jesus* is added that of *Christ,* which signifies the anointed. This name is expressive of honor and office, and is not peculiar to one thing only, but common to many; for in the Old Law priests and kings, whom God, on account of the dignity of their office, commanded to be anointed, were called Christ . . .

When Jesus Christ our Saviour came into the world, He assumed these three characters of Prophet, Priest and King, and was therefore called Christ, having been anointed for the discharge of these functions, not by mortal hand or with earthly ointment, but by the power of His heavenly Father and with a spiritual oil; for the plenitude of the Holy Spirit and a more copious effusion of all gifts than any other created being is capable of receiving were poured into his soul. This the Prophet clearly indicates when he addresses the Redeemer in these words: *Thou hast loved justice, and hated iniquity: therefore God, thy God, hath anointed thee with the oil of gladness above thy fellows* (Psalm 45:8). The same is also more explicitly declared by the Prophet Isaisas: *The spirit of the Lord is upon me, because the Lord hath anointed me: he hath sent me to preach to the meek* (Is. 61:1)

Jesus Christ, therefore, was the great Prophet and Teacher, from whom we have learned the will of God and by whom the world has been taught the knowledge of the heavenly Father. The name *prophet* belongs to Him preeminently because all others who were dignified with that name were His disciples, sent principally to announce the coming of that prophet who was to save all men . . .

[a] On Christ as Prophet see *Summa Theol.* 2a, 2ae, clxxiv, 4 ad 3; 3a, vii 8, xxxi, 2. On the Priesthood of Christ, *Summa Theol.* 3a, xxii, on Headship of Christ, *Ibid.*, 3a, viii and cf. comments on the kingdom come in Lord's Prayer.'

CHAPTER IV
CRITICISM OF RITSCHL'S
CHRISTOLOGY
Ritschl's Christology and the
Munus Triplex

In the preceding pages we have traced a history of the *munus triplex*. We began with the appearance of the institutions of prophecy, priesthood, and kingship in the Old Testament, already interacting with each other. We saw the modification of the offices as they were employed in the New Testament materials and the further development of the offices as exegetical and dogmatic formulas in the ancient and medieval Church. Finally, we examined the use of the *munus triplex* formula by Calvin in the Reformation period. This survey will provide us with a basis for our criticism of Ritschl's analysis of the history of the *munus triplex*.

Our intention in Chapter IV is to evaluate Ritschl's criticism of the *munus triplex* and the formulation of his own Christology. Then we will consider the response to Ritschl's Christology and his treatment of the *munus triplex* by other critics.

Ritschl advanced his criticism of the *munus triplex* in the course of developing his own Christological position in Chapter VI of Volume III of *The Christian Doctrine of Justification and Reconciliation*, which we have presented in Chapter II of this study. We shall consider his criticism of the *munus triplex* under the headings of Scripture, Historical and Systematic Theology.

Scripture and the *Munus Triplex*

In his criticism, Ritschl challenged the biblical authenticity of the *munus triplex*. He felt that it did not represent the self-understanding of Jesus or the witness of the New Testament writers. In addition, the *munus triplex* did not appear, to Ritschl, to preserve the distinctions in the interpretation of Christ as prophet and king which were made in the Gospels.[2] In this evaluation Ritschl moves too quickly past the roots of the offices in the Old Testament, ignoring in this case his own principle of interpretation that the New Testament is to be read with the Old Testament. He further presumes a knowledge of the intention of Jesus in making decisions which is unjustified.

The ascription of the titles Prophet, Priest, and King to Jesus was involved in the early witness to the work of Christ in the New Testament materials themselves. While there is no explicit use of the full threefold formula in the New Testament, each of the offices is used to describe and interpret the work of Christ. The background of joining the offices together extended into the intertestamental materials with examples in the *Testament of Levi*, Josephus' *Jewish Wars*, and Philo's *Life of Moses*. Ritschl's treatment of the three offices accepted them as a continuation of Jewish types but undercut their value for understanding the significance of the work of Christ. Ritschl supplied his own ethical and religious content for the offices rather than deriving the form of the offices in the Christian tradition from their earlier forms in Judaism. This betrayed the artificial character of his account of the relationship between his own formulation of Jesus' personal self-end and the biblical materials as the source of evidence for the life of Christ.[3]

Formally, Ritschl had placed the historical Jesus at the center of his theology, affirming the positive historical value of the life of Jesus for the Christian community as it is preserved in the Bible. Ritschl relied upon the image of the historical Jesus, as he presented him, to serve as the reference for his description of the continuity of the mind of the contemporary Christian with the mind of Jesus, and of God. This continuity was expressed for Ritschl in terms of a common will or purpose, the foundation of the Kingdom of God. In the notion of Jesus as the founder of the Kingdom of God, Ritschl believed that he had found a principle which collected the witness of Scripture into an intelligible whole. In focusing on the agreement of the mind of God and the mind of Christ in the foundation of the kingdom of God, Ritschl tried to deal with the character of ultimate reality in ethical and religious terms while remaining uncommited to any direct attempt at ontology *per se.*

While Ritschl's intention was to go back to Scripture for an authoritative historical witness to Jesus' person and work, the result was as much *eisegesis* as *exegesis* in its emphasis on the ethical features of the life of Jesus which Ritschl had abstracted from the Gospels. The account of Jesus as a moral agent, selecting a vocation and acting in an ethical context which was continuous with the nineteenth century in respect to the will, was not to be found in the biblical materials with the facility with which Ritschl attempted to find it. Schweitzer mentioned this aspect of Ritschl's thought in his evaluation of the work of Ritschl's son-in-law, Johannes Weiss.

Eschatology makes it impossible to attribute modern ideas to Jesus and then by way of "New Testament Theology" take them back from Him as a loan, as even Ritschl not so long ago did with such *naiveté.* Johannes Weiss in cutting himself loose from Ritschl, and recognizing that the real roots of Ritschl's ideas are to be found in Kant and the illuminist theology, introduced the last decisive phase of the process of separation between historical and modern theology. Before the advent of eschatology, critical theology was, in the last resort without a principle of discrimination, since it possessed no reagent capable of infallibly separating out modern ideas on the one hand and genuinely ancient New Testament ideas on the other.[4]

Schweitzer was wrong in concluding that Ritschl had *no* principle of discrimination. The failure of Ritschl's principle of discrimination lay in its grounding in ethics and epistemology rather than in Scripture and history. In fairness to Ritschl it must be added that no single understanding of eschatology has proved to be an infallible guide for separating out modern ideas from so-called ancient ideas. Critical theology is still without a "reagent capable of infallibly separating out modern ideas on the one hand and genuinely ancient New Testament ideas on the other."

In their form in the latest pre-Christian documents, the offices of Prophet, Priest, and King were strongly associated with eschatological and apocalyptic notions. Ritschl struggled to set aside the content of these notions when they suggested the image of Christ as a cosmic figure beyond the limits of history. He attempted to replace the content of eschatology with the notion of a common vocation expressed throughout history by Jesus and his followers. When the office of King seemed to refer to an exaltation beyond history, Ritschl led the reader to consider kingship as dominance over the world or freedom to act within history from a motive which is independent of religion, nation, or family.[5] Ritschl's eschatology stressed the fulfillment of the will of God in the foundation of the Kingdom of God. Ritschl moved away from consideration of supernatural kingship towards consideration of historical meanings but finally reduced the historical significance of kingship to the ethical problem of freedom of the individual will.[6]

In dealing with the notion of priesthood, Ritschl set aside the presentation of Christ as High Priest in Hebrews. He reinterpreted the passages in order to eliminate the sense of Christ as the objective sacrifice. Ritschl tried instead to emphasize the idea that Christ as priest brings himself into the presence of God, establishing the basis for reconciliation of men with God. Ritschl moved away from a literal interpretation of the institution of sacrifice while preserving some of the explicit personal language of the Bible in order to give authority to his ethical revision of the biblical understanding of sacrifice and the priesthood of Christ.[7] In presenting his own case, Ritschl was forced to rule meaningless most of the explicit details of creedal language and most exposition of the Christian faith which employed the doctrine of substitutionary atonement.[8] Ritschl made a careful selection of the Pauline corpus in order to mute the images in the New Testament which ran counter to his judgment of the essential meaning of the Christian faith.

While Ritschl placed great weight on the historical reality of the life of Jesus Christ which is reported in the New Testament, he did not supply an adequate account of the relationship between the Old Testament, intertestamental literature, the character of Jewish religious and political life at the end of the first century B.C. and the mind of Christ. Nor did he integrate the formation of the mind of Christ with the history of the early Christian community of the first century A.D. Ritschl remained sceptical of the possibility of such knowledge of the mind of Christ where he found it in other Christian writers, but he compromised this critical reserve in his own thought by identifying the will uncritically as the faculty which corresponded in God, in Christ, and Christians.[9]

Ritschl attempted to apply rigorous historical criticism to the New Testament materials as they contained information about the life of Christ. He did not go as far as Bruno Bauer in charging that there was no historical basis for the Gospel Story, but Ritschl's own claim to be able to reduce the data to their inherent unity does not stand up to critical scrutiny.[10] The renewed interest in the quest for the historical Jesus by contemporary biblical scholars recognizes the value of Ritschl's vision of the coherence of history, biblical theology, reason and faith, but one cannot remain within the limits of Ritschl's formulation of the problem.[11]

Ritschl's attempt to articulate his hermeneutical principles and to construct a biblically based critical theology was a valuable contribution to advancing the scholarly effort in religious studies. However, his concern for epistemological consistency moved him to de-emphasize the significance of eschatology for interpreting the biblical account of the life of Jesus and to refuse to speculate on the origin of Christ.[12] For here, as always, for Ritschl, concrete historical effects were the only source of valid Christological knowledge and the effects which were evident to Ritschl dealt with the personal acknowledgment of Jesus as Lord and conscious participation in the community of the Kingdom of God. The content of Scripture had to be evaluated in terms of human experience. Apart from a notion of human experience consistent with Ritschl's self-understanding, Scripture was not intelligible for him, although it could stand as a relic which had some irreducible continuity with the past experience of God's grace in Christ.

In respect to the *munus triplex*, Ritschl's emphasis upon discovering and expressing a unified perspective in terms of which to understand the relation of God, Christ, and the world led him to ignore the legitimate claims of the three offices to be a part of the historical matrix in terms of which the Christian witness developed and expressed itself. Consideration of the significance of the three offices and their collection into a threefold office in the Old Testament and intertestamental literature might have served to bring Ritschl to a deeper appreciation of the continuity of Jesus and the Christian tradition with Judaism as a specific historical context.

In his effort to demonstrate the universality of the Christian faith as a positive religion, Ritschl sought to view Scripture and history from a perspective which employed selection of an ethical vocation as the paradigmatic human experience. When Ritschl advanced his own proposal for unifying the witness of Scripture and revealing the unity behind the distinctions of the *munus triplex*, he struggled with alternating religious and ethical perspectives in an effort to give a logically consistent and historically accurate interpretation of the person and life-work of Jesus as the Christ. This took him even further from the witness in Scripture, which he appeared to value so highly, and left him open to the charges of *naiveté* and subjectivism which were leveled against him. Rather than prove his case, that the *munus triplex* is a distortion of the biblical material, his treatment of Scripture and his consideration of the relation of the *munus triplex* to Scripture, revealed the weakness of his own work and the effect of ethical and epistemological concerns on his use of the Bible.[13]

An effective exposition of the *munus triplex* will have to address the question of the continuity of the Christian use of the offices with Jewish eschatological and apocalyptic theology as well as the question of the distinctive presentation of the offices in the Christian tradition.[14]

Historical Theology and the *Munus Triplex*

Ritschl's presentation of the history of the *munus triplex* from Eusebius to the Reformation may be challenged for failing to give attention to the use of the offices of Christ in medieval political theory and in Roman Catholic theology.

Ritschl cited Eusebius of Caesarea as the earliest source of the application of the threefold office to Christ and regarded the Reformation dogmatics as the next significant use of the doctrine.[15] We found evidence of the application of the titles Prophet, Priest and King to Jesus in the New Testament and combination of the titles earlier than Eusebius' *Ecclesiastical History*. Use of the offices in reference to Christ occurred in Justin Martyr, *Dialogue with Trypho* (ca. 153) with similar application of the offices in Tertullian, *An Answer to Jews* (198), Cyprian, *Three Books of Testimonies against the Jews* (ca. 248) and Novatian, *Treatise Concerning the Trinity* (ca. 250)[16]. The *Constitution of the Holy Apostles* may be a source contemporaneous with Eusebius, or it may preserve earlier material. It is clear that the tradition of the *munus triplex* in Christian thought extends beyond Eusebius (ca. 323). Application of the three titles, individually and in groups, to Christ in order to indicate his unique identity as Saviour and Redeemer was a feature of the writings of the early Church Fathers. Their use of the *munus triplex* either explicitly or by reference to one of the offices carried no consciousness of employing a disputed doctrine or accepting a fabrication from a particular teacher. The *munus triplex* referred to the work of Christ as the revealer of God and regarded the life of Jesus in the Scriptures as the record of that work.

From Eusebius through Thomas Aquinas the *munus triplex* appears in both Greek and Latin authors in exegesis of the name Christ and in description of the work of Christ. Thomas Aquinas employed the *munus triplex* in his biblical commentary, *Catena Aurea*, recording its use by earlier writers.[17] On the subject of the offices of Christ, Thomas lists Rabanus, Hilary, and Chrysostom, as sources dealing with the exegesis of the name of Christ in Matthew 1:1. We found that the offices were also mentioned in Thomas' *Summa Theologica* IIIa.[18] In addition the offices are a part of the *Catechism of the Council of Trent* Part I, Article 2, Paragraphs 9, 10, and 11.[19] Implications of these offices for the believers figure in the controversy with the Reformers over the authority of the offices of priest and prophet in the Church.[20]

Ritschl however does not examine the *munus triplex* in these contexts. His major criticism of the medieval period of Christian thought in his history of doctrine has been directed at the notion of the objective merit of Christ. As it is employed by writers in the ancient and medieval period, no restriction to the doctrine of substitutionary atonement or to the objective merit of Christ is connected with the use of the *munus triplex*. This allows the role of Christ as King to refer to the *status exaltationis* and the role of Christ as priest to refer to the crucifixion as an objective offering to God. Both of these interpretations violated Ritschl's view. Since the use of the *munus triplex* in this period does not bring any direct conflict with the prevailing theological structures, Ritschl may not be interested in it as an element in dogmatics until he encounters it squarely in the Protestant tradition in Calvin. Towards the end of the medieval period and in the early Reformation period, the three-fold office was developed more extensively in the search for a right understanding of doctrine rather than serving merely as an exegetical formula.

Ritschl's failure to examine the use of the *munus triplex* more carefully in the ancient and medieval period contributes to his tendency to treat it primarily as an element of Reformation dogmatics and to obscure the question of its legitimate place in the Scriptural witness to the work of Christ. The *munus triplex* may be seen as an element in the continuity of Christian tradition which Ritschl himself sought to recover.[21]

We may also challenge Ritschl's criticism of the presentation of the *munus triplex* in Lutheran and Calvinist theology. Ritschl charged Calvin with separating the individual offices from each other by referring them to different moments in the life of Christ, and with interpreting kingship in such a fashion that it lost any meaningful relationship to history. This judgment is not supported by a careful reading of Calvin.

In his presentation of the work of Christ, Calvin took pains to show how the Christian shares fully in the work of Christ and in the benefits of his offices. Each Christian receives the power of the Holy Spirit in the preaching of the Gospel and and shares in the work of Christ. The significance of the office of King involved the implication of the office for the lives of Christians in the world. The notion of kingship has implications for the community which recognizes Christ as King. There is a reciprocal relationship.

. . .our King will never leave us destitute, but will provide for our needs until our warfare is ended. . .such is the nature of his rule that he shares with us all that he has received from the Father. Now he arms and equips us with his power, adorns us with his beauty. . .(*Institutes*, II . xv, 2).

In his criticism of the treatment of the *munus triplex* by Calvin in the *Institutes* (1559), Ritschl appears to fault Calvin for not satisfying Ritschl's own concern to limit the basis for knowledge of Christ's kingship to the earthly ministry of Jesus recorded in the Bible. Calvin employed images of the body of Christ and the unity of the Holy Spirit in order to express the openness to God that set men free from the world. This freedom was sometimes illustrated by reference to physical separation from the world. Calvin's language referred to a set of images which linked the spiritual and non-spiritual worlds in ways which were impossible or unintelligible to Ritschl's world view. Ritschl tended to regard spirit as a dimension of ethical consciousness in history. He discussed the God-man relationship in terms of purpose, end, will, and motive of action, identifying a positive relationship as reconciliation. Ritschl left the broader questions of how such a relationship fits into a coherent world view unresolved. From Ritschl's point of view, Calvin is too closely bound to a pre-Kantian world view and is using language about the work of Christ that has no significant meaning for human experience. Calvin does not limit the reference of his terminology to historical experience but asserts the efficacy and benefit of the spiritual in the midst of the worldly struggle without denying knowledge of the spiritual world. The completion of the present is seen as the arrival of the age to come (*Institutes*, II, xv, 3). Calvin moves between the images of the present world and the world to come freely, emphasizing the coming into being of the spiritual reality in concrete terms. Ritschl has cut himself off from an autonomous spiritual reality by his emphasis on the role of epistemology in validating religious experience.

While the correlation of the reign of Christ *in statu exaltationis* with the "inward perfection of believers" is strong in this area of Calvin's thought, he still maintains the idea that the power of Christ will not permit the complete destruction of the Church or of Christians (*Institutes*, II, xv, 3). There is a reference to the reign of Christ and to his power to support his subjects even worldly terms.

> In the world the prosperity and well-being of a people depend partly on an abundance of all good things and domestic peace, partly on strong defenses that protect them from outside attacks. In like manner, Christ enriches his people with all things necessary for the eternal salvation of souls and fortifies them with courage to stand unconquerable against all the assaults of spiritual enemies. From this we infer that he rules—inwardly and outwardly—more for our own sake than his. Hence we are furnished, as far as God knows to be expedient for us, with the gifts of the Spirit. By these first fruits we may perceive that we are truly joined to God in perfect blessedness. Then, relying upon the power of the same Spirit, let us not doubt that we shall always

be victorious over the devil, the world, and every kind of harmful thing. . .

Thus it is that we may patiently pass through this life with its misery, hunger, cold, contempt, reproaches, and other troubles —content with this one thing: that our King will never leave us destitute, but will provide for our needs until, our warfare ended, we are called to triumph. Such is the nature of his rule, that he shares with us all that he has received from the Father. Now he arms and equips us with his power, adorns us with his beauty and magnificence, enriches us with his wealth. These benefits, then, give us the most fruitful occasion to glory, and also provide us with confidence to struggle fearlessly against the devil, sin, and death. Finally, clothed with his righteousness, we can valiantly rise above all the world's reproaches; and just as he himself freely lavishes his gifts upon us, so may we, in return, bring forth fruit to his glory (*Institutes*, II, xv, 4).

Calvin believes that the warfare he describes is in part visible and waged within the realm of history.[22] The first fruits of the Spirit are present with the people of God: perception of relationship to God; confidence in victory over the world; patience in life; and righteousness in face of the reproaches of the world. The outcome of the warfare is already to be seen for Calvin.

Now Christ fulfills the combined duties of king and pastor for the godly who submit willingly and obediently; on the other hand, we hear that he carries a "rod of iron to break them and dash them all in pieces like a potter's vessel (Ps. 2:9)." We also hear that "he will execute judgment among the Gentiles, so that he fills the earth with corpses, and strikes down every height that opposes him (Ps. 110:6)." We see today several examples of this fact, but the full proof will appear at the Last Judgment, which may also be properly considered the last act of his reign (*Institutes* II, xv, 5).

Ritschl attacked the value of referring the Kingship of Christ beyond the limits of history in dealing with the biblical material.[23] He presses the attack further in challenging the validity of Reformation theology which bases its Christology on the authority of such language and uses extra-historical references to the kingship of Christ in expressing the significance of the work of Christ.

I have already pointed out that the formula which describes Christ as exalted to the right hand of God, either has for us no meaning, since Christ as exalted is beyond our ken, or else offers an occasion for every form of extravagance, unless regard be had to the fact that between Christ and the community of believers, which He designed by His words, deeds, and patience to establish, there is an abiding relation whereby Christ continues to be the ground of its existence and specific character. If by His kingly Prophethood and Priesthood Christ founded His community, then its present maintenance, through the continued exercise of these functions in His exalted state, can only be rightly judged in the light of what is recognized to have been in the content of these functions in His historical life.[24]

If Ritschl was correct in refusing to consider the meaning of religious language apart from the meaning which the language has for the community that uses it, and to point to the effects of revelation as evidence of the reality of revelation, then he has done Calvin a disservice in his criticism.[25] For Calvin was concerned to preserve the continuity of the work of Christ with the transformation of mankind which Ritschl charges him with neglecting. Calvin expresses the transformation of men through the work of Christ in the traditional language of the Bible and the creeds. Ritschl demonstrated the relativity of various epistemologies within the theology of a positive religion in *Theologie und Metaphysik* and in his introduction to the third edition of Volume III of *The Christian Doctrine of Justification and Reconciliation*, but he does not provide for a translation of concepts from one system to another in this case.[26] The eschatological language uses images of time which suggest different ages in history correlated with different levels of reality. Expositions of metaphors which use space and time to suggest the spiritual value of Christ's kingship as part of the world to come or the Kingdom of Heaven, although based on the language of the New Testament, are dismissed by Ritschl. When Calvin employs this kind of language in his exposition of kingship, Ritschl finds that it threatens his (Ritschl's) description of personal independence by appearing to treat human salvation ex-

clusively from the side of God. Ritschl's ethical concern to present
a description of man as a free and active participant with God in
justification and reconciliation, and his epistemological concern to
refer all knowledge of Christ's activity *in statu exaltationis* to "the
abiding influence of His historical manifestation," appear as the
criteria in terms of which Calvin is found wanting.

The complete presentation of the three *munera Christi* in the
Institutio of the year 1559 (vol. ii, p. 15) marks a change for the
worse in this respect, that the practical bearing of the Kingship
and Priesthood of Christ, in the transference of these attributes
to believers, has disappeared. Which shows that the religious
interest has suffered at the hands of the purely dogmatic method,
which treats human salvation exclusively from the side of
dependence upon God, without keeping in view the practical
consideration that in Christianity our religious dependence upon
God is to form the basis of our personal independence. . .Calvin
still gives the same definition of Christ's kingship, so far as
subject-matter is concerned, that he has previously given, namely,
that Christ's kingship verifies itself in our assurance of eternal
salvation, in our victory over sin, in our patience in face of the
evils of the world. The scope of the *regnum Christi* in this relation he expressly limits to the *status exaltationis.*[27]

Ritschl's failure to deal with the appearance of the *munus triplex*
in Catholic tradition and his slighting of its importance for Calvin
results in an evaluation of the *munus triplex* which ignores its potential as a common element in Protestant and Catholic theology which
could serve to illuminate a continuity in two major streams of Christian thought.

Another aspect of Ritschl's approach to Christology that is revealed
in his treatment of the *munus triplex* is his narrow definition of Christian doctrine as an ideological concern. In the late medieval period
the *munus triplex* became an element of political theory. This is an
important move, reflecting the influence cf Christian thought in shaping and defining the social institutions of Christendom. While he does
acknowledge the importance of the historical context for the shaping of the doctrine of atonement (JR, I, p. 15), he does not consider
the movement of the *munus triplex* into more concrete form until

he examines the different interpretation of kingship supplied by the Puritans, and there he regards it as an unjustified departure from dogmatic to political use.[28]

In order to give a more complete and representative evaluation of the *munus triplex* from the perspective of historical theology than Ritschl has done, it will be important to regard the *munus triplex* as part of the shared tradition of Catholic and Protestant thought and to be prepared to consider more seriously its actual function in the history of Christianity rather than its failure to conform to Ritschl's epistemological concerns.

Systematic Theology and the *Munus Triplex*

Ritschl's objections to the value of the *munus triplex* for systematic theology may be considered under two headings, concern for internal unity and concern for external intelligibility.

In his concern for internal unity Ritschl measures the doctrine against his own understanding of the Christian faith and criticizes the *munus triplex* for failing to reflect in its structure the priority of Jesus' kingship as the most important of the offices. Ritschl bases his judgment that the kingship is the most important office on the evidence of the New Testament.[29] The distinction between Jesus' shared identity with the prophets of Israel and his unique identity as the founder of the Kingdom of God is not preserved in the form of the *munus triplex* as Ritschl receives it. The relationship of the offices which is preserved in the simple listing of the titles does not reflect the actual subordination of the offices of prophecy and priesthood to kingship which Ritschl finds in the Bible and in the intention of Jesus.[30] Ritschl's criticism of the *munus triplex* in this case involves his judgment that he knows what the intention of Jesus was, that he can document that intention as the inherent unity of the witness in the Bible, that he knows what the essential form of the *munus triplex* has been apart from the statement of it by any theologian and, that he, Ritschl, is in a position to pronounce a verdict upon it. We have shown how selective his view is in providing a history of the *munus triplex* and we have suggested that his claim to know the intention of Jesus on the basis of the New Testament has not been substantiated by the critical tradition in biblical scholar-

157

ship. On this basis we are on the alert not to accept readily a further judgment from Ritschl about the *munus triplex* without examining it carefully.

The munus triplex is regarded by Ritschl as systematically defective because it allows the distinction of Jesus' life into two formal categories, the *statu exaltationis* and the *status exinanitionis*. For Ritschl the *status exaltationis*, dealing with the resurrected and exalted Christ, can only be known in terms of the *status exinanitionis*, dealing with the humiliated and suffering Christ, based on the New Testament record of Jesus' public ministry. Direct knowledge of the exalted Christ is a violation of Ritschl's epistemology. The kingship of Christ, frequently presented in Christian theology as the reign of Christ in Heaven, can only be known to Ritschl through the world dominating patience of Jesus' historical life, namely, his publicly visible life and death. Ritschl argues that Jesus cannot be supposed to have regarded his own suffering as anything but an intensification of his public life. The view of Jesus' life which Ritschl finds in the Bible is that of a unitary life-work in which all words and deeds are equally available to the community of faith and not distributed in three separate compartments corresponding to the three offices.

The *munus triplex* is not then, in Ritschl's view, consistent with the form or content of the witness to the work of Christ which Ritschl finds in the Bible. But as we have seen in Chapter III, the *munus triplex* is quite properly a part of the Christian theological tradition, based on Old Testament sources, employed along with other Christologies in the attempts of the New Testament writers to describe and interpret the work of Christ, and developed further in the writings of major theologians. The character of the form and content of the *munus triplex* as a doctrine may be discussed in more specific terms in respect to Ritschl's or Calvin's presentation of the *munus triplex*. If this is done, it becomes clear that Ritschl is objecting to the use of the *munus triplex* in a particular form as a complete, balanced, and systematic solution to the Christological enterprise. We may share Ritschl's conclusion that the presentation of the *munus triplex* in the Calvinist tradition is not the final answer to Christological questions, but we must also recognize that this is not a conclusion which follows simply from Scripture or theological tradition as Ritschl has presented it.

In his concern for external intelligibility Ritschl tried to clarify the presentation of the Christian faith in terms of an epistemological position which would recognize the freedom and independence of the individual person. Ritschl sought to make explicit in his critical work the variety of epistemological and metaphysical systems which have been associated with the Christian faith in order that these systems could be seen clearly and evaluated. Ritschl drew his own guidelines for epistemology within the Kantian tradition and hoped to show how a coherent theory of knowledge, built upon the notion of value judgments, could remove the speculative misconceptions of past Christian thought. Removal of false conceptions would reveal what was essential to the experience of the work of Christ in reconciliation for the believer, and what was the residue of a particular ontological system.

Ritschl found the notions of sacrificial atonement and the objective merit of Christ to be examples of such misconceptions. By making common human experience a regulative notion and by giving an account of the work of Christ in historical and ethical terms as a moral agent, engaged in a community-forming enterprise, motivated by love, he sought to give a positive expression of the social, public, and historical significance of the Christian faith. In Christ's life alone were the other-wordly and transcendental characteristics of divinity manifest. But even in the life of Christ, the divine characteristics were revealed only in terms of phenomena of religious experience, namely, faith, patience, humility, prayer. The affirmation of Christ's divinity is a judgment concerning the effect of his actions upon the believer, that Christ has the value of God for him. The kingship of Christ is the image in terms of which the early Christian community was able to express its understanding of the divinity of Christ.

That I speak of Christ at all only in so far as His personal character as the Bearer of the revelation of God comes into account, surely no one who has read what I have written will deny. At the least, therefore, it is a proof of incompetence and hasty judgment when my opponents maintain that I regard Christ as a mere man, and deny His Godhead.

But if Christ by what He has done and suffered for my salvation is my Lord, and if, by trusting for my salvation to the power of what He has done for me, I honour Him as my God, then that is a value-judgment of a direct kind. It is not a judgment which belongs to the sphere of disinterested scientific knowledge, like the formula of Chalcedon. When, therefore, my opponents demand in this connection a judgment of the latter sort, they reveal their own inability to distinguish scientific from religious knowledge, which means that they are not really at home in the sphere of religion. Every cognition of a religious sort is a direct judgment of value.[31]

This is an example of the epistemology in terms of which Ritschl tried to give a positive account of the experience of revelation, as an alternative to subjective idealism and naturalism, and as a positive content for dogmatic theology.

His own metaphysical perspective was grounded on the personal experience of Jesus as the Christ, the revealer of God. Ritschl took refuge in the reality of this experience for himself and for the Church in order to avoid more theoretical and speculative issues. He pointed to the role of a theory of cognition in expressing a positive religious experience rather than attempting to support directly a particular form of metaphysics.

The function of a value judgment, as understood by Ritschl, is to state the value of a sensation for the self and to determine the cause of the sensation and its relationship to other causes perceived in terms of their effects.[32] Concomitant value judgments (*begleitenden Werturtheilen*) lead to scientific theoretical knowledge about the world. Independent value judgments (*selbständigen Werturtheilen*) are perceptions of moral ends. Religious knowledge is made up of independent value judgments which relate to man's moral attitude to the world and his pleasure in the dominion over the world given world to him by God. When Ritschl identifies Jesus as having the value of God for him, he is reporting on his independent value judgment of Jesus as the cause of his (Ritschl's) salvation.

The result of Ritschl's analysis of religion on the basis of his epistemology was to raise a question which threatened the very perspective from which Ritschl presented his account of Christian experience. If common human experience is important as a regulatory notion which set limits between individual fantasy and public fact in cognition while providing content for religious knowledge, what becomes of the exclusive claims made by Ritschl on behalf of Jesus and the Christian community? One alternative set of answers leads toward the general study of the history of religion as the proper basis for the study of Christianity and denies the claims of Christianity as the exclusive or most perfect form of the revelation of God for men (a direction characterized by the work of Troeltsch); the other alternative is to focus on the Christian experience which exists within the limits of a specific community and to deny that it is an instance of generic human experience This risks leaving Christianity and ultimately religious consciousness unintelligible to anyone who is not a member of the specific community (a direction which may be characterized by the early work of Barth).

When this dilemma is expressed in terms of Christological categories, either Jesus is important as an example of the high degree of perfection in humanity but not discontinuous with human experience, or he is important as the occasion of a unique experience being made available in a limited way to human experience. The alternatives are to some degree mutually exclusive. Either alternative surrenders the identity of ethical purpose and religious affirmation which Ritschl found in the person and life-work of Jesus Christ. Ritschl does not want to surrender to a biblicism which would proclaim Jesus as the standard for human life without any consciousness of the role of human experience in apprehending Jesus and extracting his person from the textual and hermeneutical complexities of the New Testament witness.[33] At the same time Ritschl is wary of yielding to a speculativism which would present Jesus as an example of a cosmic principle or an element in a metaphysical system which would reduce the value of the historical life of Jesus in the Bible as the unique source of revelation for the Christian faith.

In respect to the *munus triplex*, Ritschl found that the treatment which the offices had received in the New Testament was not an adequate systematic Christology. At the same time, the systematic adequacy of a Christology had to deal with the biblical events and the biblical categories of expression. This called for a modification of the form and content of the *munus triplex* to reflect Ritschl's ethical and epistemological concerns without sacrificing the faithfulness of the witness to the work of Christ. For Ritschl, the uniqueness of Christ could be presented both historically and systematically. The final objective validity of the systematic statement would lie in the reality of the effect of the person of Christ upon the world.

Reformulation of the *Munus Triplex*

Ritschl's reformulation of the *munus triplex* called for the representation of Christ *in statu exaltationis* to be known only as the abiding influence of his historical manifestation (*als Ausdruck der permanenten Wirkung seiner geschichtlichen Erscheinung*).[34] This meant one should regard the words and actions of Jesus in the New Testament as the one common ground, illustrating the performance of all the offices and guaranteeing their historical reality. This replaced the complex of eschatological and cosmological notions associated with prophecy, priesthood and kingship in their biblical contexts with Ritschl's own sense of historical continuity. In personal terms this was understood to be the experience of consciousness of a common purpose or ethical vocation, namely, the foundation of the Kingdom of God.

Ritschl sought to indicate the priority of the office of kingship which he found in the Gospel witness to the work of Christ by modifying both prophecy and priesthood to reflect their participation in the goal of the Kingdom of God. Royal prophecy and royal priesthood were seen as aspects of the one historical ministry of Jesus as the founder of the Kingdom God. Ritschl tried to avoid any false understanding of the work of Christ as prophet and priest which might threaten the unity of history. He defined the execution of the office of royal prophet as the expression of the revelation of *God to man* as His presence with man through the acknowledgement of a common vocation. The royal priest is identified as the one who realizes the response of *man to God* by being a man in fellowship with God.[35] For Ritschl, Jesus Christ is the historically unique royal prophet and royal priest who is the first to realize these offices, which, taken together, represent for Ritschl's epistemological and ethical concern, the complete revelation of God and the basis for reconciliation with man.[36]

The designation of the offices as "offices" is changed to functions or activities in order to reflect the judgement that the community of the Kingdom of God is organized according to loving conduct and not by legal rights. Ritschl reads John 18:36 ". . . My kingship is not of this world;" to mean that Christ's kingdom is exempt from legal rights. He does not recognize the text as asserting an extra-historical location of the Kingdom, nor does he consider what the actual claim of legal rights to objective reality may be. The importance of the offices of prophet and priest for the community as legal forms is due to the historical character of the community and not to divine intervention in a particular instance. A juxtaposition of love and law is accepted but not organized into a consistent ontology

> That particular officials are duly licensed to administer Word and sacrament follows not from the religious character of the community as such, in which, consistently with Christ's vocation as Prophet, all must be regarded as "taught of God," but from the earthly and historical conditions of the existence of the community. If, on the contrary, a duly licensed office as such is the organ of Christ's lordship, then the declarations of Christ Himself, that His Kingdom is not of this world, and that His disciples are not to rule but to serve (Mark 10:42-45) are made of none effect.[37]

By these changes Ritschl accomplished a presentation of the threefold office of Christ which expressed a unified historical view organized around an individual personal experience available to Ritschl himself. From his own perspective, Ritschl saw himself revealing what he conceived to be the inherent unity of the offices, grounded in Scripture, historically defined, and systematically complete. This met the requirements of his epistemological and ethical criteria as he applied them.

In his reworking of the *munus triplex* Ritschl made it clear that he found for himself the divinity of Christ manifest in the authoritative teaching and action of Jesus as royal prophet and in the reconciling response to God the Father by Christ as the royal priest. However, the objective reality of this usage is still in question. Ritschl could only propose an alternation of perspective to affirm the subjective reality of religious judgments and the objective reality of judgments, but he would not supply a theoretical resolution of the dialectic.[38] By leaving the question open, in the area of human experience, with a positive definition of religion as a historical reality and not a speculative enterprise, Ritschl preserved the living character of religious experience and the positive effect of the events of the life of Jesus upon the experience of the individual Christian. The weakness of this approach is that it depends upon the judgment of the individual so completely that the contributions of the Bible, the Church, and general human experience to the individual are threatened. Ritschl's evaluation of the history of the *munus triplex* and reformulation of the doctrine involved the distortion of the biblical witness to the person and work of Christ in an effort to render it consistent and intelligible in Ritschl's ethical and historical categories, the selective misrepresentation of the continuity of the *munus triplex* in the history of doctrine, and a lack of appreciation of the difference in context that accompanies the doctrine at various stages in its appearance in the history of religious thought. The *munus triplex* quite properly has its biblical, medieval catholic, Calvinist, and Ritschlian forms, without faulting the interpretation of Calvin for not solving the epistemological problems of Ritschl.

By a clearer view of the historical basis of the *munus triplex* and the diversity of its exposition in the tradition of Christian thought, we hope to enrich the appreciation of the role of this doctrine in giving expression to the relationship between the self-consciousness of the religious individual and the experience of the grace of God in history, preserved in the biblical witness to the life of Jesus. The continuity of faith and history to which Ritschl pointed in his critical approach to theology can be seen more strongly illustrated in the history of this doctrine than Ritschl himself perceived.

Ritschlian Christology and Its Critics

The effect of Ritschl's work in organizing, evaluating and interpreting the history of the Christian faith was as diverse as his work was far-ranging. The questions raised by Ritschl himself and those provoked by his thought were profound. They examined the basis of the Christian faith in history and experience as well as reflected upon the broader implications for Church life. The term *Ritschlian* came to stand for many things, some drawn from Ritschl himself, others supplied from the state of historical and critical studies in religion among the university faculties of his day, but which came to the attention of the wider public in association with his name.[39] Ritschl-

ianism meant for some the whole body of German theology expressed in higher criticism of the Bible, a challenge to the "Biblical world
view" as the most appropriate for the believing Christian, an attempt
to replace straight-forward Bible reading and fervent public and private
prayer with a philosophical and metaphysical teaching that was a
perversion of the religious conscience. Others found Ritschlianism
to be a positive attempt to distinguish between scientific and religious
ways of reasoning and speaking in order to allow each to proceed
unhampered, representing an acceptance of rational historical thinking
in dealing with the history of the Christian faith in place of ignorance
and superstitious belief in unexamined or spurious traditions in
Church life. In a narrower sense Ritschlianism referred to a specific
argument concerning the relationship of a particular theory of cognition to any adequate ontology required by the study of religious
experience.

C. E. Luthardt, from the conservative Lutheran point of view, was
quick to oppose the divergence of Ritschl from the usual reading of
Pauline and Johannine materials in the New Testament and to ob-
ject to Ritschl's interpretation of Luther's doctrine of atonement.
Luthardt supported Frank's doctrine of the Absolute in the face of
Ritschl's agnostic criticism and rejected Ritschl's attempt to dodge
questions of the origin of the person of Christ and the reality of his
Godhead beyond the limits of human experience.

According to Ritschl an image of the person or work of Christ
must have had to be set forth after the method of biblical
theology and from this basis as the authoritative revelation of
God for the Christian community, all members of the Christian world and viewpoint would establish under them first the
necessary concept of God. Indeed, if Christ were to appear sud-
denly in the world in a Marcionite fashion, unexpected and unan-
nounced and without advance preparation, then this method
would be correct. If, however, Christ has his historical preparation, then Christ would not be a *deus ex machina* in dogmatic
theology either, solitary, unexpected, and would not be encountered without connection with our other thoughts and conceptions. We must keep this in view and show all statements which
prepare us are informed from this perspective just as God has

prepared not only the Old Testament salvation-history but has also ordered the creation and the entire course of human life before Christ.[40]

The notions of the pre-existence of Christ and the exaltation of Christ are crucial to Luthardt's conception of the biblical and metaphysical significance of the Christian faith and he will not allow Ritschl to disengage them from the life of Christ.

Otto Pfleiderer, a representative of the liberal theologians, examined Ritschl's philosophy of religion. In *Development of Theology in Germany Since Kant* (1890) Pfleiderer makes short shrift of Ritschl's epistemology as an adequate solution to the problem of the relationship of metaphysics and theology.

> On a closer inspection, however, this, his famous theory of cognition, is seen to be only a dilettante confusion of the irreconcilable views of subjective idealism, which resolves things into phenomena of consciousness, and common-sense realism, which looks upon the phenomena of consciousness as things themselves, admitting no distinction between phenomena as perceived by us and the being of things in themselves;[41]

He finds Ritschl's treatment of the doctrine of the work of Christ and his reworking of the *munus triplex*, while aiming at a single comprehensive conception of Christ's work, to be inconsistent with the usual orthodox meaning of the deity of Christ.

> Even if we agree with Ritschl's rejection of the theory of satisfaction, we cannot approve of his unsympathetic judgment of the Pauline and orthodox doctrine of the atonement; we cannot but see in this an illustration of that Rationalistic dogmatism which is neither able nor willing to appreciate objectively, from a given religious point of view, the historical and psychological conditions of dogmatic conceptions, or to admit their relative validity for such a point of view. In respect of this intolerant dogmatism, Ritschl's theology marks a return to the weakest side of that Rationalism which he has so severely censured.[42]

Pfleiderer finds that Ritschl is not successful in overcoming the dualism which he encounters in the course of his theological interpretation of religious experience. The dualism is expressed in distinguishing between realms of Nature and Spirit, ethical and religious points of view, and moral freedom and religious dependence. On the one hand, such distinctions appear to give Ritschl the opportunity to show how traditional language of religious experience has valid subjective meanings even if it does not prove readily intelligible to a scientific and empirical point of view. However, the reality of the Christian faith in history must also be expressed in objective terms, and here Pfleiderer finds Ritschl cannot defend himself from Feuerbach's criticism of religion as the projection of human wishes.[43]

I. A. Dorner, representative of the mediating theologians, in *System of Christian Doctrine* (1882) judges Ritschl's Christology to be directed too much toward the "common consciousness of the present."

> What is characteristic of his Christology consists in this, that in order to commend again or to make accessible a higher estimation of the person of Christ to the common consciousness of the present, he cuts off from the established Christology everything which could bring it into collision either with the natural sciences, or with the laws of historical writing or with historical criticism. Therefore not merely is the pre-existence of Christ combated *retrospectively* but even the so-called early history is abandoned to criticism; indeed a dogmatic assertion on the person of Christ, or its peculiar original constitution, is not ventured for a moment. . . And *prospectively* he renounces the whole Christological eschatology,—the Second Advent, the doctrine of Christ's personal judgment of the world.[44]

Dorner also finds Ritschl's attempts to establish the compatibility of the ethical and religious views of the world to be problematic. He identifies Ritschl's exposition of the problem as a pure theory of immanence, holding that "all human morals are identical with the Divine life, without its becoming clear how the permanent distinction between God and the creature still maintains its right."[45]

The threefold office of Christ is employed by Dorner in his own Christology. He follows Ritschl in treating the person and work of Christ together but he gives the earlier background of the doctrine more weight in assessing its positive and intrinsic value. He is able to develop the threefold office in the structure of his own dogmatic theology.

In point of fact, the excellency of the doctrine of Offices is not merely the plastic character of the expression, easily yielding a clear sense but also its *historic* and *intrinsic* worth. The former lies in this, that the beginnings of this division are found already in the ancient Church, and that the word *christos*, Anointed, is early referred to the fact of His being King, Prophet, Priest. Just so the division has New Testament support (Acts 2:22; Rev. 1:5, 3:14; John 8:36[1]*basileus*; cf. Eph. 1: 7, 20; Col. 1:12-20; Phil. 2:5-11;[2] *archiereus*; cf. Heb. 7-9). This triple division is of special value, because it sets in vivid light the continuity between the O.T. theocracy and Christianity; for it is these three offices through which the former was founded and preserved...Now in Christ—this is the meaning of the triple division—the threefold office was united, not merely in the way of addition...in such a way that they mutually penetrate, and each one of the three, rightly understood, carries the two others in itself, but in its own fashion. Thus Christ's entire official action forms a unity as a true mirror of His person; but observation is directed to this one collective activity, or vitality of His Messianic person, which forms a finished whole under three definitely distinguishable points of view.[46]

Dorner goes on to develop the threefold office as a doctrinal safeguard for the Christian faith, insuring that all aspects of the work of Christ are considered. For Dorner, the pre-existence of Christ is acknowledgment of the continuity of the incarnation with the revelation of God as possible, necessary and real, a link between the Trinity and Christology.

For Christian faith knows God to be dwelling and living in Christ truly, perfectly, and in unique manner, and humanity in Him as united with the Deity eternally, as the Deity is in Him. But this knowledge only harmonizes with the eternal ground of the possibility of becoming man in the special mode of being (Hypostasis) which He has eternally in Himself, and which is perfectly revealed in Christ.[47]

The resurrection of Christ is the realization of unbroken continuity in the living and working fellowship of Christ with his Church, really present in the fullest sense and bearing promise for the future.

In brief, in this fact we are able to view Christianity in its relation to the history and future of humanity. It is there made known not as a vague idea or mere string of dogmas and a mere system of doctrine. This fact is a witness to the actual effect which Christianity has produced and is still producing. Hence the hope and strength of Christianity lie in its substantial reality.[48]

The exaltation of Christ represents for Dorner the acknowledgment that Christ is never separated from his work but sustains it and is the source of its development. This is worked out in terms of the threefold office and its implications for the life of the Church. Dorner preserves his own balance in adapting the traditional doctrinal forms to his own perspective without rejecting their insights into the value of the life of Christ for other Christians. Ritschl's stricter approach to defining the work of Christ as founder of the community with a common religious vocation met the epistemological standards which he had set himself but at the cost of devaluing his appreciation of dogmatic content.[49]

Ritschl's critics attacked his biblical theology with respect to the accuracy of his exegesis, his historical theology with respect to the validity of his judgments, and his systematic theology with respect to the adequacy of its basis and development. As a school of thought, Ritschlianism was not identified by a strict dogmatic system or obedience to the findings and formulations of the master. It came to represent, rather, a common interest in issues and problems on the theological scene which carried the stamp, more or less self-consciously, of Ritschl's influence. Wilhelm Herrmann, Julius Kaftan and Adolph Harnack are most prominent among those who pursued Ritschl's constructive concerns. The expansion of literature in all fields of theology and the character of critical problems has made it difficult for anyone to occupy a position of leadership in as many areas as Ritschl did in his time. It was in historical and systematic theology that his most persistent influence has been felt, and where the Ritschlian school, insofar as the term applies, can be found.

Wilhelm Herrmann was sceptical of the label "Ritschlian," but in *The Communion of the Christian with God* (1906) set out three positive assertions for theology that demonstrate his own development of Ritschl's emphasis on the life of Jesus as the source for knowledge of God and on the effects of Jesus' life as the objective evidence of Christian experience.

1) The objective power which is the enduring basis of the religious experiences of a Christian is not any sum of thoughts concerning faith, however obtained, but is the man Jesus.
2) The thoughts concerning faith arise within that communion with God into which the personal power of Jesus lifts us.
3) It is not the possession of any prescribed sum of such thoughts, recorded though they may be in Holy Scripture, that makes a man a Christian, but the faculty of producing such thoughts, and of cherishing them as the truth grasped by his own consciousness.[50]

What stands out clearly in Herrmann is the concern for the immediate subjective, personal contact with Jesus. This contact is seen as a mutual contact between persons at an intimate level. For Ritschl this was limited primarily to the consciousness of a common vocation, a matter of the will in establishing motives for action. In Herrmann the language is more vivid, conveying a sense of personal encounter. The intensity of the encounter and its effect on the Christian becomes *the reality* which makes other historical questions secondary for Herrmann.

It is thus, therefore, that the inner life of Jesus becomes part of our own sphere of reality, and the man who has experienced that will certainly no longer say that, strictly speaking, he can know only the story of Jesus as a real thing. Jesus Himself becomes a real power to us when He reveals His inner life to us; a power we recognise as the best thing our life contains.[51]

Ritschl was sensitive to the fact that critical issues in the New Testament made a consistent view of the divinity of Christ or the details of his earthly ministry problematic without an interpretative principle. In Herrmann the impact of the person of Jesus is portrayed as reshaping the observer, moving the historical event of the life of Jesus from the first century in Galilee to the present. At the same time, the emphasis on the place of the community as the mediator of the effects of Jesus to the individual, which Ritschl maintains, is obscured in the individualistic style of Herrmann.

Help lies for each of us, not in what we make of the story, but in what the contents of the story make of us. And the one thing which the Gospels will give us as an overpowering reality which allows no doubt is just the most tender part of all: it is the inner life of Jesus itself.[52]

Herrmann recorded his view of the self-conscious independence of the Ritschlians in the presence of their mentor in "Albrecht Ritschl, seine Grösse und seine Schranke," in *Festgabe von Fachgenossen und Freunden A. von Harnack* (1921).

Ritschl wanted to be the head of a school, and expected that those who attached themselves to him would respect him as such. He could fly out violently when one of us whose relationship to him had become particularly valued, disagreed with a proof, [or held] that he was mistaken on a simple historical question. Schleiermacher on the other hand expected right away from those who wanted to be his pupils that they would go their own ways. Ritschl indeed appeared not to have noticed that he did not attain Schleiermacher's greatness in this respect. We are grateful to him for that which he has given to us. However, we would not do justice to him if we were to allow ourselves to refrain from recognizing the limits in which he remained behind the humane, open greatness of Schleiermacher.[53]

Julius Kaftan in *Dogmatik* (1920) follows Ritschl in presenting the relationship of God and Christ in terms of will, but he expresses this in terms of the threefold office without requiring the revision which Ritschl employed.

The salvation of man is on the one hand God's gift and action through Jesus Christ, and on the other hand it is the work of the man Jesus, who through his own free agreement with the will of the Father and his proven obedience even to the death on the cross, has made possible the judging and blessing revelation of God for our salvation. This work of his human obedience will clearly illustrate in the image of the threefold office what he needed to accomplish in the world as the perfect Prophet, Highpriest, and King.[54]

Kaftan finds that attempts to separate the offices are pedantic, but he distinguishes between the notion of the exaltation of Christ over the community as its Lord and the notion of his kingship defined in terms of the formation of the community.

We touch however on the Lordship of the Exalted One in this kingdom, that is, over his community, not under the idea of the royal office of Jesus. For there we would violate the point of view from which this formulation of the doctrine of the threefold office is drawn, namely, that it concerns the perfect human obedience of the Saviour. In the act, this Lordship of the Exalted One is such that he exercises it in unity with the Father through the Spirit, so that he is not present to faith as a distinguishable self. As such he is the man, who through his doing and suffering leading the people, has established the kingdom. The idea of his kingly Lordship remains there with his kingdom establishing activity on which it depends.[55]

In his consideration of the proof of Christianity in *The Truth of the Christian Religion* (1894), Kaftan warns against trying to distinguish the historical from the ideal Christ. The revelation of God in Christ becomes the *historical reality*.

The distinction drawn between a historical and an ideal Christ, by means of which an attempt has been made to prove that it is impossible in principle for a contradiction to arise here, must in all its forms be definitely and for ever rejected, because if really carried out it involves as its precise issue the destruction of our faith in the Christian revelation. All depends on the fact, that, in that faith we have to do not merely with an idea, with a thought, but with a *historical reality*: the historical person of Jesus Christ, His relation to God, has been essentially different from what is seen in the case of all other men; He is the Son who knows the Father, through the knowledge of whom all men are meant to come and can come to the knowledge of God. This fact is *the foundation of the Christian faith and Christian hope.*[56]

Adolph von Harnack is the Ritschlian whose own name is perhaps most familiar today. His concentration on the history of the New Testament community and the ancient Church established an eminence for him in his own right. The critical concern of Ritschl about the place of metaphysics in the Christian faith found expression however in Harnack's judgment in the *History of Dogma* (1894-99) that the *Hellenic spirit* is an addition to the New Testament in the doctrinal formulations of the early Church.[57] In *What Is Christianity?* (1900), Harnack examined the importance of the ethical point of view in the Christian faith, which had formed one pole of the experience of Christianity for Ritschl.[58] Harnack recalls Ritschl's contribution in the closing summary of the *History of Dogma* and draws on Ritschl's parallel of the ethical and religious in his characterization of the goal of evangelical theology.

> It would appear, finally, that in his description of the gospel, the most disdainfully treated theologian of the age—Ritschl— has given expression in a powerful way—though within the limitations that belong to every individual—to the outcome of two hundred years work on the part of evangelical theology in endeavoring to understand the Reformation, and to the products of criticism of doctrinaire Lutheranism...Therefore the goal of all Christian work, even of all theological work, can only be this—to discern ever more distinctly the simplicity and the seriousness of the gospel, in order to become ever purer and stronger in *spirit*, and ever more loving and brotherly in *action*.[59]

Harnack discusses the work of Christ in relation to the threefold office only in his account of the Socinian movement and its modification of the formula which drew all the effective powers of Christ under the prophetic office and turned the priestly office against the Church Harnack does not press the historical analysis of the threefold office any further, relying upon Ritschl heavily as a source. The elements of the *munus triplex* which are developed are very close to what Harnack has reported are the ideas of Christ's work which were influential in the early Christian communities but these ideas are not considered in relation to the history of the *munus triplex*. The elements of the historical life of Jesus are discussed in relation to the contesting Christologies (Adoptionist, Pneumatic, and Logos) but not in respect to the *munus triplex*.

In his review of Gustav Ecke's *Die Theologische Schule Albrecht*

Ritschls, Harnack gives his own summary of Ritschl's theological concerns.

First, Ritschl wanted no fragmentary theology but a tight, unified and compact conception; what did not fit into this he shut out, dismantled or dismissed as "individual"...second, while Ritschl wanted a clear theology, that is clearly stating faith, he sought in no sense to know anything from "natural theology," which he declared an artificial product, arbitrarily abstracted from philosophy, but he wanted himself to remain exclusively in history...and finally, third—Ritschl was a Protestant, that is, an anticatholic theologian of such keenness and determination as we have not seen since Flacius, Chemnitz and the days of the old Protestant orthodoxy.[60]

The concern for a unified, consistent theology, free from dependency upon natural theology derived from philosophy or upon ecclesiastical authority stands out for Harnack as the basis of judgment from which Ritschl operates. His aim, as Harnack saw it, was for a renewed faith freed from the aberration of the past.

Ritschl wanted a new sound Protestant orthodoxy purified of Catholicism and Pietism. It should live again in the moral sense but also in the mind and in the act. All uncertain, emotional and sentimental elements should be shut out of it. He believed himself to have found this universally valid form and he kept watch over it as Flacius did his.[61]

After Ritschl's death, the Ritschlian school was rapidly dissolved in the strife of the German academic arena and interest in Ritschl was to be quite restricted until the renewal of interest in the major figures in the formation of liberal theology in the 1960's. Interest in Ritschlian theology and its interpretation passed to Great Britain at the turn of the century in the work of Alfred E. Garvie, *The Ritschlian Theology* (1899), with Robert Mackintosh, *Albrecht Ritschl and His School* (1915), and R. S. Franks, *A History of the Doctrine of the Work of Christ* (1918), keeping track of the effect of Ritschlian thought and attempting to apply its methods.[62] Opposition to Ritschlian theology was registered by James Orr in *The Ritschlian Theology and the Evangelical Faith* (1897) and James Denney in *Studies in Theology* (1895).[63]

174

Garvie gives a brief survey of the influence of Ritschl on British theology in the nineties, and the critical response to Ritschl's Christology is mixed.[64] Garvie finds Ritschl's inductive method, of starting from the work of Christ to reach an appreciation of the worth of Christ, to be better than referring only to the external authority of Scripture or the apostolic witness. Ritschl's method allows recognition of the subjective religious consciousness of the individual Christian. However, Garvie finds that Ritschl is guilty of artificial and arbitrary exegesis in setting aside the New Testament basis for the conception of the personal pre-existence of Christ.

In regard to Ritschl's modification of the *munus triplex*, Garvie questions Ritschl's wisdom in trying to rework the doctrine at all as adequate to the person and work of Christ.

The question may be raised, however, whether if any modification is to be made in the traditional doctrine, the three categories alike should not be set aside; for all alike carry with them misleading associations, and are insufficient to express all that Christ is and does. Although used in the Holy Scriptures, do not they belong to the temporary forms of expression, and not to the permanent contents of our Christian faith? Are not the moral and spiritual facts which they express more fully and truly expressed in the categories of Son and Brother, which are not taken from the Old Testament, but are Christ's own terms? However, accepting Ritschl's own term King as descriptive of the work of Christ, he does well in insisting on the fact that in the state of humiliation Christ already exercised a moral end and a spiritual dominion over the world and mankind, and that we are to expect the same genuinely moral and spiritual features in His dominion in the state of exaltation. Not only is the Jesus of history the interpretation of the Christ of faith, but He is the only interpretation; but the Christ of faith is *actor* in as well as *spectator* of Christian history, a truth which Ritschl fails to state with the clearness which should save him from being misunderstood.[65]

Garvie finds that Ritschl has fixed the attention on phenomenal aspects of reality to the neglect of the noumenal. The notion of the divine nature of Christ in Ritschl's treatment of Christ's person is replaced by a description of the correspondence between the direction of Christ's will and God's final purpose, accepted by Christ as his own self-end. Ritschl's approach is important as a corrective to misplaced emphasis on the traditional notions of Christ's person and work and his relationship to God which obscure the historical Jesus, but Ritschl's formulation is not in itself an adequate replacement.

> We cannot escape the double estimate of Christ, first from the standpoint of His personal perfection, and then from the point of view of His divine revelation; and Ritschl's treatment here is of very great value. His representation of the "manifest" divinity of Christ, if not altogether adequate, yet does lay stress on the features of primary importance. His prohibition of any deeper investigation of the problem must be, howevor, set aside; and his own essays in that direction, inconsistently made, must be pronounced as altogether inadequate.[66]

Robert Mackintosh finds that the Ritschlian synthesis was premature. The spirit and aim of the movement may be creditable but the actual constructive work needs repair. The aversion to speculative doctrines is extended to the point of obscuring any attempt at a clear doctrine of God. Mackintosh advocates an alliance with a more positive metaphysic without yielding the role of Christianity as a religion to "reveal God's Fatherly heart towards us," and suggests that Hegel has taught the importance of establishing provisional positions while searching for affirmations that are relatively true.

> . . . feeling certain that no future evolution of thought will destroy our assertions—rather it will transmute them into worthier forms—yet also feeling certain that the form in which we hold and treasure truth is not the highest possible.[67]

The result of this counsel is to encourage the Ritschlians to admit the limitation of knowledge in matters of religion, but in terms of the over-all character of knowledge, rather than to assert a dualism which proclaims the certainty of the historical revelation of God in Christ while refusing to consider the origin of the historical person of Christ. It was a strength of Ritschl's faith that he could refer to the grace and truth of Christ in history as a fact and in that fact find himself reconciled with God. His ethical concern caused him to consider how that fact would affect the life of the individual Christian within the community of faith. Mackintosh favors the notion of a gradual evolution of faith and knowledge towards an ultimate harmony at the cost of surrendering claims to present certainty. Ritschl prefers to admit periods of uncertainty while affirming the complete reality when it is present to him in Christ.

On the specific issue of the *munus triplex*, Mackintosh reports Ritschl's judgment but does not comment on it.

R. S. Franks acknowledges his debt to Baur, Ritschl, Harnack, Kaftan and Kattenbusch in his preface to *A History of the Doctrine of the Work of Christ* (1918). Franks points to four great syntheses in the history of doctrine represented by Greek theology, Medieval scholasticism, Protestant orthodoxy, and modern Protestant theology. The essence of Protestantism is that faith in Christ alone achieves what had been accomplished in the Medieval system by a whole series of doctrines which involved among other things works and sacraments.

In Protestantism accordingly the doctrine of the work of Christ, when it has finally reached its full development, even more than in the Greek theology, is the practical summary of the whole Christian religion, the different parts of the doctrine once more co-operating to express the total ethico-religious character of Christianity. . .the modern Protestant synthesis differs only from that of the older Protestantism in that it seeks to make more plain the inner unity of Christian doctrine; and accordingly seeks to reduce the orthodox Protestant doctrine of the work of Christ itself to simpler terms.[68]

The chief examples for Franks of the modern synthesis are Schleiermacher and Ritschl.

In the German Protestant theology of the nineteenth century, and especially in the work of Schleiermacher and Ritschl, we have to recognize the fourth great doctrinal synthesis, which, as over against the Greek, the medieval, and the seventeenth century Protestant synthesis, we may call "the modern synthesis." This new synthesis has taken up into itself the truth of the evangelical experience of the Reformers, of the Socinian criticism, and of the accommodation doctrine of the *Aufklärung*, combining them by means of the new philosophy of self-consciousness, which, emerging first in the form of the Kantian criticism, presently reveals itself in the doctrines of Hegel and Schleiermacher as a principle of immanent union and interpenetration of the opposites of common logic, and thus as the principle of a higher logic adequate to the subject matter of theology.[69]

Franks points to Schleiermacher's theology as having an initial advantage over Ritschl's positivism by virtue of having a metaphysical basis. He finds that Ritschl's formulation of religious truth in terms of value judgments is unsatisfactory unless the judgments refer to reality. Ritschl's strong points in respect to Schleiermacher are his close connection between the New Testament material and the knowledge of the personality of God as revealed in Jesus Christ, and his notion of a biblical and historical context for the Kingdom of God. In dealing with the work of Christ, Franks supports Ritschl in the subordination of the category of Representation to that of Revelation, the shift away from emphasis on punishment, and the view of the sacraments as validated by, not preceding, communion with Christ.[70]

In regard to the *munus triplex*, Franks considers it to be part of Calvin's contribution to the Protestant synthesis.

What, however, concerns us most of all in Calvin's theology, is the emergence of a new doctrine of the work of Christ, distinct from either the patristic or the medieval, viz. the doctrine of the threefold office. This doctrine, the really characteristic Protestant doctrine of the work of Christ, is highly synthetic in character. It has not merely the value of presenting the whole work of Christ in a single view, but also of presenting it in such a manner that it shows how it terminates in the production of faith (*fiducia*) through the Gospel. It is thus of an eminently practical character: the objective aspect of the work of Christ is here duly completed by the subjective aspect. . . [71]

Franks sees in the *munus triplex* a formula that provides both a theoretical structure and significant historical content for the discussion of the work of Christ.

The Greek scheme of revelation by the Logos and of the destruction of sin and death by the Incarnation, is like the doctrine of the threefold office conceptual. But the Greek Fathers were not able to control by their formulae the whole historical material of the life of Christ: although the Logos doctrine is of considerable utility in this direction. It was therefore a real advantage when first Alexander of Hales and then Thomas began to work into the theology of the Incarnation more of the historical details. By so doing they indeed made their doctrine less synthetic than the Greek and ran the risk of making theology appear, as the Nominalists said, to be an aggregate science only. But they prepared thereby for a richer synthesis, conceptual like the Greek synthesis and indeed more of a unity than that, since all its elements run back into the one idea of the "Anointed" representative of God,—a synthesis, moreover, which could more fully than the Greek synthesis include and control the whole historical material of the Gospels. The Protestant synthesis of the threefold office then includes the advantages of both the prior great stages of the doctrine of the work of Christ.[72]

From Franks' point of view, Ritschl is working on extremely important ground in his criticism of the threefold office.[73] Since Franks has already approved the doctrine in its formulation by Calvin, the effect of Ritschl's work is seen as bringing the doctrine closer to the characteristic emphasis of the modern synthesis and further improving the doctrine. Ritschl stresses the immanental character of revelation within the terms of humanity, a positive connection with the Bible as the witness of the faith of the community, and the preference of Abelardian to Anselmic doctrine as the paradigm for atonement. Franks goes on in *The Atonement* (1934) to follow Troeltsch and Heim in the search for a metaphysical basis for religion, regarding Ritschl as having provided what was finally a biblical theology, related to individual experience but inadequately related to the rest of knowledge.[74]

Among Ritschl's outright critics, James Orr found that Ritschl could not avoid metaphysical discussion in defense of his position that God is known in His actions and manifestations and not in terms of His essential nature.

God is for us "the complex of all the divine modes of action," through which He becomes known to us. In like manner, a "non-metaphysical," that is a "religious" interpretation is sought for the divine "attributes," which Ritschl will have us regard as derivative aspects of the single attribute of love, viewed by him as inclusive of the notion of a "world-end." For the efficient realisation of this end, God must be conceived of as the Creator and Preserver of the world, as being able to dispose of all things by His power, as having all wisdom to execute His purposes, etc. But these affirmations of religion are not to be translated into "theoretic" forms.[75]

Orr's reaction is that such an attempt at "nominalism or phenomenalism is unthinkable if we are to retain our hold on God as a real Being at all."[76] Actions and manifestations have meaning only as expressions of a "nature" or character. It is a drawback of Ritschl's theology that it will not allow movement from will to nature. Ritschl's restatement of the meaning of the death of Christ is "a lame and inconsequential attempt"[77] supported only by "*a tour de force*" of exegesis which tries in vain to evade the testimony of the New Testament (Gal. 3:13; I John 2:2, 4:10; and Heb. 2:17).[78] Orr finds in Ritschl a shift from the *individual* to the *community* as the object of forgiveness which suggests to Orr that Ritschl accepts a theory of imputed righteousness which he has denied in respect to the objective merit of the work of Christ, but which he accepts in terms of a false distinction between individuals and the community.[79]

Orr notes Ritschl's modification of the Church formula of the threefold office to suit his own system but remains critical of the exposition which Ritschl gives to the doctrine. Orr objects to regarding the kingly office as presenting the acts of Christ without relating them to a notion of a divine nature, he criticizes Ritschl's presentation of the priestly office for an unbiblical erosion of the doctrine of sacrifice, and the exposition of the prophetic office as the action of one who represents God to his people but whose significance is not completed in a theology which fails to relate nature and will. Ritschl's suppression of the origin of the person of Christ is indefensible to Orr. In his final summation of his judgment on the Ritschlian theology he says:

180

...we still feel bound to speak of it as an imperfect and mutilated, in many respects wholly inadmissible, version of the Christian Gospel—a system which will not bear to be put in comparison in permanent vitality with the older evangelical creed it seeks to displace...[80]

In closing Orr charges that Ritschl is faithful neither to the apostolic witness, the biblical record nor the needs of the contemporary Church.

James Denney in *Studies in Theology* (1895) links the British and American interest in Ritschlian theology. His book is the publication of lectures given at the Chicago Theological Seminary. In *Studies in Theology* Denney surveys briefly what he proposes as a systematic statement of the Christian faith and comments on the contemporary theological scene in general and on the deficiencies of Ritschlian theology in particular. Denney is not satisfied that Ritschlian theology is an accurate bearer of the New Testament witness. The apostolic writings develop an explicit Christology that is not content "to recognise that Christ had for their hearts the religious value of God" but rather were "under the teaching and guidance of the Spirit, to set Christ in such a relation, objective and real, to God and the world, as justified that judgment of the heart."[81] He further regards Ritschl's statement of the uniqueness of Christ (Cf. *Unterricht in der christlicher Religion*, Paragraph 22) as inconsistent with any form of Christianity in its causal assertion.[82] Denney bases his criticism of the adequacy of Ritschl's thought on his own conception of the authoritative apostolic witness. Nevertheless, Ritschl has provoked similar distrust of his work from liberal and conservative critics alike. As an example of the distance between Ritschl and the orthodoxy he (Denney) champions, Denney focuses on the notion of the death of Christ as the acceptance of the divine condemnation of sin.

I have indicated, in a summary way, what the New Testament "theory" of Christ's work is. His death is conceived as putting away sin, because in that death our condemnation came upon Him. That is the apostolic interpretation, the apostolic theory of atonement. That is the ultimate fact which gives significance to Christ's death, and makes it a sin-anulling death. It is a death in which the divine condemnation of sin comes upon Christ, and is exhausted there, so that there is thenceforth no more condemnation for those that are in Him.[83]

Denney supports Ritschl's criticism of the *munus triplex* which holds that all of the elements of the life and experience of Christ manifest his various functions as prophet, priest, and king, and that the primary function is his kingship.[84]

> Christ's fulfillment of His vocation was all of a piece; in all that He did and bore from beginning to end, He freely accepted His Father's will and made it His own. Active and passive obedience interpenetrate in this willing fulfillment of His vocation, and they neither can be nor should be separated from each other. By introducing the conception of vocation, or at least by giving it a dominant place in the interpretation of Christ's life, Ritschl has given unity to a department of theology which had suffered much from excessive analysis; and by viewing everything afresh from the historical and ethical standpoint, he has vivified what had become a rather lifeless subject, at least in books.[85]

Negatively, Denney finds that Ritschl employs an inadequate conception of Christ's person which refuses to examine the origin of Christ's person and therefore tacitly acknowledges that "Jesus is in the world exactly as we are."[86] Ritschl's formulation of the divinity of Christ functions for Denney as a denial of divinity. It is for Denney a denial both of the witness of the first Christians and of the witness of Christ Himself. This inadequate doctrine leads to a second failure in the statement of Christ's vocation which ignores the resurrection and Pentecost.

> What Ritschl's theory amounts to is, that Christ redeemed us from death as the debt of nature, by showing us how to trust God's love even in that extremity; what the apostolic doctrine shows is how Christ redeems us from death as the wages of sin by dying *our* death Himself, and bearing our sins for us.[87]

Finally, in refusing to bring Christ's death into specific relation to sin, Ritschlian theology invalidates the past witness of the Christian faith and its relevance to human need.

> It is extremely important, Ritschl says, to maintain the distinction between our individual religious reflection on the one hand,

and the form of theological knowledge *sub specie aeternitatis*
on the other. But to maintain this distinction by saying that wrath,
curse, penalty, etc., are ideas or things which from the divine
point of view (*sub specie aeternitatis*) do not come between God's
love and sinful men, seems to me precisely equivalent to saying
that the *real experiences* through which men are prepared to
welcome redemption are after all not *real*, but merely illusions.
Christ redeems us simply by undeceiving us...Our sin, our evil
conscience, our sense of condemnation, are absolutely real
things; and in the New Testament work of redemption they are
treated *as* real, and not as illusions.[88]

Denney's positive suggestion is for a correction of Ritschlian theology
by reference to the New Testament, recovering the notion of sacrificial
atonement.

The conception of Christ's vocation, on which the whole
scheme depends, can be enlarged so as to include a death which
is not what ours is, but what ours could not be—a real propitiation for the sin of the world, regarded as itself real.[89]

This would provide for Denney, a clear distinction between what Christ
was and what mankind is which would restore to the Ritschlian
theology a real and objective difference between humanity and divinity. It would also open the way for recovery of the other "biblical"
elements which had been lost to Ritschlian positivism such as the pre-
existence of Christ, the resurrection and the eschatological accounts
of the exaltation and the final Judgment.

In the course of this brief survey of the early reaction to Ritschlian
theology and its view of the person and work of Christ we have found
criticism from liberal and conservative sides of Ritschl's attempt to
find a workable solution to the problem of the relationship of
metaphysics to theology. The critics call either for a more consistent
positivism and more thorough criticism of the mythological character
of religious language or for a return to a fuller acceptance of traditional formulations of the relation between biblical language and
philosophical notions. The criticism of the *munus triplex* tradition
regarded it, in most cases, to be a helpful attempt to express the work
of Christ in biblical categories. But the relevance of the biblical

material to the work of Christ, as Ritschl formulated it, was challenged on exegetical grounds as selective and arbitrary, and on systematic grounds as incomplete and strangely inconsistent. Ritschl's historical theology was judged to be a departure from the apostolic norms as well as from the recovery of those norms in Reformation theology to which Ritschl claimed allegiance. Ritschl's constructive work was challenged as well, as not close enough to the Bible, to traditional confessional language, nor to the experience of orthodox Christians to be valid. His systematic work was found to be inescapably metaphysical, despite his formal disclaimers, and incomplete in its consideration of origins of religious knowledge and experience and their relationship to the rest of human knowledge and experience.[90]

The dividing line between the earlier exposition of Ritschl and the interpretation of Ritschlian theology and the more contemporary works of criticism and analysis falls in 1942 with the publication of Gösta Hök's *Die elliptische Theologie Albrecht Ritschls: Nach Ursprung und Zusammenhang.*[91] Hök included a bibliography of the important materials in print to 1942 and was able to work with the unpublished papers and notes from Ritschl's library then in care of his son Otto Ritschl. Although Hök did not receive much attention from British and American readers at publication, his work has figured as the basic bibliographical collection on Ritschl for continental theologians until the publication of Rolf Schäfer's *Ritschl: Grundlininen eines fast verschollenden dogmatischen Systems* (1968).[92]

Hök presents a genetic analysis of Ritschl's thought, from his early essays and lectures to the published revisions of his major works, which focuses on the concept of religion.[93] Hök distinguishes between a Rationalistic approach to religion which is based on the knowledge of God and his will for man mediated through reason, and a Supernaturalistic approach to religion which is based on the revelation of God and retains its autonomy and authority apart from man and Nature, although present in Nature as a positive historical fact. Hök cannot place Ritschl immediately in either category. The relationship between the notions of transcendence and immanence is problematic.

Finally, we ask, is Ritschl's God transcendent? He is in terms

184

of his revelation in religion. This cannot be accounted for only as a product of the development of the human spirit. It cannot be derived in any other way. He is also transcendent in respect to the universal essence and development of man. That proves his relation to Nature. However, is he not, in spite of all, immanent and grounded in that unity which is composed of the human spirit and Nature? We do not know God in himself as Absolute according to Ritschl. We know him simply in his actions or revelation in the human spiritual life, in positive religion, and in Nature. Isn't he then immanent?[94]

In Hök's view, Ritschl attempts to involve both perspectives through his concept of religion, developing corresponding notions of the end of religion in *transformation*, as the goal of complete development, and in *blessedness*, as the full appreciation of the transcendent.

With Ritschl objective historical revelation is combined in part with the notion of transformation and in part with the notion of blessedness. Both notions are found in the lectures and in *Justification and Reconciliation*. In the lectures the notion of the transformation of the inner will dominates completely, and in *Justification and Reconciliation*, the notion of blessedness dominates while the historical revelation is interpreted as redemption.[95]

The unification of this dual perspective remains a problem for Ritschl, affecting his Christology and his epistemology. Hök finds Ritschl combining the notion of a transcendent God with an immanent Christology.[96]

This transcendent revelation given in a this-worldly manner also accounts for the way in which Ritschl develops his Christology. The revelation is not tied to the activity of Jesus as Master in any way, only to what he was. His person is that which is normative. God's Word is not a spoken word but the Son of God himself. . . In this the spiritually perfect Man reveals himself. Christ's suffering and death do not have separate meanings; they are only the highest form of human obedience and reveal God in that way. Ritschl indeed goes so far that he accepts this revelation was completely necessary apart from whether sin came to

the world through Adam or not. The appearance of Christ is
not an accidental means, that God applied in order to redeem
men, and that was necessary because man had accidentally sinned; it is the highest revelation, that necessarily had to come,
whether man had sinned or not. He has come to reveal God as
universal End while he established the Kingdom of God, and
he revealed God through that, in order that men see his obedience even to the death and so learn to know God. The Christology remains immanent and free from all the supernatural, as
it refers to Jesus as the perfect Man. As a consequence of that,
the concept of God which arises through the mediation of this
man is somewhat immaterial although Ritschl had especially
stressed the transcendence of God in contrast to his prede-
cessors.[97]

Karl Barth, in his historical survey of Protestant theology in the
nineteenth century and in his dogmatic work as well, is critical of
Ritschl's presentation of the person and life-work of Christ. Barth
does advocate the consideration of the person and work of Christ
together and himself employs the *munus triplex* in the development
of *Church Dogmatics*, IV, in dealing with the doctrine of reconciliation.[98] Barth regards Ritschl as making a return to Kant and Luther
on an essentially ethical basis which does not represent a departure
from the liberal tradition but only a variation in its course of thought.
Barth portrays Ritschl as one who sought to overcome the rationalism
of the Enlightenment but who fell at last into line with its emphasis
on the fulfillment of human life.

Barth surveys the history of the *munus triplex* in *Church Dogmatics*,
IV, 3, 1, pp. 13-38, dealing with the transition from the twofold to
threefold forms. Barth locates the shift with Calvin and judges that
the addition of the prophetic office is an appropriate one. He points
to the anticipation of the move in Paul's recognition of Christ as the
mediator, in ransom and witness.[99]

Hans Vorster in "Werkzeug oder Täter? Zur Methodik der Christologie Albrecht Ritschls," in *Zeitschrift für Theologie und Kirche*,
points to the translation in Ritschl's thought of the traditional doctrine of the two natures of Christ, divine and human, into the religious
and ethical aspects of experience in which dependence and in-

dependence of action become the basic categories.[100] The biblical basis of Ritschl's Christology is important as the ground of his attempts to free Christology from the control of a particular metaphysical approach. The selective and inadequate exegesis may be set aside while the value of the starting point is preserved. Ritschl's criticism of the effect of traditional Christology was that its account of the work of Christ from the religious perspective tended to reduce the ethical description of Christ's obedience to a mechanical level, that of a marionette. As a standard for human behavior, the account of Christ must be that of the historical Jesus and his actions. Ritschl's attempt to resolve the contradiction is to regard Jesus' obedience as an active, independent category in which Christ chooses God's self-end as his own self-end and therefore endures the crucifixion as a positive demonstration of his own decision to adhere to his vocation. However, the adequacy of Ritschl's shift toward ethical categories remains in question.

The correct start in understanding Jesus as the author of his own actions and the attempt to correct the hidden docetism of classical Christology fails in that in its place steps a hidden Ebionitism. In the expulsion of the old historical concepts the religious judgment remains the function of a rejected background. Religion becomes an ideology. Ritschl has made Jesus himself the theme and principle of Christology. He has opened the door in the ethical judgment. That is his service. In the account of the religious judgment he has retained the causal structure of the old metaphysics and merely modified it by drawing on the consciousness of Jesus in place of his Being. The criticism of Ritschl's Christology has nothing to add, as most people see it, to the account of ethical judgment but rather to the religious. The questionable point of his Christological doctrine is the withdrawal of history from it.[101]

Hermann Timm in *Theorie und Praxis in der Theologie Albrecht Ritschls und Wilhelm Herrmanns* (1967) reviews Ritschl's life and work from the perspective of Christian ethics with an interest in the relationship between the theoretical formulations of theological judgments and their more concrete effects in history. Timm considers the personal histories of the theologians as well as their interpretation of historical events.[102] He works to recover Ritschl's historical positivism about the life of Jesus and the foundation of the Kingdom of God from the wreckage of *Kulturprotestantismus*. The interest in the "new quest" for the historical Jesus has placed Ritschl in a central position with his constructive linking of the historical effects of the life of Jesus to the formation of the community of faith. The positive character of religion as a historical reality, which Ritschl maintained, and not a theoretical a priori, is crucial for the practical concerns of Christian ethics.[103] The development of the notion of the Kingdom of God in terms of its practical effects on the lives of its members is important for the analysis of the Christian community in relation to its concrete expression in an organic community life as part of a rational social structure.

Ritschl understood his theology as scientific theory of religious practice, that is, as a doctrine of world view. He addressed the problem of providing a helpful intellectual basis for the religious and ethical self-realization of humanity. The human spirit remains unaware of its practical sovereignty, a creature, that is, disturbed by that which is different from himself, by Nature, that he has not created. Man might always preserve automatically his lordship over Nature, yet that still does not answer the question if his doing so were according to the determination of Nature. A negative response to question would unavoidably have ethical defeatism to follow. However, God has prepared a positive answer to this uneasy question for humanity through the life and work of Jesus Christ; it must only be worked out scientifically from Christian theology. This provides the proof for the actual deification of mankind in the Kingdom of God through the acceptance of an absolute Being, for whom the creation of Nature and the creation of a universal spiritual kingdom represent two successive moments following each other in the realization of its self-end. The Ritschlian theology is its practical definition according to a universal eschatological theory of the Kingdom of God as a correlate of the self-end of God.[104]

Philip Hefner in *Faith and the Vitalities of History* (1966) is concerned to redress the balance of criticism of Ritschlian thought by concentrating on Ritschl's historical works rather than following the lead of most Ritschl studies in concentrating on the systematic works.[105] He aims to show how Ritschl's understanding of historical continuity resulted in the historical judgments which Ritschl made and the comments Ritschl had on the Bible, early Christianity, Catholicism, the Reformation, Lutheranism, and pietism. Hefner distinguishes Ritschl's approach to the problem of continuity in the various historical manifestations of Christianity from that of his mentor, F. C. Baur. Where Baur was concerned with the *Idee, Geist,* or spirit of the Church as an ontological category, Ritschl's concern was personal and religious, dealing with the character of the personal relationship which exists between God and man, namely, reconciliation. The historical expression of this personal relationship is the teaching of Jesus.

Ritschl's historical investigations push continually *not* towards the elucidation of the ontological career of *Geist,* but rather towards an illumination of the personal relation between God and man, the relation of reconciliation. Like Baur, Ritschl locates this problem of reconciliation initially in the distinction between spirit and letter (or matter), as it is expressed in Jesus' own understanding of his relationship to the Mosaic law. Ritschl, too, understood that Jesus' preaching modified the literal external applicability of that law in a way that gave pre-eminence to a spiritual authority over a literal or material one. Ritschl expressed this in terms of man's acknowledging the ultimate claims which his own highest end places upon him; these ultimate claims are found in those parts of the Mosaic law which embody the highest end, namely, love for God and man...The *Grundprincip* of Christianity for Ritschl (and for his theology, as noted below) is the assertion that the God-man relation of reconciliation is grounded in the spirit (in faith, or trust in God) rather than in the literal or legal works which man can effect in his own behalf.[106]

Hefner does not press Ritschl on his claim to be able to present Jesus' own self-understanding or the historical relationship of that understanding to the apostolic community and its continuity in turn with first century Judaism. Ritschl and Hefner are more concerned with the continuity of Jesus' self-understanding and that of the community of Jesus' followers than with the continuity of the history of the human community prior to the formation of the primitive Christian community and subsequent to it.[107] Ritschl's intentions were indeed quite catholic within the limits of the Christian community but his correlation of the continuity of that community with history must lead to further continuity or make it clear that Christian history is limited and therefore does not deal with universal reality. Hefner acknowledges this in respect to the problem of historical diversity and the notion of grace.

Ritschl's insistence on a certain *Lebensfuehrung* or *Froemmigkeit* as the identifying category of the Christian historical continuity specifically undermines this grace, because it makes God's redemptive grace accessible within only *one* configuration of the human psyche. Only by running roughshod over the realities of human diversity and historical relativism is Ritschl able to affirm a continuity even of the *Lebensfuehrung*. If he had honestly wrestled with what we now know about the relativism of time and place, the idiosyncrasies of race and nation, he would have had to admit that this psychical configuration to which grace is alone accessible was very likely a present reality only to those who shared the idiosyncrasies of a Paul or a Luther or a Ritschl.[108]

Rolf Schäfer in *Ritschl: Grundlinen eines fast verschollenen dogmatischen Systems* (1968) presents a survey of important work on Ritschl since Hök's study in 1942 and an updated bibliography listing the more recent work together with the older materials which have proved to be of continuing importance.[109] Of 161 entries; 141 are in German, 14 in English, and 6 in French and Latin.[110] Publication dates since 1942 appear for about 40 articles or monographs, approximately 25 per cent of the total. Four of the most recent German citations are unpublished dissertations. Through the cooperation of Ritschl's grandson, Dietrich Ritschl, Schäfer had access to original manuscripts from which he has attached selections.

Schäfer begins his own consideration of Ritschl's work with an examination of his Christological starting point. Jesus's proclamation of the Kingdom of God is to be understood in the context of the Old Testament notion of the authority of God over the people of the Covenant.[111] The change which Jesus makes is to view the Kingdom of God as a supranational ethical reality which is contemporaneous with Ritschl's consciousness. This removes Jesus' self-understanding and the content of the notion of the Kingdom of God from any subordination to Jewish religion or any other suggestion of historical origin or parallelism, according to Ritschl's view. He avoids speculative notions of the highest good or pure idealism by defining good in terms of judgments by the community of the Kingdom of God. As founder of the community, Jesus performs an objective historical act which is at the same time uniquely his own and of utmost religious importance without violating the character of human causality. Ritschl makes contact with the historical criticism of the New Testament by drawing on the Markan tradition for support of his image of the self-consciousness of Christ and his proclamation. We have criticized Ritschl's use of the New Testament in regard to the notions of priesthood and sacrifice, but Schäfer finds Ritschl to be on solid ground and commanding an important contact point for contemporary discussion, namely, the historical significance of Jesus' life and its meaning for the community that followed him.

While Ritschl subordinated the proclamation of Jesus to his actions and understood it as a part of this whole, the proclamation of the Kingdom still retained the character of grace and of the Gospel unprejudiced to its ethical content. Through that Ritschl avoided the intellectual misunderstanding of Jesus' message which sought only ethical or apocalyptic instruction. Finally, Ritschl has already excluded individualism in this start for the individual disciple is always ruled by the community founded by Jesus; his relationship will never appear to be private concerning Jesus and him alone but is mediated through the community as a whole.[112]

Schäfer examines in turn the proclamation of the Kingdom of God, the actions, the forgiveness of sins, the resurrection, the messianic consciousness, and the relationship to the community which are ascribed to Jesus by the New Testament and interpreted by Ritsch. The form of Jesus' person emerges from the historical material, known in its effect on the life of the Christian community.[113] It is on the basis of this historical image that Ritschl can proceed.

191

The image of the historical Jesus, as the New Testament shows him as founder of the community, contains, for Ritschl, all the guiding concepts which control his dogmatic theology. The passage from the New Testament to valid doctrine in the present is easy for Ritschl because for him the community is a continuous whole for all times.[114]

Ritschl's Christology is subordinated to the doctrine of God in his dogmatic structure. This is in keeping with the relationship of Christian knowledge to revelation and the context of the broader history of the revelation of God to the specific historical event of the revelation of Christ. However, the logical order in the experience of the individual suggested by Ritschl is from his experience of Christ to his knowledge of God's will. The historical order of the Jewish community as the predecessor of the Christian community in the revelation of God prevails although there is a haunting paradox that the experience of Israel is somehow not authentic for itself until the Christian community was formed. The correlation of history, *Heilsgeschichte*, and religious experience is meant to be positive, but it is inconsistent here with history providing the chronological order of events while the epistemological order is reversed and the order of religious significance is in question.[115] Schäfer tries to locate the ultimate unity in the divine viewpoint, and to find it expressed in dogmatic theology.

Now the Christology must be understood as a part of the whole: the Person and work of Christ summon the will of God and are invoked in that issuing from the Being of God and in the relation leading toward the end of the kingdom. It is the task of the dogmatic theology to represent the meaning and effect of the person and work of Christ from the standpoint of God.[116]

Schäfer describes Ritschl's treatment of *munus triplex* in relation to the states of Christ, *in exaltationis* and *in exinanitionis* as dealing with two schemata of tradition in respect to their usefulness for Christology. In Ritschl's view no separation of status can be known without violating the manner in which Christ is known to man.

For if Christ as the Exalted One can only be known as he is revealed in his historical form, then whoever exceeds that must boast of a special revelation. If Lordship over the world is ascribed to the Exalted One, then this must be according to the Humiliated One.[117]

In line with this, the *munus triplex* must be restated in order to correct the tendency to allow the office of kingship to refer to the exaltation of Christ apart from his historical life, and to prevent the description of the office of priest from referring to the passion apart from the deeds and teachings of his earthly ministry. Each of the offices has reference to the historical life of Jesus, and no single office or event stands apart from the whole.

In Jesus of Nazareth, God goes the last and decisive step with mankind to the Kingdom of God. Jesus is the perfect Man, the Model, through whom God creates the new humanity in the community. The perfection of Jesus is that he held the untroubled place of the Son of the Father and remained as the Exalted; in addition he completely fulfilled the will of God, comprehended in love, and not only is the historical Model, but works in the present through the message coming from him.[118]

Christ is the royal prophet and royal priest. These two perspectives express his function as the revealer of God's will to men and the one who establishes man's response to God.

Schäfer says that although the artificial division of the words and deeds of Christ remains, the person and work of Christ form a consistent whole. His kingship receives a biblical basis from which it can be comprehended, and the Exalted One can be known from his historical form in the community. The principle is set out by Ritschl that all dogmatic statements must be rooted in the historical revelation. Therefore, while the person and work of Christ are the same in regard to the humiliation and the exaltation, pietistic deductions based on the exaltation alone are excluded and the historical Jesus remains present in the world for its salvation. Schäfer directs his attention to the way in which the soteriological process is related to the notion of the whole world in Ritschl's thought.

The *munus triplex* is called on to demonstrate the *grace* and truth of God in the person and work of Christ. This demonstration must be in terms of the historical experience of the community to be valid. As Christ is founder and Lord of the Kingdom of God for men, he occupies the place of God for men. The definition is empty, however, without the witness of the community. This emphasis allows Ritschl to keep in balance the relationship between the religious consciousness of the individual and his personal ties to Jesus as the representative of God, and the awareness of the individual of the community in terms of which Jesus is known to him.

What God is and where the Godhead of Christ is, can only be found through the analysis of what is given in revelation. The whole definition, then, of the Godhead, whether of Christ or of God, presupposes the community as the context of the thought . . . where there is no community, it is senseless to speak of God.[119]

Schäfer's judgment is that Ritschl grounds his theology in the notion of a biblical revelation and only develops such philosophical notions as value judgments, a concept of religion in general, and epistemological theory, in the course of his examination, of the basic phenomenon of his religious experience, Jesus Christ.[120] Schäfer finds the key to understanding Ritschl in the relationship of the notions of Scripture, religion and revelation to value judgments and epistemology.

We have seen that Ritschl takes the material of his dogmatic theology from the New Testament: the foundation of the community is the central idea which is developed in its many implications. This historical complex of revelation with the present, which also belongs to systematic theology, will require that the religious component in the reconciliation of the community, the ethical, appear in striving towards the Kingdom of God. Historical revelation and contemporary experience come together in interaction.[121]

The problem is that Ritschl supplies his own formulations for what is important in what the experience of the community must have been. He is infiltrating the objectivity of the biblical witness of the first community to the effect of Jesus with his own clarification of that witness. Ritschl is ready to set aside the dogmatic interests of traditional orthodox theology which differ with his approach as sincerely intended, but mistaken. In order to reconcile Scripture and tradition Ritschl has to supply his own harmonizing notion, related to a general view of religion and functioning in fact, though Ritschl would deny it in theory, as a theoretical standard for evaluating the positive historical revelation. Ritschl's theology finally does not rest on positive historical revelation alone but upon an interpretation of that revelation which involves the value judgments of the early Christian community and of Ritschl in respect to the religious and historical character of revelation.[22] The diaspora of the Ritschlian school after his death follows these various concerns. The extent to which they represent the present concerns of theology in making the historical witness of Christianity intelligible in the modern world in terms of immanence and transcendence, is the extent to which, Schäfer believes, Ritschl is a man of the present age.[23]

David L. Mueller's book, *An Introduction to the Theology of Albrecht Ritschl* (1969), views Ritschl's theology from the perspective of the doctrine of justification and reconciliation, following the outline of the development in the third volume of *The Christian Doctrine of Justification and Reconciliation*.[23] Mueller shows how Ritschl grounds the historical work of Christ both within the divine eternal will and within the ministry of Jesus as vocation. Mueller finds the historical basis of Ritschl's Christology is clearly the primary one.

The only legitimate approach in Christology is from the historical to the suprahistorical, from below to above. The attempt to bypass this order of knowing indicates a failure to comprehend that theological statements are value judgments based upon faith's understanding of the revelation in Jesus; as such, they are not to be confused with scientific statements established a priori. Therefore, Ritschl maintains his earlier viewpoint in saying: "We know God only by revelation, and therefore also must understand the Godhead of Christ if it is to be understood at all, as an attribute revealed to us in His saving influence upon ourselves."[125]

Mueller finds that Ritschl joins other nineteenth century theologians in contending that the interpretation of Jesus must begin with the Jesus of history rather than the Christ interpreted only by dogmatics. Here, Ritschl's distinctive position is that he proposes to deal with Christ as the subject of religion, described in terms of ethical categories. The principal notion is vocation, and Ritschl presents the offices of royal prophet and royal priest as they reveal Christ's vocation as the revealer of God and the founder of the Kingdom of God (representing God to man, and man to God). The critical response to Ritschl, characterized by Mueller, forms around six basic perspectives for interpreting Ritschl's thought; as epistemology, as theology of redemption, as a Christology, as an anthropology, as a doctrine of God, and as a doctrine of Christian perfection.[26] Mueller credits Ritschl with developing a new historical hermeneutic as the basis for interpreting the Christian faith. This hermeneutic incorporates the subjective pole represented by the faith of the community and the individual within the system. and suggests an ethical formulation of an existential basis for theology in history which may prove important in the future.

In respect to Christology, Mueller charges that Ritschl allows a theological reductionism which is dictated by his epistemology to affect his Christology. Ritschl's understanding of the deity of Jesus as seen in the light of his saving work is not the understanding of Christ held by the Reformers, especially Luther, whom Ritschl claims as his model. Ritschl replaces the traditional doctrine of the incarnation with the notion of Jesus' relationship to the Father defined in terms of harmony of will, perfect trust, actions motivated by love, and personal freedom of action in respect to the world. He moves too quickly toward a concentration upon the effects of God's redemptive activity upon man's subjectivity. The result is to avoid the description of the objective significance of the Christian faith beyond the limits of the historical community.

The greatest difficulty for Ritschl comes at the point of relating his doctrine of justification and reconciliation to the death and resurrection of Jesus. Interpreting Jesus in terms of his vocation is helpful in depicting his historical ministry. However, the early church did not interpret Jesus primarily in the light of his earthly ministry before the cross and resurrection; on the contrary, the activity of God in the latter events was the basis for the church's confession of Jesus as Lord. . . Because his Christology has lost its ontological basis in the preexistence of the Son and his continuing life by virtue of his resurrection, the manner in which God is present in Jesus is not adequately treated.

It would seem, therefore, that a Christology divorced from the understanding of God as triune creates as many new problems for Ritschl as the former doctrine which he treats as too speculative. . .The inadequate development of the teleological pole in his thought made his theology more anthropocentric than he intended. Instead of seeing creation, history, and the church moving toward the goal intended by God, Ritschl increasingly restricted his gaze to the individual's quest for self-realization. A more comprehensive perspective was available to him in the stress upon man's faith in divine providence, but there is little appreciation of God's purposive activity in man's present history. This deficiency stems from Ritschl's depreciation of creation and the natural order and leads him to develop an eschatology without any cosmic dimension.[27]

Our examination of the response to Ritschl's Christology has found an appreciation of his constructive attempt to base the knowledge of God for the Christian community upon the life of Jesus in the New Testament, and appreciation of his concern to express the role of the individual in the interpretation of Scripture, in the evaluation of theological traditions, and the experience of the significance of justification and reconciliation. At the same time, we found support for our contention that Ritschl's own Christology involved a misevaluation of the biblical authenticity, historical continutiy, and systematic value of the *munus triplex*, due to Ritschl's ethical and epistemological concerns. His reformulation of the *munus triplex* carried it further from its biblical roots and traditional interpretations in Catholic and Reformation theology.

In the next chapter we shall attempt to employ the positive results of our study in a consideration of the constructive problem in Christology, reexamining the *munus triplex* in the light of Ritschl's objections and the criticism of his approach which we have noted. Finally, we hope to offer some suggestions about the availability of the doctrine of the *munus triplex* for the Church today.

NOTES CHAPTER IV

1. A. Ritschl, RV, III, 403-409; JR, III, 427-433. Compare with RV, I, 3; JR, I, 3.

2. *Ibid.*

3. *Ibid.*

4. Schweitzer, *The Quest of the Historical Jesus,* p. 252.

5. A. Ritschl, RV, III, 424-425; JR, III, 450 ff.

6. Ibid.

7. A. Ritschl, RV, III, 446-448; JR, III, 474-476.

8. A. Ritschl, RV, III, 449; JR, III, 478.

9. A. Ritschl, RV, III, 424-425; JR, III, 451-452.

10. A. Ritschl, RV, III, 408-409; JR, III, 432.

11. Cf. Deegan, "Albrecht Ritschl on the Historical Jesus"; Perrin, *The Kingdom of God in the Teachings of Jesus;* and Robinson, *A New Quest of the Historical Jesus.*

12. A. Ritschl, RV, III, 426; JR, III, 451.

13. Ritschl's claim that the biblical data themselves do not warrant setting the three offices side by side as of equal worth for interpreting the work of Christ is justified. His claim of finding a further inherent unity is not supported by a general acceptance of his exegesis. A fact which may explain why Volume II of *Rechtfertigung und Versöhnung* remains untranslated.

14. We have tried to suggest this in Chapter III.

15. A. Ritschl, RV, III, 393-394; JR, III, 417-418.

16. See above, pp. 65 ff.

17. See above, pp. 67 ff.

18. *Ibid.*

19. See above, pp. 88 ff.

20. Cf. Gerrish, "Priesthood and Ministry in the Theology of Luther," pp. 404-422 and Williams, *Wilderness and Paradise in Christian Thought,* pp. 184-192.

[21] A. Ritschl, RV, I, 15-16; JR, III, 15-16.

[22] See above, n. 19.

[23] Cf. A. Ritschl, RV, III, 394-395; JR, III, 418-419; RV, III, 383-384; JR, III, 406.

[24] A. Ritschl, RV, III, 407-408; JR, III, 431.

[25] Cf. A. Ritschl. RV, I, 15; JR, I, 15; RV, III, 1-3; JR, III, 1-3.

[26] Cf. Mueller, *An Introduction to the Theology of Albrecht Ritschl,*. pp. 38-46.

[27] A. Ritschl, RV, III, 403-404; JR, III, 427.

[28] *Ibid.*

[29] A. Ritschl, RV, III, 396-397; JR, III, 419-420.

[30] A. Ritschl, RV, III, 400-403; JR, III, 424-427.

[31] A. Ritschl, RV, III, 368; JR, III, 397.

[32] A. Ritschl, RV, III, 14-25, 193-201; JR, III, 14-25, 203-211; *Theologie und Metaphysik,* pp. 23ff.

[33] A. Ritschl, RV, III, 1-6; JR, III, 1-6.

[34] A. Ritschl, RV, III, 408-409; JR, III, 432.

[35] A. Ritschl, RV, III, 438; JR, III, 465.

[36] A. Ritschl, RV, III, 453-454; JR, III, 482.

[37] A. Ritschl, RV, III, 409-410; JR, III, 434.

[38] A. Ritschl, RV, III, 33-34; JR, III, 33-34.

[39] Ritschlianism. Cf. A. E. Garvie, "Ritschlianism," *Encyclopedia of Religion and Ethics,* ed. by J. Hastings (Edinburgh: T. & T. Clark, 1905), pp. 812-820; E. Schott, "Ritschl, A. B.," *Die Religion in Geschichte und Gegenwartm* Dritte Auflage (Tübingen: J. C. B. Mohr, 1961), pp. 1114-1119; "Ritschl, A. B.," *Lexikon für Theologie und Kirche,* Zweite Auflage, VII (Freiburg: Herder, 1913), 1324-1325; and "Albrecht Ritschl," by Otto Ritschl in Hauck, *Realencyklopädie für protestantische Theologie und Kirche,* Dritte Auflage, VII (Leipzig: J. C. Hinrichs, 1906), 22-34.

[40] C. E. Luthardt, "Zur Beurtheilung der Ritschl'schen Theologie," *Zeitschrift für kirchliche Wissenschaft und kirchliches Leben,* II (1881), 625. My translation.

[41] Otto Pfleiderer, *The Development of Theology in Germany Since Kant* (London: Sonnenschein, 1890), p. 183.

[42] *Ibid.*, p. 192.

[43] Cf. on this problem Otto Pfleiderer, "Die Theologie der Ritschl'schen Schule," *Jahrbücher für protestantische Theologie.* 1891, pp. 323 ff.

[44] I. A. Dorner, *A System of Christian Doctrine* (4 vols.; Edinburgh: T. & T. Clark, 1882), III, 274-275.

[45] *Ibid.*, p. 279.

[46] *Ibid.*, pp. 387-388.

[47] *Ibid.*, p. 285.

[48] *Ibid.*, IV, 137.

[49] *Ibid.*, pp. 142ff.

[50] Wilhelm Herrmann, *The Communion of the Christian with God* (London: Williams and Norgate, 1906), p. 47.

[51] *Ibid.*, p. 74.

[52] *Ibid.*, p. 75. Cf. also W. Herrmann and Adolph Harnack, "The Real Mind of Jesus," in *Essays on the Social Gospel* (London: Williams and Norgate, 1907), pp. 186-225 and Wilhelm Herrmann, *Systematic Theology* (New York: Macmillan, 1927), p. 50. "If, however, we long for a Being to whom we may surrender ourselves, the self-evidencing picture of Jesus' inner life drawn in the New Testament is capable of gripping us with all the power of a personally experienced reality."

[53] Wilhelm Herrmann, "Albrecht Ritschl, seine Grösse und seine Schranke," *Festgabe von Fachgenossen und Freunden A. von Harnack* (Tübingen: J. C. B. Mohr, 1921), pp. 405-406. My translation. Herrmann gives another sympathetic portrait of Ritschl in "Faith as Ritschl Defined It," in *Faith and Morals* (London: Williams and Norgate, 1910), pp. 7-17. For Herrmann, Ritschl was primarily responsible for a recovery of the spirit of the work of Luther from destructive interpretation. "Of the two propositions—Faith saves a man, and Faith is a submission to the authority of a revelation. . . Ritschl maintained both. That made him incomprehensible to most of his contemporaries; but it also puts him in the frontrank of those who have wanted to rescue and preserve the work of Luther from forms that are falling to pieces."

[54] Julius Kaftan, *Dogmatik* (Tübingen: J. C. B. Mohr, 1920), pp. 563-564, 571. My translation.

[55] *Ibid.*, p. 574.

[56] Julius Kaftan, *The Truth of the Christian Religion* (Edinburgh: T. & T. Clark, 1894), p. 404. He adopts this position even though it entails, in theory, that Christianity could be proved false by historical research.

[57] Adolph Harnack, *History of Dogma* (London: Williams and Norgate, 1894), I, 45-49; 122-127; IV, 272, and *Outline of the History of Dogma* (London: Hodder and Stoughton, 1893), p. 5, n. 6.

[58] Adolph Harnack, *What Is Christianity?* (London: Williams and Norgate, 1923), p. 7.

[59] Harnack, *History of Dogma,*. VII, 272, 274. Harnack makes oblique use of the *munus triplex* in discussing the threefold issue of Christian thought in Catholic, Protestant and Rationalist forms. Like Herrmann, Harnack encounters the person of Christ directly in the biblical accounts and is reluctant to find heterodox doctrinal interests at this stage which might obscure the experience of the person of Christ in subjectivism or relativism.

[60] Adolph Harnack, "Ritschl und seine Schule," *Reden und Aufsätze*, II (Giessen: J. Richer, 1904), 352-353.

[61] *Ibid.*, pp. 354-355.

[62] Alfred E. Garvie, *The Ritschlian Theology* (Edinburgh: T. & T. Clark, 1899); Mackintosh, *Albrecht Ritschl and His School;* and Franks, *A History of the Doctrine of the Work of Christ.*

[63] James Orr, *The Ritschlian Theology and the Evangelical Faith* (London: Hodder and Stoughton, 1897); James Denny, *Studies in Theology* (London: Hodder and Stoughton, 1895).

[64] Garvie, *The Ritschlian Theology,* pp. 264ff.

[65] *Ibid.*, pp. 276-277; 284-285.

[66] *Ibid.*, p. 296.

[67] Mackintosh, *Albrecht Ritschl and His School,* p. 254.

[68] Franks, *A History of the Doctrine of the Work of Christ,* I, 5-8.

[69] *Ibid.*, II, 364-365. Cf. pp. 349-351. "In fact the modern purpose to reduce the system of Christian theology to the unity of a single principle, nowhere receives a more notable exemplification than in the work of Ritschl. He has endeavored to bring every part of Christian theology under the control of the central idea of the Christian conception of God as revealed in Christ, with its twofold development in the notions of the Kingdom of God and reconciliation. He rejects the orthodox dogmatic system, including all modern repristinations of the same, on the ground

that it is not a unity, but is developed from different and inconsistent principles. . . . Ritschl has particularly attacked the principle of the Divine twofold retribution of rewards and punishments according to merit, as being unfit for use in Christian doctrine. It is in his view an idea of Hellenic religion which was first firmly established within Christianity by the Apologists. . . . As has already been observed, Ritschl defines the Divine righteousness as the consistency of the Divine grace: this position as well as the distinction between punishment and affliction he inherits from Socinianism. He stands, in fact, to the criticism of Socinus and the *Aufklärung* in the same relation as Luther does to that of Duns and the Nominalists."

[70] *Ibid.*, pp. 368-369.

[71] *Ibid.*, I, 441.

[72] *Ibid.*, p. 444.

[73] *Ibid.*, II, 346-347.

[74] Cf. R. S. Franks, *The Atonement* (London: Oxford University Press, 1934), pp. viii-ix.

[75] Orr, *The Ritschlian Theology and the Evangelical Faith,* pp. 108-110.

[76] *Ibid.*

[77] *Ibid.*, p. 131.

[78] *Ibid.*, pp. 154-155.

[79] *Ibid.*, pp. 169ff., 210.

[80] *Ibid.*, p. 234. Cf. James Orr, *Ritschlianism: Expository and Critical Essays* (London: Hodder and Stoughton, 1903).

[81] Denney, *Studies in Theology,* pp. 17-18.

[82] *Ibid.*, pp. 65-66.

[83] *Ibid.*, p. 108.

[84] *Ibid.*, pp. 140ff.

[85] *Ibid.*

[86] *Ibid.*

[87] *Ibid.*, p. 143.

[88] *Ibid.*, p. 145.

[89] *Ibid.*, p. 146.

[90] Further response to Ritschl and Ritschlian theology is described in F. Kattenbusch, *Von Schleiermacher zu Ritschl* (Giessen: J. Richer, 1892); H. Stephan, "Albrecht Ritschl," *Die Religion in Geschichte und Gegenwart,* Zweite Auflage (Tüubingen: J. C. B. Mohr, 1927) and materials listed, n. 39. above. In England the course of Ritschlian theology is assessed by H. R. Mackintosh, "Ritschlianism Old and New," *London Quarterly Review,* CXXI (January, 1914), 25-50; *Types of Modern Theology: Schleiermacher to Barth* (New York: Charles Scribners, 1937), pp. 138-180, and more recently, Thomas Langford, *In Search of Foundations: English Theology 1900-1920* (New York: Abingdon, 1969), pp. 219-233. In the United States the interest in Ritschlian theology may be seen in C. M. Mead, *Ritschl's Place in the History of Doctrine* (Hartford: Hartford Seminary Press, 1895); A. T. Swing, *The Theology of Albrecht Ritschl,* and "Recent Ritschlianism," *Outlook,* LXVIII (June, 1901), 361-362; E. A. Cook, "Ritschl's Use of Value Judgments," *American Journal of Theology,* XXI (October, 1917), 345-353; and in W. C. Kierstead, "Theological Presuppositions of Albrecht Ritschl," *American Journal of Theology,* X (1906), 423. In this period, the literature explores the over-all effect of Ritschlian thought upon orthodoxy, the specific place of value judgments in epistemology and ontology, and Ritschl's account of the history of the doctrine. His own Christology and its relationship to the *munus triplex* is not examined in any detail. The bulk of the material is exposition of Ritschl's thought to a new audience. In French, the material on Ritschlian theology includes A. Sabatier, *Outlines of a Philosophy of Religion* (London: Hodder and Stoughton, 1897); H. Schoen, *Les origens historique de la théologie de Ritschl* (Paris: Fischbacher, 1893); G. Baldensperger, "La théologie d'Albert Ritschl," *Revue de théologie et ohilosophie, XVI (1883), 511-529, 617-634; and Maurice* Goguel, *La théologie d'Albert Ritschl* (Paris: Fischbacher, 1905). For more recent publications cf. Chapter I, p. 1, n. 1.

[91] Gösta Hök, *Die elliptische Theologie Albrecht Ritschls: Nach Ursprung und innerem Zusammenhang* (Uppsala Universitets Arsskrift, 1942:3).

[92] Rolf Schäfer, *Ritschl: Grundlinien eines fast verschollenen dogmatischen Systems* (Tübingen: J. C. B. Mohr, 1968).

[93] Hök, *Die elliptische Theologie Albrecht Ritschls,* pp. 7-9. My translation.

[94] *Ibid.*, pp. 35-36.

[95] *Ibid.*, p. 248.

[96] *Ibid.*, p. 39.

[97] *Ibid.*, pp. 38-39.

[98] Karl Barth, *Protestant Thought from Rousseau to Ritschl* (New York: Harper, 1959), pp. 390-398, and *Church Dogmatics,* IV, 1, 381-383.

203

⁹⁹ Barth, *Church Dogmatics*, IV, 3, 1, 11. Most recent commentators on Ritschl attempt to defend him from Barth's overdrawn portrait. The most interesting outcome is the analysis of parallels between Barth and Ritschl which reveals their basic agreement. Cf. Deegan, "The Ritschlian School, The Essence of Christianity and Karl Barth"; Hefner, "Albrecht Ritschl and His Current Critics"; Jersild, "The Judgment of God in Albrecht Ritschl and Karl Barth"; "Natural Theology and the Doctrine of God in Albrecht Ritschl and Karl Barth"; and Pickle, "Epistemology and Soteriology."

¹⁰⁰ Hans Vorster, "Werkzeug oder Täter? Zur Methodik der Christologie Albrecht Ritschls," *Zeitschrift für Theologie und Kirche*, LXII (May, 1965), 46-65.

¹⁰¹ *Ibid.*, p. 65

¹⁰² H. Timm, *Theorie und Praxis in der Theologie Albrecht Ritschls und Wilhelm Herrmanns* (Gütersloh: Mohn, 1967), p. 40, n. 19. My translation.

¹⁰³ *Ibid.*, p. 55.

¹⁰⁴ *Ibid.*, pp. 73-74.

¹⁰⁵ Hefner, *Faith and the Vitalities of History*, p. 27.

¹⁰⁶ *Ibid.*, p. 28. Ritschl maintains a more positive position in respect to the participation of the individual self in reconciliation than Hefner acknowledges here. In light of Hefner's interest in the importance of historical continuity in Ritschl's thought, it is surprising that he did not examine *Rechtfertigung und Versöhnung*, II more closely in order to check on Ritschl's assessment of the continuity or lack of it in the pre-Christian and Christian lifestyle of the early followers of Jesus.

¹⁰⁷ *Ibid.*, pp. 44, 86, 113-115. Hefner regards *Lebensführung* as bound to history and expressed in historical events but he does not try to derive it from specific grounds in the life of Christ.

¹⁰⁸ *Ibid.*, pp. 106-107.

¹⁰⁹ Schäfer, *Ritschl*, pp. 46-51.

¹¹⁰ *Ibid.*, p. 51.

¹¹¹ Cf. Hefner, *Faith and the Vitalities of History*, pp. 167-182.

¹¹² Schäfer, *Ritschl*, p. 240.

¹¹³ *Ibid.* The personal relationship here is less the direct, intimate communication described by Herrmann and more a reserved and professional association appropriate to a business interview or the examination of an applicant for an appointment.

[114] *Ibid.*, p. 67.

[115] *Ibid.*, p. 102, n. 1.

[116] *Ibid.*, pp. 102ff. Schäfer does press Ritschl here about restricting the possibility of a natural theology, or arguing the historical uniqueness of Jesus' person in history while accepting the historical order of Judaism superseded by Christianity as part of the reality disclosed in revelation. Ritschl's concept of history seems to shift. In relation to Nature, history is seen as characteristic of the spirit, as conscious of itself in time. In relation to man, history includes natural events occurring in time, which is seen as a continuum of objects and persons. In relation to Christ, the historical sequence may be viewed as continuous with the human consciousness and at the same time with the divine will. This is another case, like the historical origin of the person of Christ, where Ritschl's lack of interest in the broader metaphysical implications of his approach sets his work adrift. He needs either to be more consistent in providing a historical sequence of effects and their causes which relates the person of Jesus to the history of religion and politics in Israel or else more inclusive in his metaphysical judgments about what can be known and legitimately regarded as real. Schäfer finds Ritschl inconsistent in his treatment of the Old Testament as the source of *echte Offenbarung* (p. 103). This is another way of pointing to the inconsistency of Ritschl's approach.

[117] *Ibid.*, p. 104.

[118] *Ibid.*, p. 105.

[119] *Ibid.*, p. 109.

[120] *Ibid.*, p. 154.

[121] *Ibid.*, p. 156.

[122] *Ibid.*, p. 159.

[123] *Ibid.*, p. 186.

[124] Mueller, *An Introduction to the Theology of Albrecht Ritschl.*

[125] *Ibid.*, p. 58.

[126] *Ibid.*, p. 90.

[127] *Ibid.*, pp. 174-175, 179.

CHAPTER V
CONCLUSION: THE CONSTRUCTIVE PROBLEM
Reexamination of the *Munus Triplex*

Ritschl judged the doctrine *munus triplex* to be a distortion of the biblical evidence regarding the life of Christ, a failure in preserving the historical unity of the life of Jesus and in presenting the significance Christ's life. From a systematic standpoint, he found the doctrine to be a defective formula for preserving distinctions in the work of Christ because it offers no notion of unity and allows the offices to become separated from each other in respect to their reference to the life of Christ *in statu exinanitionis.* He judged the importance of the doctrine was its application by Reformation theologians in bringing together the person and work of Christ, and regarded the notion of offices associated with the doctrine to be so open to abuse by self-aggrandizing clergy that he replaced the word *office (Amt)* with *personal vocation (persönlicher Beruf)* in order to protect the availability of the offices for all Christians[1].

His own criticism notwithstanding, Ritschl proceeded to recast the form of the doctrine, referring all activities of Christ as Prophet, Priest, and King to one historical ground, the *status exinanitionis.*[2] The offices were united by the notion of Christ's vocation, expressed in terms of his being the founder of the Kingdom of God and the perfect revealer of God. Ritschl preserved the distinction of the priestly and prophetic activities while expressing the distinction in terms of the relationships of prophetic revelation from God to man and of priestly response from man to God.[3]

We found in our examination of Ritschl's biblical criticism of the *munus triplex* that his own dogmatic commitment to the uniqueness of the revelation in Jesus Christ did not allow him to explore the history of the institutions of prophecy, priesthood and kingship within the Old Testament extensively in order to consider the positive historical influence which these notions had on the mind of Jesus as a member of the Jewish tradition. Ritschl can admit the value of the offices of Christ only after he has replaced the content of the offices with his own formulation of how they are executed by Christ. The ethical character of his definitions is so consistent with his empirically oriented epistemology that it strikes down traditional notions of Christian thought about relating the offices to the work of Christ without giving an account of the broader unity that functions to preserve the meaning of the offices outside of the Ritschlian framework. This failure to secure a consistent ontology, history, or hermeneutic is evident in Ritschl's approach to the Old Testament, the New Testament, and the history of doctrine.

Ritschl's use of the Bible as the source for historical information about the impact of Jesus upon the circle of his followers is problematic, if the language of the disciples about Jesus and Jesus' own words must be read without considering their historical context and regarding them as conditioned by that context. Ritschl acknowledges that "it is a false assumption that a uniform doctrine of the Godhead of Christ can be exegetically constructed from the New Testament," yet he also claims to be capable of "reducing the different data before us to their inherent unity."[4] He rejects biblical obscurantism which would regard the Bible uncritically, admitting only one point of view, but he is also unwilling to separate systematic theology from the Bible and to let purely historical norms apply to historical material or to acknowledge fully the speculative responsibilities of systematic theology in providing an ontology. Internal coherence and external intelligibility are both important. This leaves Ritschl steering a perilous course in which he regards the Bible as a legitimate source of historical knowledge, when treated critically, that supplies knowledge of God through participation in the work of Christ in the experience of the believer, but relies upon the experience of the believer to validate the reality of that knowledge for himself.

The difficulties which we have encountered in correlating Ritschl's account of the doctrine of sacrifice and priesthood with material in the Old Testament and his presentation of the self-consciousness of

Christ with critical studies on the life of Jesus in the New Testament, lead us to reject his judgment of the limited historical importance of the *munus triplex*. We want to stress the greater historical value of the *munus triplex* as a doctrine which involves basic religious, political and social categories in its presentation of the religious consciousness of the people of God in the Judeo-Christian tradition. The majority of criticisms of Ritschl's position which we surveyed supports this judgment.

In the light of this reexamination of the history of the *munus triplex*, we regard *munus triplex* as a doctrine that has authentic biblical roots, in both Old Testament and New Testament understandings of the various offices, but we recognize that the precise definition of the content and form of the doctrine at various stages in its history is a joint function of the surviving traditions of the period and the specific interpreter of the history, be it Ritschl or ourselves. The individual value judgment of an observer concerning the meaning and importance of a doctrine must be related to further terms of reference in order to communicate the judgment to other minds. Ritschl's dissatisfaction with the accuracy of the *munus triplex* as stated by Calvin is more precisely Ritschl's dissatisfaction with the ability of the formulation of the doctrine supplied by Calvin and Reformation theology to express the positive correlation between the New Testament and the mind of Christ which Ritschl himself held. The individual offices and their association together are a part of the Old Testament tradition, in its text, and in the tradition of its interpretation. This forms part of the history of the doctrine prior to the New Testament witness to the effect of Jesus' ministry upon how the Christian community came to view these institutions. We must not lose sight of the fact as we deal with the biblical material that we are working with material that carries with it an interpretative framework as part of itself, which interacts with our own interpretative structures. Ritschl has cautioned us not to regard the *munus triplex* without being aware of its distinctively Christian significance. By referring to its earlier roots we are balancing Ritschl's emphasis and broadening the historical base in terms of which the *munus triplex* is to be understood.

We found in our examination of Ritschl's historical account of *munus triplex* that he ignored to a large degree the occurrence of the formulation in theological writing between Eusebius and Calvin. The association of the *munus triplex* with the doctrines of substitutionary atonement and the notion of the objective merit of Christ during this time invalidated the doctrine, in Ritschl's judgment. His understanding of the proper content of the doctrine of justification and reconciliation and of the definitition of the subjective appropriation of grace as fellowship with God in a common vocation suggested a different content for the *munus triplex*. His objection to the *munus triplex* in the ancient and medieval Church was systematic as well as historical. Ritschl was looking for a more consistent unity between the form and content of the *munus triplex* and other aspects of Christian doctrine than he found in the history of doctrine.

The fact that Ritschl feels that he can correct the content of the doctrine and clarify its form, relating his version of *munus triplex* to the inherent unity of the Christian faith, indicates that he has made an implicit acceptance of the biblical basis and doctrinal potential of the doctrine in the presentation of the Christian faith even in face of his criticism. This raises a question in regard to Ritschl's theory of religion. Briefly, the central issue is how his description of Christianity as a positive religion, perceived as a historical phenomenon, is related to his general theory of religion. Does Ritschl's account of the meaning of the Christian faith control the notion of religion, or does Ritschl have a general theory of religion which controls his account of what is authentic in the Christian faith? Since we found that the biblical material was organized by his ethical and epistemological concerns, the latter seems to be the case. His attempt to remain aloof from speculative questions has failed. In regard to the *munus triplex*, he is able to find it important in understanding the Christian faith for some periods of Church history and not for others. In order to treat it as part of the historical phenomena of the Christian tradition and still make judgments about its suitability, a further standard of judgment is in operation. In Ritschl's case a more careful attempt to address the issue of an ontological basis for religion might have produced a clearer understanding of the limits of individual value judgments in history and resulted in a fairer treatment of the history of the *munus triplex* in Christian thought.

The *munus triplex* is a doctrine which reflects the distinctive theological interests of succeeding periods in Church history without completely submitting to the doctrinal interests of those periods. It is independent because of its authentic historical base in the biblical material and because of the diversity of its interpretation when viewed from a historical rather than a doctrinal or epistemological perspective. In the course of our study we have observed Ritschl's theological method in relation to the doctrine of the person and life-work of Christ. He has provided us with a critical but selected history of the *munus triplex* and a constructive reformulation of the doctrine in the course of presenting his own Christology. He claimed to have found in the New Testament the historical record of the work of Jesus Christ as royal prophet and royal priest. We found that Ritschl's epistemology controlled his evaluation of what was important in the history of doctrine, and that the content of his dogmatic theology—the work of Jesus as the founder of the Kingdom of God—was viewed by Ritschl as the historical event to which he looked as the objective standard for validating his epistemology. While the exposition of Ritschl's views on the historical and systematic value of the *munus triplex* has served to demonstrate his theological method and to direct our attention to important periods in the history of that doctrine, it has also raised fundamental methodological questions.

Ritschl's presentation of the relationship between his epistemology and his dogmatic theology risks being dismissed as a circular argument. Religious knowledge, as described by Ritschl, is based on the value judgment of the effect of Jesus upon the believer. Some objective standard is required to avoid regarding *any* and *every* personal feeling as the result of Jesus' action. Ritschl believes that he is in possession of such a standard in the content of his dogmatic theology, namely, the witness of the Christian community to the work of Jesus as the Christ. However, the biblical materials to which Ritschl turns for historical evidence of an objective character are themselves results of the value judgments of the early Christian community and include material which does not conform to Ritschl's epistemological standards. Since he has neither articulated a consistent ontology himself nor acknowledged any direct revelation apart from the life of Jesus, Ritschl lacks a further objective standard. Efforts to erect such a standard in the Bible, in the institution of the papacy, in the establishment of councils and creeds, in the self-consistency of doctrinal systems, and in the experience of the individual have had some measure of success in the history of Christian thought, but the question of the objective reality of religious consciousness is still open.

The *munus triplex* is a part of the biblical, historical, and systematic heritage of the Christian faith and an expression of the character of the impact of religious experience upon men and the historical institutions, concepts, persons, and feelings in terms of which this awareness is expressed. The importance of stages in the history of the doctrine may be noted and provisional judgments offered about its origin in history and its value in expressing and interpreting religious experience, but the limits of these judgments must be clarified by reference to the experience of the judge.

Besides offering a broader historical base for *munus triplex* and a more sympathetic appreciation of its different formulations within the history of doctrine, we must adopt a more restricted view of the ability of *munus triplex* to exhaustively represent the understanding of the person and lifework of Christ for the entire Christian faith in any one of its formulations. Its value for Christian tradition is as part of the historical record of the witness of the Christian community to past events, as an example of the interpretation of past events reflected through the experience of theologians within the history of doctrine, and finally as a source for suggesting, shaping and expressing continuing religious experience in terms of the work of Christ.

The Availability of the Doctrine of the Offices of Christ Today

Study of the *munus triplex* as a record of the representation of the work of Christ as Prophet, Priest and King has brought us to consider the continuity of Christian experience with the religious traditions of Israel and to consider the significance of the witness of the Christian community to the new experience of Jesus as the Christ. We have seen religious experience interpreted in terms of a series of philosophical and theological systems which were used in an attempt to clarify and define the nature of that experience. Ritschl directed our attention to the continuity which he found within the Christian witness to the will of God for the salvation of his people, the will of Christ for fellowship with the Father in reconciliation, and the will of the individual Christian to share in bringing that reconciliation to mankind. The *munus triplex* as Ritschl presented it expressed the understanding of the vocation of Christ as royal prophet and royal priest and offered the vocation of Christ to men.

The contribution of our study has been to provide a critical assessment of Ritschl's treatment of the *munus triplex*, from the perspective of historical theology. Three factors cluster together in support of our criticism. First, Ritschl's exegesis of the Old and New Testaments drew immediate objection from his peers in all parties—conservative, liberal and mediating—because of his failure to deal with the meaning of passages more carefully in terms of their proper historical context. Second, his key category for integration of the biblical witness with his systematic work, the kingdom of God, was effectively challenged by the criticism of Weiss and Schweitzer. Their work revealed, to the theological world, the historical distance which existed between the kingdom of God in its eschatological sense, in the first century, and its ethical sense, in the nineteenth century. Third, the richness of the Christian tradition, which recognizes several theories of the person and work of Christ, has been narrowed by Ritschl's ethical and epistemological criteria. In this respect, our criticism has pointed toward the possibility of a broader interpretation of the *munus triplex* as a Christological doctrine.

NOTES CHAPTER V

[1] A. Ritschl, RV, III, 409; JR, III, 434.

[2] A. Ritschl, RV, III, 408; JR, III, 432.

[3] A. Ritschl, RV, III, 409; JR, III, 433.

[4] A. Ritschl, RV, III, 408; JR, III, 432.

BIBLIOGRAPHY

Abba, Raymond. "Priests and Levites." *Interpreter's Dictionary of the Bible.* 1964. Vol. III.

Acton, H. B. "Georg Wilhelm Friedrich Hegel." *The Encyclopedia of Philosophy.* 1967. Vol. III.

Albertus Magnus. *Opera Omnia.* Paris: n.p., 1890.

Alcuin. *Interpretationes nominum Hebraicorum progenitorum Domini nostri Jesu Christi.* Patrologiae Cursus Completus Series Latina, Vol. C. Edited by J. P. Migne. Paris: 1844-1880.

Alexander of Roes. *"Memoriale de prerogativa Romani imperii."* Edited by George Hunston Williams. Selected Texts Church History 183, Harvard University, 1964. (Mimeographed.)

_____. *"Notici seculi."* Edited by George Hunston Williams. Selected Texts Church History 183, Harvard University, 1964. (Mimeographed.)

Ambrose of Milan. *De Nabuthe Jezraelita. Sermo contra Auxetium. De Mysteriis. Epistolae. De Fide.* Patrologiae Cursus Completus Series Latina, Vols. XIV-XVII. Edited by J. P. Migne. Paris: 1844-1880.

Augustine of Hippo. *Enarratio in Ps. 26:2. Epistola Ioannis ad Parthos.* Patrologiae Cursus Completus Series Latina, Vols. XXXII-XLVII. Edited by J. P. Migne. Paris: 1844-1880.

Baldensperger, Gerhard. "La théologie de Albrecht Ritschl." Revue de Théologie et de Philosophie. XVI (1883), 511-529; 617-634.

Barr, James. *The Semantics of Biblical Language.* London: Oxford University Press, 1961.

Barth, Karl. *Church Dogmatics,* IV, 1, 2, 3. English translation by G. W. Bromiley. Edinburgh: T. & T. Clark, 1956.

_____. *The Epistle to Romans.* English translation from the sixth German edition by Edwyn C. Hoskyns. London: Oxford University Press, 1933.

_____. *Protestant Thought from Rousseau to Ritschl.* English translation from *Die protestantische Theologie im 19. Jahrhundert* by Brian Cozens. New York: Harper, 1959.

Baur, Ferdinand C. *Die christliche Lehre von der Versöhnung in ihrer geschichtlichen Entwicklung von der ältesten Zeit bis auf die Neuste.* Tübingen: Osiander, 1838.

McCulloh

Beardslee, John W., III, ed. *Reformed Dogmatics.* New York: Oxford University Press, 1965.

Blaser, Klauspeter. *Calvins Lehre von den drei Amtern Christi. Theologische Studien,* CV (1970), 1-51. Edited by Max Geier *et al.* Zurich: EVZ-Verlag, 1970.

Bosc, Jean. *The Kingly Office of the Lord Jesus Christ.* Edinburgh: Oliver & Boyd, 1959.

Bowlin, Ruth E. "The Christian Prophets in the New Testament." Unpublished Ph.D. dissertation, Vanderbilt University, 1958.

Bright, John. *A History of Israel.* Philadelphia: Westminster Press, 1959.

Bucer, Martin. *In sacra quator evangelia enarrationes.* Citation in George Hunston Williams. *Wilderness and Paradise in Christian Thought.* New York: Harper & Row, 1962.

Calvin, John. *Catechismus Genevensis.* Corpus Reformatorum, Vol. XXXIV. Edited by Guilelmus Baum, *et al.* Brunsvigae: Schwetschke, 1869. English translation by J. K. S. Reid. *Calvin: Theological Treatises.* Library of Christian Classics, Vol. XXII. Philadelphia: Westminster Press, 1954.

Calvin, John. *Commentarius in Epistolam Pauli ad Romanos.* Corpus Reformatorum, Vol. LXXVII. English translation by John Owen. *Calvin's Commentaries.* Edinburgh: Calvin Translation Society, 1849.

_____. *De fugiendis impiorum illicitis sacris.* Corpus Reformatorum, Vol. XXXIII. English translation by H. Beveridge. *Calvin, Tracts Relating to the Reformation,* Vol. III. Edinburgh: Calvin Translation Society, 1844.

_____. *L' Harmonie des trois evangelists.* Corpus Reformatorum, Vol. LXXIV. English translation H. Beveridge. *Commentary on a Harmony of the Evangelists Matthew, Mark and Luke.* Edinburgh: Calvin Translation Society, 1845.

_____. *Institutio Religionis Christianae.* Corpus Reformatorum, Vol. XXIX. English translation by J. T. McNeill *et al. Calvin: Institutes of the Christian Religion.* Library of Christian Classics, Vols. XX XXI. Philadelphia: Westminster Press, 1960.

_____. *Instruction in Faith.* Edited and translated by Paul T. Fuhrmann. London: Lutterworth Press, n.d.

_____. *Responsi ad Sadoleti Epistolam.* Corpus Reformatorum, Vol. XXXIII. English translation by H. Beveridge. *Calvin, Tracts Relating to the Reformation,* Vol. I. Edinburgh: Calvin Translation Society, 1844.

_____. *Theological Treatises,* Library of Christian Classics, English translation J. K. S. Reid. Philadelpia: The Westminster Press, 1960.

Cathechism of the Council of Trent for Parish Priests. English translation by J. A. McHugh and C. J. Callen. London: B. Herder, 1934.

Charles, R. H. *The Apocrypha and Pseudepigrapha of the Old Testament.* London: Oxford University Press, 1913.

Constitution of the Holy Apostles. E. T. by A. C. Coxe. *Ante Nicene Fathers,* Vol. VII. Buffalo: The Christian Literature Co., 1886.

Cook, E. A. "Ritschl's Use of Value Judgments." *American Journal of Theology,* XXI (October, 1917), 345-53.

Cross, Frank M., Jr. *The Ancient Library of Qumran.* New York: Anchor Doubleday, 1961.

Cullmann, Oscar. *Christology of the New Testament.* Philadelphia: Westminster Press, 1959.

Cyprian. *Testimoniorum contra Judaeos.* Patrologiae Cursus Completus Series Latina, Vol. IV. Edited by J.P. Migne. Paris: 1844-1880.

Cyril of Jerusalem. *Testimoniorum contra Judeos.* Patrologiae Cursus Completus Series Graeca, Vol. XXXIII. Edited by J. P. Migne. Paris: 1857-1866.

Dabin, Paul. *Le sacerdoce royal des fidèles dans les livres saints.* Paris: Librarie Blaudard et Gay, 1941.

_____. *Le sacerdoce royal des fidèles dans la tradition ancienne et moderne.* Paris: De Brouwer, 1950.

Davies, Paul E. "Jesus and the Role of Prophet." *Journal of Biblical Literature,* LXIV (1945), 241-254.

Deegan, Dan. "Albrecht Ritschl as Critical Empiricist." *Journal of Religion,* XLIV (April, 1964), 149-160.

_____. "Albrecht Ritschl on the Historical Jesus." *Scottish Journal of Theology.* XV (June, 1962), 133-150.

_____. "Philip Hefner, *Faith and the Vitalities of History.*" *Scottish Journal of Theology (Fall, 1968), 336-339.*

_____. "The Ritschlian School, the Essence of Christianity and Karl Barth." *Scottish Journal of Theology,* XVI (December, 1963), 390-414.

Denny, James. *Studies in Theologyy.* London: Hodder and Stoughton, 1895.

216

Dorner, I. A. *History of Protestant Theology.* English translation by G. Robson. Edinburgh: T. & T. Clark, 1871.

————. *A System of Christian Doctrine.* Vols. I-IV. English translation by A. Cave, *et al.* Edinburgh: T. & T. Clark, 1882.

Dowey, E. A., Jr. *The Knowledqe of God in Calvin's Theology.* New York: Columbia University Press, 1952.

Ebeling, Gerhard. *Luther An Introduction to His Thought.* English translation by R. A. Wilson. London: Collins, 1970.

Ecke, Gustav. *Die theologische Schule A. Ritschls und die evangelische Kirche der Gegenwart.* Berlin: Reuther & Reichard, 1897.

Ehrenfeuchter, E. "Albrecht Ritschl in der Sicht eines Bonner Kollegen." *Jahrbuch der Gesellschaft für niedersachsische Kirchengeschichte.* LX (1962), 146-150.

Engall, I. *Studies in Divine Kingship in the Ancient Near East.* Uppsala: Universitets Arsskrift, 1943.

Ernesti, Johann August. *Gedanken über einige Stücke in der Lehre von Jesu Christo.* Leipzig: n.p., 1775.

Eusebius of Caesarea. *Ecclesiastica Historiae.* Patrologiae Cursus Completus Series Graeca, Vols. XIX-XXIV. Edited by J. P. Migne. Paris: 1857-1866. English translation by Kirsopp Lake. *Ecclesiastical History.* Loeb edition. Cambridge: Harvard University Press, 1959.

Fabricius, Cajus. *Die Entwicklung in Albrecht Ritschls Theologie von 1874 bis 1889.* Tübingen: J. C. B. Mohr, 1909.

Farmer, H. H. *The Word of Reconciliation.* New York: Abingdon, 1966.

Flavius Josephus, *Bellum Iudaicae.* English translation by Traill. London: Routlege, 1851.

Florovsky, Georges. "Scripture and Tradition: An Orthodox Point of View." *Dialog,* II (1963), 288ff.

Frankfort, H. *Kingship and the Gods.* Chicago: University of Chicago Press, 1948.

Franks, R. S. *The Atonement.* London: Oxford University Press, 1934.

Franks, R. S. *A History of the Doctrine of the Work of Christ.* London: Hodder and Stoughton, 1918.

Bibliography

Fuller, R. H. *A Critical Introduction to the New Testament.* London: Duckworth, 1966.

Garvie, Alfred E. "Ritschlianism," *Encyclopedia of Religion and Ethics.* Edited by J. Hastings. Edinburgh: T. & T. Clark, 1905. Vol. X.

_____. *The Ritschlian Theology.* Edinburgh: T. & T. Clark, 1899.

Gerrish, Brian A. "Priesthood and Ministry in the Theology of Luther." *Church History,* XXXIV (December, 1965), 404-422.

Gils, Félix. *Jésus Prophète.* Louvain: Publications Universitaire, 1957.

Glick, G. Wayne. *The Reality of Christianity.* New York: Harper & Row, 1967.

Goguel, Maurice. *La théologie d'Albert Ritschl.* Paris: Fischbacher, 1905.

Guthrie, George P. "Kant and Ritschl: A Study in the Relation Between Philosophy and Theology." Unpublished Ph.D. dissertation, University of Chicago, 1962.

Harnack, Adolph. *History of Dogma.* English translation from third edition by Neil Buchanan, *et al.* London: Williams and Norgate, 1894.

_____. *Outline of the History of Dogma.* English translation by E. K. Mitchell. London: Williams and Norgate, 1893.

_____. "Ritschl und seine Schule." *Reden und Aufsätze.* Giessen: J. Richer, 1904. Pp. 352-353.

_____. *What Is Christianity?* English translation by T. B. Saunders. London: Williams and Norgate, 1923.

Hefner, Philip. "Albrecht Ritschl and His Current Critics." *The Lutheran Quarterly,* XIII (May, 1961), 103-112.

Hefner, Philip. "Baur Versus Ritschl on Early Christianity." *Church History,* XXXI (September, 1962), 259-278.

_____. *Faith and the Vitalities of History.* New York: Harper & Row, 1966.

_____. "The Role of Church History in the Theology of Albrecht Ritschl." *Church History,* XXXIII (September, 1964), 338-355.

Hegel, George Friedrich Wilhelm. *The Phenomenology of Mind.* English translation by J. B. Baillie. New York: Harper & Row, 1967.

Heick, Otto. *A History of Christian Thought.* Vol. II. Philadelphia: Fortress Press, 1966.

Herrmann, Wilhelm. "Albrecht Ritschl, seine Grösse und seine Schranke." *Festgabe von Fachgenossen und Freunden, A. von Harnack zum siebzigster Geburtstag dargebracht.* Tübingen: J. C. B. Mohr, 1921.

_____. *The Communion of the Christian with God.* English translation from second edition by J. S. Stanyon. London: Williams and Norgate, 1906.

_____. "Faith as Ritschl Defined It." *Faith and Morals.* English translation by D. Matheson, *et al.* London: Williams and Norgate, 1910.

_____. "The Real Mind of Jesus." *Essays on the Social Gospel.* Herrmann, W. and Harnack, A. London: Williams and Norgate, 1907.

_____. *Systematic Theology.* English translation by Nathaniel Micklem and K. A. Saunders. New York: Macmillan, 1927.

Hilary of Poitiers. Citation in Thomas Aguinas. *Catena Aurea.* Edited by John Henry Newman. Oxford: Oxford University Press, 1841-45.

Hodgson, Peter C. *The Formation of Historical Theology.* New York: Harper & Row, 1966.

Hök, Gösta. *Die elliptische Theologie Albrecht Ritschls: Nach Ursprung und innerem Zusammenhang.* Uppsala: Universitets Arsskrift, 1942.

Hooke, S. H. "Genesis." *Peake's Commentary on the Bible.* Edited by Matthew Black. London: Nelson, 1962.

_____. *Myth and Ritual.* London: Oxford University Press, 1933.

The Holy Bible. Revised Standard Version. New York: Nelson, 1952.

Jansen, John F. *Calvin's Doctrine of the Work of Christ.* London: James Clark, 1956.

Jersild, Paul. "Judgment of God in Albrecht Ritschl and Karl Barth." *The Lutheran Quarterly, XIV (November, 1962), 328-346.*

_____. "Natural Theology and the Doctrine of God in Albrecht Ritschl and Karl Barth." *The Lutheran Quarterly.* XIV (August, 1962), 238-257.

John Chrysostom. Citation in Thomas Aquinas. *Catena Aurea.* Edited by John Henry Newman. Oxford: Oxford University Press, 1841-45.

Justin Martyr. *Apologia prima pro Christianis.* Patrologiae Cursus Completeus Series Graeca, Vol. VI. Edited by J. P. Migne. Paris 1857-1866. English translation by T. B. Falls. *Saint Justin Martyr.* Washington: Catholic University Press, 1948.

_____. *Dialogus cum Tryphone Judaeo.* Patrologiae Cursus Completeus Series Graeca, Vol. VI. Edited by J. P. Migne. Paris 1857-1866. English translation by T. B. Falls. *Saint Justin Martyr.* Washington: Catholic University Press, 1948.

Kaftan, Julius. *Dogmatik.* Tübingen: J. C. B. Mohr, 1920.

_____. *Die Wahrheit der christlichen Religion.* English translation. *The Truth of the Christian Religion.* Edinburgh: T. & T. Clark, 1894.

Kant, Immanuel. *Kritik der practischen Vernunft.* Riga: J. F. Hartnack, 1788. English translation by L. W. Beck. *Critique of Practical Reason.* New York: Liberal Arts Press, 1950.

_____. *Kritik der reinen Vernunft.* Riga: J. F. Hartnack, 1781. English translation by Norman Kemp Smith. *Critique of Pure Reason.* New York: St. Martin's Press, 1961.

_____. *Die Religion innerhalb der Grenzen der blossen Vernunft.* Leipzig: Erich Koschny, 1875. English translation by T. H. Greene, H. H. Hudson. *Religion within the Limits of Reason Alone.* New York: Harper and Row, 1960.

Kantorowicz, Ernst H. "Mysteries of State." *Harvard Theological Review,* LVIII (1955), 65-91.

Kattenbusch, Ferdinand. *Von Schleiermacher zu Ritschl.* Giessen, J. Richer, 1892.

Keirstead, W. C. "Theological Presuppositions of Albrecht Ritschl." *American Journal of Theology,* X (July, 1906), 423.

Koenig, Robert Emil. "The Use of the Bible in Albrecht Ritschl's Theology." Unpublished Ph.D. dissertation, University of Chicago, 1953.

Krauss, A. "Das Mittlerwerk nach dem Schema des *Munus Triplex.*" *Jahrbücher für deutsche Theologie,* XVII (1872), 595-655.

Langford, Thomas. *In Search of Foundations: English Theology 1900-1920.* New York: Abingdon, 1969.

Lessing, Gotthold. *Lessing's Theological Writings.* Edited by Henry Chadwick. Stanford: Stanford University Press, 1967.

Lichtenberger, F. *History of German Protestant Theology in the 19th Century.* English translation by W. Hastie. Edinburgh: T. & T. Clark, 1889.

Lietzmann, Hans. *A History of the Early Church.* English translation by B. L. Woolf. New York: Meridian Press, 1963.

Livingston, James C. *Modern Christian Thought: From the Enlightenment to Vatican II.* New York: Macmillan, 1971.

Lotze, Rudolph Hermann. *Microcosmus.* 4th ed. English translation by E. Hamilton, Constance Jones. Edinburgh: T. & T. Clark, 1897.

Luthardt, Christoph E. "Zur Beurtheilung der Ritschl'schen Theologie." *Zeitschrift für kirchliche Wissenschaft und kirchliches Leben,*. II (1881), 625.

_____. *Zur Kontroverse über die Ritschl'sche Theologie.* Leipzig: n.p., 1886.

Luther, Martin. *De libertate christiana.* Werke, Vol. VII. Weimar, Hermann Böhlau, 1883. English translation by W. A. Lambert and H. J. Grimm in J. Dillenberger, ed. *Martin Luther: Selections from His Writings.* New York: Anchor Doubleday, 1961.

_____. *Von weltlicher Oberkeit wie weit man ihr Gehorsam schuldig.* Werke, Vol. XI. Weimar, Hermann Böhlau, 1883. English translation by W. A. Lambert and H. J. Grimm in J. Dillenberger, ed. *Martin Luther: Selections from His Writings.* New York: Anchor Doubleday, 1961.

McKeating, H. "The Prophet Jesus." *Expository Times,* LXXIII (1961), 4, 50ff.

Mackintosh, H. R. "Ritschlianism Old and New." *London Quarterly Review,* CXXI (January, 1914), 25-50.

_____. *Types of Modern Theology: Schleiermacher to Barth.* New York: Chas. Scribners, 1937.

McNeill, J. T., ed. *Calvin: Institutes of the Christian Religion.* Library of Christian Classics, Vols. XX-XXI. Philadelphia: Westminster Press, 1960.

Mead, C. M. *Ritschl's Place in the History of Doctrine.* Hartford: Hartford Seminary Foundation Press, 1895.

Mowinckel, Sigmund. *He That Cometh.* New York: Abingdon, 1954.

Mueller, David L. *An Introduction to the Theology of Albrecht Ritschl.* Philadelphia: Westminster Press, 1969.

Muilenburg, James. "Old Testament Prophecy." *Peake's Commentary on the Bible.* Edited by Matthew Black. Revised edition. London: Nelson, 1962.

Mure, G. R. G. *The Philosophy of Hegel.* London: Oxford University Press, 1965.

Niesel, Wilhelm. *The Theology of Calvin.* Philadelphia: Westminster Press, 1956.

Novatian. *De Trinitate.* Patrologiae Cursus Completus Series Latina, Vol. III. Edited by J. P. Migne. Paris: 1844-1880.

Obermann, Heiko A. "Quo Vadis, Petre?" *Harvard Divinity School Bulletin, July, 1962.*

Orr, James. *The Ritschlian Theology and the Evangelical Faith.* London: Hodder and Stoughton, 1897.

_____. *Ritschlianism: Expository and Critical Essays.* London: Hodder and Stoughton, 1903.

Osiander, Andreas. *Schirmschrift zum Augsburger Reichstag,* 1530. In *Quellen und Forschungen zur Geschichte des Augsburgischer Glaubensbekenntnisses.* Berlin: n.p., 1911. Cited. Jansen, J. F. *Calvin's Doctrine of the Work of Christ.* London: James Clark, 1956.

Pannenberg, Wolfhart. *Jesus-God and Man.* English translation by L. L. Williams, *et al.* London: SCM Press, 1968.

Parker, T. H. L. *Calvin's Doctrine of the Knowledge of God.* Grand Rapids: Eerdmans, 1959.

Passant, E. J. *A Short History of Germany 1815-1945.* Cambridge: Cambridge University Press, 1969.

Perrin, Norman. *The Kingdom of God in the Teaching of Jesus.* Philadelphia: Westminster Press, 1963.

Peter Lombard. *Book of Sentences.* English translation by E. R. Fairweather. *A Scholastic Miscellany: Anselm to Ockham.* Library of Christian Classics, Vol. X. Philadelphia: Westminster Press, 1956.

Petrus Chrysologus. *Sermo lix.* Edited by J. P. Migne. Patrologiae Cursus Completus Series Latina. Vol. LII.

Pfleiderer, Otto. *Development of Theology in Germany Since Kant.* English translation by J. F. Smith. London: Sonnenschein, 1890.

_____. *Die Ritschl'sche Theologie.* Braunschweige, 1891.

_____. "Die Theologie der Ritschl'schen Schule." *Jahrbuch für protestantische Theologie.* 1891, 323ff.

Philo Judaeus. *Opera. De vita Moses.* English translation by C. D. Yonge. London: Bohn, 1855.

Pickle, Joseph W., Jr. "Epistemology and Soteriology: A Study in the Theologies of Albrecht Ritschl and Karl Barth." Unpublished Ph.D. dissertation, University of Chicago, 1969.

Randall, John Herman, Jr. *The Making of the Modern Mind.* Cambridge: Houghton Mifflin, 1954.

Reimarus, H. S. *Apologie oder Schutzschrift für die vernünftigen Vereher Gottes.* Gotthold Lessing, ed. *Wolfenbüttel Fragments.* Cited in *Lessing's Theological Writings.* Edited by Henry Chadwick. Stanford: Stanford University Press, 1956.

Reist, B. A. "Life in the Old Boys Yet." *The Christian Century,.* LXXXIII (September 28, 1966), 1179-1180.

"Religionsgeschichte Schule." *Die Religion in Geschichte und Gegenwart,* Dritte Auflage, Bd. 5.

Ringgren, Helmer. *Israelite Religion.* Philadelphia: Fortress Press, 1965.

Ritschl, Albrecht B. *Die christliche Vollkommenheit.* Leipzig: J. C. Hinrichs, 1924. English translation by Archibald Duff, Jr. Bibliotheca Sacra. XXXV (January, 1878), 656-680.

_____. *Die christliche Lehre von der Rechtfertigung und Versöhnung,.* 3 Bd. Bonn: Adolph Marcus, 1870-74. English translation Vol. I., *A Critical History of the Christian Doctrine of Justification and Reconciliation.* Edinburgh: Edmonston and Douglas, 1872. English translation Vol. III., of third German edition, *The Christian Doctrine of Justification and Reconciliation.* Clifton, New Jersey: Reference Book Publishers, 1966.

_____. *Das Evangelium Marcions und das kanonische Evangelium des Lucas.* Tübingen: Osiander, 1846.

_____. *Geschichte des Pietismus.* Bonn: A. Marcus, 1880-86.

_____. *Theologie und Metaphysik.* Bonn: A Marcus, 1881.

_____. *Three Essays.* Translated by Philip Hefner. Philadelphia: Fortress Press, 1972.

_____. *Unterricht in der christlichen Religion.* Bonn: Adolph Marcus, 1895. English translation by Alice Swing. *Instruction in the Christian Religion.* In A. T. Swing. *The Theology of Albrecht Ritschl.* London: Longmans, Green and Co., 1901.

"Ritschl, Albrecht Benjamin." *Lexikon für Theologie und Kirche,* Zweite Auflage, Bd. 8.

Ritschl, Otto. *Albrecht Ritschls Leben.* Freiburg: J. C. B. Mohr, 1892.

_____. "Albrecht Ritschl." *Realencyklopëdie für protestantische Theologie und Kirch.* Dritte Auflage, Bd. 7.

223

_____. "Albrecht Ritschls Theologie und ihre bisherigen Schicksale." *Zeitschrift für Theologie und Kirche,* XVI (N. F., 1935), 43-61.

Robinson, James M. *A New Quest of the Historical Jesus.* London: SCM Press, 1959.

Schäfer, Rolf. *Ritschl: Grundlinien eines fast verschollenen dogmatischen Systems.* Tübingen: J. C. B. Mohr, 1968.

Schleiermacher, Friedrich. *Der christliche Glaube nach der evangelischen Kirche.* Berlin: G. Reimer, 1835. English translation by D. M. Baillie and others. *The Christian Faith.* Edinburgh: T. & T. Clark, 1929.

_____. *Uber die Religion: Reden an die bildeten unter ihren Verächtern.* Berlin: G. Reimer, 1835. English translation by John Oman. *On Religion: Speeches to Its Cultured Despisers.* London: Kegan, Paul, French, Drübner & Co., 1893.

Schoen, Henri. *Les origens historique de la théologie de Ritschl.* Paris: Fischbacher, 1893.

Schott, E. "Ritschl, A. B." *Die Religion in Geschichte und Gegenwart,* Dritte Auflage. Vol. V.

Schweitzer, Albert. *Von Reimarus zu Wrede.* Tübingen: J. C. B. Mohr, 1906. English translation by W. Montgomery. *The Quest of the Historical Jesus.* New York: Macmillan, 1962.

Sellen, E. and Fohrer, G. *Introduction to the Old Testament.* New York: Abingdon, 1968.

Shepherd, Massey U. Jr. "Priests in the New Testament." *Interpreter's Dictionary of the Bible.* 1964. Vol. III.

_____. "Prophet in the New Testament." *Interpreter's Dictionary of the Bible.* 1964. Vol. III.

Southern, R. W. *The Making of the Middle Ages.* New Haven: Yale University Press, 1953.

Stephan, H. "Albrecht Ritschl," *Die Religion in Geschichte und Gegenwart,* Zweite Auflage. Vol. IV.

Stinnesring, W. F. "I and II Samuel." *The Oxford Annotated Bible.* Edited by H. G. May and B. M. Metzger. New York: Oxford University Press, 1962.

Strauss, David F. *Das Leben Jesu kritisch bearbeitet.* Tübingen: J. C. B. Mohr, 1835. English translation by George Eliot, from 4th ed., *The Life of Jesus Critically Examined.* London: Sonnenschein, 1848.

Swing, Albert T. "Recent Ritschlianism." *Outlook,* LXVIII (June, 1901), 361-362.

————. *The Theology of Albrecht Ritschl.* London: Longmans, Green & Co., 1901.

Taylor, A. J. P. *The Course of German History.* London: Hamilton, 1945.

Taylor, Vincent. *The Names of Jesus.* New York: St. Martin's Press, 1953.

Tertullian. *Adversus Judaeos.* Patrologiae Cursus Completus Series Latina, Vol. II. Edited by J. P. Migne. Paris: 1844-1880. English translation by A. C. Coxe. *Ante Nicene Fathers,* Vol. V. Buffalo: The Christian Literature Co., 1886.

Testament of Levi. English translation by R. H. Charles. *Apocrypha and Pseudepigrapha of the Old Testament.* London: Oxford University Press, 1913.

Tillich, Paul. *Perspectives on 19th and 20th Century Protestant Theology.* New York: Harper and Row, 1967.

————. *Systematic Theology,* Vol. I. Chicago: University of Chicago Press, 1950.

Thomas Aquinas. *Catena Aurea.* Edited by John Henry Newman. Oxford: Oxford University Press, 1841-45.

————. *Summa Theologia,* III. English translation by Fathers of the Dominican Province. New York: Benziger Bro., 1917.

Timm, Hermann. *Theorie und Praxis in der Theologie Albrecht Ritschls und Wilhelm Herrmanns.* Gutersloh: Mohn, 1967.

Torrance, T. F. *The School of Faith.* London: James Clark, 1959.

Troeltsch, Ernst. *Die Soziallehren der christlichen Kirchen und Gruppen.* Tübingen: J. C. B. Mohr, 1912. English translation by Olive Wyon. *The Social Teaching of the Christian Churches.* New York: Harper. 1931.

Ullmann, Walter. *A History of Political Thought in the Middle Ages.* Baltimore: Pelican, 1965.

Van Buren, Paul. *Christ In Our Place.* Edinburgh: Oliver & Boyd, 1957.

————. *The Secular Meaning of the Gospel.* New York: Macmillan, 1963.

Vorster, H. "Werkzeug oder Täter? Zur Methodik der Christologie Albrecht Ritschl." *Zeitschrift für Theologie und Kirche,* LXII, 1 (May, 1965), 46-65.

Walker, Williston. *A History of the Christian Church.* Revised edition. New York: Chas. Scribners Sons, 1959.

Weinel, H. and Widgery, A. *Jesus in the 19th Century*. Edinburgh: T. & T. Clark, 1914.

Weiss, Johannes. *Die Predigt Jesu vom Reiche Gottes*. Göttingen: Vandenhoeck & Ruprecht, 1892. English translation by R. H. Hiers and D. L. Holland. *Jesus' Proclamation of the Kingdom of God*. Philadelphia: Fortress Press, 1971.

Welch, Claude. *God and Incarnation in Mid-nineteenth Century German Theology*. New York: Oxford University Press, 1965.

Williams, George Hunston. *Wilderness and Paradise in Christian Thought*. New York: Harper & Row, 1962.

_____. Selected Texts in Church History 183. Harvard University, 1964. (Mimeographed.)

Willis, E. David. *Calvin's Catholic Christology*. Leiden: E. J. Brill, 1966.

Wright, G. E. and Fuller, R. H. *The Book of the Acts of God*. New York: Anchor Doubleday, 1960.

Wrzecionko, Paul. *Die philosophischen Wurzeln der Theologie Albrecht Ritschls*. Berlin: Topelmann, 1964.

Young, Franklin W. "Jesus the Prophet: A Reexamination." *Journal of Biblical Literature,* LXVIII (1949), 285-299.

von Zahn-Harnack, Agnes. *Adolph von Harnack*. Berlin: Hans Bolt, 1936.

INDEX